Routledge Revivals

The Present State of Russia

The Present State of Russia

Volume I

Friedrich Christian Weber

First published in 1968
by Frank Cass and Company Limited

This edition first published in 2021 by Routledge
2 Park Square, Milton Park, Abingdon, Oxon, OX14 4RN

and by Routledge
605 Third Avenue, New York, NY 10017

Routledge is an imprint of the Taylor & Francis Group, an informa business

© 1968 Taylor & Francis

All rights reserved. No part of this book may be reprinted or reproduced or utilised in any form or by any electronic, mechanical, or other means, now known or hereafter invented, including photocopying and recording, or in any information storage or retrieval system, without permission in writing from the publishers.

Publisher's Note
The publisher has gone to great lengths to ensure the quality of this reprint but points out that some imperfections in the original copies may be apparent.

Disclaimer
The publisher has made every effort to trace copyright holders and welcomes correspondence from those they have been unable to contact.

A Library of Congress record exists under LCCN: 68104209

ISBN: 978-1-032-22152-6 (set)
ISBN: 978-1-032-21872-4 (Volume 1) (hbk)
ISBN: 978-1-003-27038-6 (Volume 1) (ebk)
ISBN: 978-1-032-21874-8 (pbk)

Book DOI 10.4324/9781003270386

RUSSIA THROUGH EUROPEAN EYES
No. 2
General Editor: Dr. A. G. CROSS, University of East Anglia

THE PRESENT
STATE OF RUSSIA

THE
PRESENT STATE
OF
RUSSIA

BY

FRIEDRICH CHRISTIAN WEBER

IN TWO VOLUMES

VOLUME I

FRANK CASS & CO. LTD.

1968

Published by
FRANK CASS AND COMPANY LIMITED
67 Great Russell Street, London WC1

First edition   1722–23
New impression   1968

Printed in Great Britain by
Thomas Nelson (Printers) Ltd., London and Edinburgh

THE PRESENT STATE OF RUSSIA.

In Two Volumes.

BEING
An Account of the Government of that Country, both Civil and Ecclesiastical; of the CZAR's Forces by Sea and Land, the Regulation of his Finances, the several Methods he made use of to civilize his People and improve the Country, his Transactions with several Eastern Princes, and what happened most remarkable at his Court, particularly in relation to the late CZAREWITZ, from the Year 1714, to 1720.

The whole being the Journal of a Foreign Minister who resided in *Russia* at that time.

WITH
A Description of *Petersbourg* and *Cronslot*,
AND
Several other Pieces relating to the Affairs of RUSSIA.

Translated from the High-Dutch.

To which is added
A general MAP of the *Czar's* Dominions, according to the latest Observations.

LONDON:

Printed for W. Taylor in *Pater-noster-Row*. W. and J. Innys at the West-End of St. *Paul's*, and J. Osborn in *Lombard-street*. MDCCXXIII.

THE TRANSLATOR's PREFACE.

IT is now almoſt two Years ſince I undertook to write an Introduction to the Hiſtory of Ruſſia, and I had made ſome Progreſs in it, when this Book was publiſhed in Germany. The Attention and Countenance which the Publick has of late given to whatever could inform them of the preſent State of that Country, made me immediately reſolve to ſuſpend

my

The Translator's

my *Design*, and to enter upon the *Translation* of this Book, as the newest Account given by a Gentleman, whose Character procured him the best Opportunity of informing himself with Exactness of the Affairs of a Country, which within these few Years has been so surprizingly improved.

As it would be superfluous to say any thing in Commendation of the Book it self, the Value of which I leave to the Reader's Judgement; I shall confine myself to acquaint him only with certain Circumstances relating to the part I have taken in publishing it in English.

I undertook the Translation of it with the Author's Knowledge, and consulted him about several Difficulties.

I own that I took the Liberty of leaving out a few things which either have appeared in Print before, or were, as I apprehended, unsuitable to the Taste of an English Reader; as for Instance, some humorous Verses which would not bear a Translation, and besides contained nothing material but what was already related before. On the other hand, I have inserted some things which I took from Extracts of Letters written by the Author when in Russia,

PREFACE.

Ruſſia, *that were communicated to me by a Perſon of Honour.*

I think it is neceſſary likewiſe to give the Reader ſome Information concerning the ſeveral Pieces annexed to this Account.

Firſt, the Deſcription of Petersbourg *and* Cronſlot *appears not to be the Author's, but publiſhed before by one M.* Schûtz *in* High-Dutch, *though our Author has adapted it to his own Obſervations.*

The Journal of the Travels to China *was communicated to our Author by M.* Lange *himſelf, who lately has been ſent a ſecond time to that Country, and is ſtill there, as I have been informed by a Gentleman in the* Czar's *Service, who is acquainted with M.* Lange, *and told me at the ſame time, that the latter was not pleaſed with the publiſhing of his Journal, he looking upon it as an incomplete Draught which he took during the Fatigue of his long Journey, with an Intention of bringing it into better Order before he communicated it to the World. Be that as it will, I am of opinion our Author obliged the Publick, by imparting to them ſuch a Piece of Curioſity how imperfect ſoever. At the End of this Journal was a very*

The Translator's *very lame Extract of a Description of* China, *communicated to* M. Lange *by the Jesuits there, out of which I took the Character of the present Emperor* Kamhi, *and left out the rest, because it contained nothing besides what* Kircherus, Martinius *and other* Chineze *Missionaries have said before more at large.*

The melancholy Account which M. Müller, *the Author of the Description of the* Ostiacks, *gives in his Preface of his way of Life in his Captivity, is the Reason why I here acquaint the Reader, that that Gentleman's Circumstances have mended since, he being at present honourably employed at* Petersbourg *in one of the new Boards or Offices established by the* Czar, *as I have lately learnt from a* Livonian Gentleman, *who knew him in* Russia.

The Manifesto relating to the criminal Proceedings against the late Czarewitz, *is not entire in the* High-Dutch *Original, and in some places it is hardly even intelligible. I have therefore given the whole as it was printed in* French *at the* Hague *by the* Czar's *express Orders.*

The Discourse, concerning the War between Russia *and* Sweden, *was at first*

PREFACE.

first intended to be inserted by our Author, but as the tranflating of it from the Ruffian *would have retarded the publifhing of his Book, he left it out. It has fince been printed in* High-Dutch, *and I have joined it to the* Swedifh *Deduction to which it refers, though I was obliged to retrench the long Preface and the Hiftorical Documents belonging to it, for fear of fwelling the Bulk of that Volume too much.*

I have followed the Author in annexing to his own Account M. LeBrun's *Obfervations on* Ruffia, *the rather becaufe that part of his Travels has not yet been tranflated into* Englifh. *I cannot forbear taking notice that this Gentleman's Obfervations appear in many refpects not fo accurate as it were to be wifhed; however as they contain feveral remarkable Particulars, I have given an Abftract of them juft as they are.*

The Annotations at the end of fome Pages printed between two Crotchets [ ] *are not of the refpective Authors, but my own, taken either from the publick News, or from credible Authorities.*

I have

The Translator's

I have been advised to explain the Russian *Coin and their Measure of Distance of Places, by comparing them with those used in* England. *I have therefore annexed to this Preface a List of the Terms that relate thereto, and other difficult Words that occur either in this or other Books and Maps of* Russia, *with the Explanation of them, which I have taken from good Authorities. It was not easy for me to bring the Orthography of the* Russian *proper Names to an exact Uniformity; I have therefore writ them according to the respective Authors I had before me, thinking it presumptuous to do any thing by guess in a Language to which I am a Stranger.*

I have added to this English *Edition a new Map of the* Czar's *extensive Dominions, which I have drawn according to the latest Observations, and adapted to this Account. I shall mention some Particulars in which it differs from others.* Azoff *and* Tobolsky *are placed in other Latitudes than in the Maps of* Russia *and* Siberia, *drawn up by the late M.* Nicholas Witsen, *the learned Burghermaster of* Amsterdam, *who by about thirty Years Experience and Correspondence, and with a Princely Expence, settled*

PREFACE.

settled the Geography of the Czar's *Dominions, till then almost unknown to their own Sovereign as well as to the rest of* Europe, *with such Accuracy, that* Isbrand Ides, *the* Russian *Ambassador to* China, *made use of M.* Witsen's *Map of* Siberia *as a Guide in his Journey to* Peking *. If one compares that Map with this, it will appear that M.* Witsen *gave to the Northern Part of* Asia *a much larger Extent than it has since been found in reality to have. The Description of the* Ostiacks *appears to suppose that* Nova Zemla *is not an Island but a Peninsula, consequently that there is no Passage through the Streights of* Waigats *into the* Icy Sea *or* Tartarian Ocean: *A Point much disputed among former Geographers, and even long denied by M.* Witsen, *till he was convinced by an Experiment made by the* Czar's *particular Orders †. I have marked in this Map the Limits regulated in the Treaty of* Nipchou *in the Year* 1689 *between the Dominions of* China *and* Russia *by the* 48th *Degree of Northern Latitude on*

---

* *See* Isbrant Ides's *Travels, pag.* 90.
† *See* Philosoph. Transact. N° 101. *p.* 3 & N° 193. *p.* 494.

one

The Translator's

one side, and the 55th more Eastward‡. *The Limits between the* Swedish *and* Russian *Dominions, as they were settled in the late Peace at* Nystat, *are likewise designed as far as the narrow Compass of so general a Map would permit. Want of Room is also the Reason why I could not mark every Place that is mentioned in this Book, particularly the several Canals, which the Czar has attempted or caused to be made for Communications between divers Rivers and Seas. The situation and shape of the* Caspian Sea, *and another smaller Sea next to it, hitherto not observed by any Geographer, is a Curiosity for which I am beholden to M.* De la Motraye, *who now has a Relation of his Travels in the Press, ready to be published in* French *and* English *by Subscription, in which besides other curious Observations, he promises an Historical Account of the late Transactions between the* Ottoman Porte, *the* Czar, *and the late King of* Sweden, *particularly the famous Actions on the River* Pruth *and at* Bender, *as also the Siege of* Fre-

---

‡ *See Father* Le Gobien's *History of the Empire of* China, *Lib.* II. *in the Annotation; and* Dionysius Kao's *short Description of* China, *annexed to* Isbrant Ides's *Travels, pag.* 195. *in the* English *Edition*

dricks-

PREFACE.

dricks Hall, *where the said King was killed, to the greater part of which Affairs he has been an Eyewitness. In this Relation he is to communicate a Map of the* Caspian Sea *at large, according to the Degrees of Longitude and Latitude, with the several Places situate on and near its Coasts, as the same was drawn by the* Czar's *Orders. The Reader will probably expect to find in this Map the River* Daria, *which carries Gold Sand, taken notice of in this new Account of* Russia, *and so frequently mentioned since in the publick Advices from* Russia. *But I have not been able to get any certain Information about its situation either from Maps or Persons that have been in those Parts. Our Author indeed affirms in one Place* †, *that it runs out of the Country of the* Calmucks *into the* Caspian Sea *on the Northside, but as he says in* * *other Places, that the* Czar's *Forces who were sent to take Possession of that River, march'd through the great* Step *or* Desart, *and were defeated by the* Kibick Tartars, *or the Subjects of the* Can *of* Shirvan, *these Circumstances render the Situation of that River more*

---

† p. 154.   * p. 197, 199.

doubtful.

The Translator's

doubtful. For if it runs through the Country of the Calmucks, *its situation must be East of* Astracan, *and those* Kibicks *probably are a Tribe of the* Calmucks *inhabiting about the great* Step *that lies on that side. But if the Country of* Shirvan *is the same with the* Persian *Province of that Name, the River* Daria *must be not only West of* Astracan, *but even discharge itself into the* Caspian Sea *on the West-side; and the latest Advices actually seem to place it thereabouts, beyond* Terki *on the Frontiers of* Georgia. *We must therefore leave this Difficulty to be cleared up by newer Observations; in the mean time if I may venture upon a Conjecture, it is probable* Daria *is not so much the proper Name of that River, as a Word denoting in the Language of the Inhabitants any River in general; which Conjecture seems to be supported by the Termination of the Rivers* Antidarie, Sivdarie, *and* Araundarie, *mentioned in the new Map of the* Caspian Sea; *consequently it may be that the said River is marked in the ordinary Maps, though by another Name.*

So much I thought proper to mention concerning the Translation of this new Account of Russia; *before I conclude,*

PREFACE.

clude, I shall add, that, as to my former Design of writing an Introduction to the History of that Country, I intend to resume the same, having now for near two Years past studied that Subject and prepared the necessary Materials, being a Collection of all sorts of printed Books, Manuscripts, and Extracts in divers Languages. Though I have found that History full of the most remarkable Revolutions, and withal as entertaining as any other whatsoever; it is certain that we have not yet had any tolerable Compendium of the whole, which chiefly proceeds from this Reason, that the Russians have no Historians of their own, and that consequently the Transactions of that Nation must be gathered from the Histories of their Neighbours, the Poles, Livonians, Prussians, Swedes, and the Relations of Ambassadors of those Princes and States, who upon account of Trade or other Concerns had Intercourse and Correspondence with them, as for instance, England, the United Provinces, Germany and Denmark; nay, even the Histories of the Eastern Empire under the Christians as well as under the Turks, of all Asia in general, and particularly of China

The TRANSLATOR's

of late, must be consulted, if one will speak with certainty of the Russian Affairs. But this has either been thought by some Writers too great a Trouble to undergo, or their being unacquainted with the History and Geography of so many Nations, and with the different Languages necessary for that purpose, has rendered that Task too difficult for them; and so all that we have had hitherto of the Russian History, is either imperfect in the most material Circumstances, or only relates to some particular Revolution or Period of Time. Besides it is usual with those Authors to pass over in Silence almost whole Centuries of the ancient History of Russia, the Transactions of which Times they look upon as entirely buried in Oblivion; though, since Christianity was introduced in Russia, there are not so great Chasms in their History, as is commonly pretended, but what may be in some measure filled up with the scattered Remains that are to be met with chiefly among the Polish Historians, and in the History of the Tartars. This latter is inseparably linked with the History of Russia, forasmuch as the Russians were for some Centuries subject

and

PREFACE.

and tributary to the Tartars, *but afterwards in their turn conquered their Conquerors, and are at present possessed of an immense Tract of Land which formerly made Part of the vast* Tartarian *Empire, the History of which has been lately cleared up in the Lives of* Genghiz-Can *and* Tamerlan, *which M.* Petis de la Croix *has collected from Oriental Authors. My Design therefore is to gather from good Authorities whatever I can meet with relating to the History of the* Russian *Nation and the extensive Dominions that at present obey the Czar, and only to relate Facts in the most natural Order, without enlarging upon the tedious Particulars of Sieges, Battels, Solemnities and the like, or filling up whole Pages with Treaties of Peace, Manifestoes, Letters, and Negotiations, the usual Method of those who love to be voluminous. As a great part of the Books I shall have Recourse to, are written in* High-Dutch, *my Knowledge of that Language will be of particular advantage to me in executing this Design, in which I shall think myself greatly encouraged, if the present Translation meets with a good Reception, and I flatter myself with Hopes,*

The Translator's PREFACE.

Hopes, that any Persons who have Memoirs relating to this Subject, will be willing to favour me with the Communication of them, which shall be duly acknowledged.

AN

THE PRESENT STATE OF RUSSIA.

VOL. I.

CONTAINING

I An Account of the Government of that Country, both Civil and Ecclesiastical; of the CZAR's Forces by Sea and Land, the Regulation of his Finances, the several Methods he made use of to civilize his People and improve the Country, his Transactions with several Eastern Princes, and what happened most remarkable at his Court, particularly in relation to the late CZAREWITZ, from the Year 1714, to 1720.

The whole being the Journal of a Foreign Minister who resided in *Russia* at that time.

II. A Description of *Petersbourg* and *Cronslot*,

WITH THE

Plan of the first, and the Prospect of the latter.

LONDON:

Printed for W. Taylor in *Pater-noster-Row*. W. and J. Innys at the West-End of St. *Paul*'s, and J. Osborn in *Lombard-street*. MDCCXXIII.

THE AUTHORs PREFACE.

IT must be owned not only by all who have been in Russia themselves, but also by those who have any Notion of the Affairs of the North, that for about these twenty Years past Russia has been entirely reformed and changed. The extending of its Limits; the building of the City of Petersbourg, and making the Harbour at Cronflot; the regulating of its Forces according to the German Establishment, and the inuring them to Hardships by continual Exercise; the building of a whole Fleet, with Timber fetched as far as Cafan, and manning it with Peafants transformed

The Author's

formed into Sailors; the founding of Academies for teaching Navigation and other Sciences; the reforming and modelling of the publick Administration by establishing new Courts of Judicature and Offices for the Revenue; the introducing of Arts and Manufactures; the changing the Succession, and the other Transactions relating to the Czarewitz; *and last of all the reducing of the Clergy to an absolute Obedience, the reclaiming them from their former Ignorance, and obliging them to apply themselves to solid Learning: All these things, I say, are such Events and Improvements, as must needs surprize those who have seen them happen, and leave Posterity to doubt whether it was possible that such a Revolution could be brought about in so few Years among a People formerly so rude and unpolished, and at the same time so refractory to all Culture; that a City containing above sixty thousand Houses could be raised in a Place where in the Year* 1701, *no Habitations were to be seen but two Fishermens Cottages; and a Fleet built on that Coast, consisting of forty Men of War, and some hundreds of Gallies; in short, that the Czar should so far succeed in his Endeavours for the Welfare of his Country and the Improvement of his Dominions, that nothing now seems wanting but that his Subjects should renounce their Hatred towards Foreigners, that trading People should be allowed more Liberty to go to and return from his Country, and a Method be found out to remedy the*
excessive

PREFACE.

excessive Dearness of Necessaries in his new Metropolis.

It is indeed matter of wonder, that the curious World has hitherto had so little Information of all these Transactions, particularly with relation to those Events that have happened within Russia: If we except the History of the Czar's Life which came out in High-Dutch above 10 Years ago, there is only Captain Perry, who in his Account of Russia, has given an impartial, though not a full Idea of the present State of that Country; but as he owns himself that it was not his Intention to write a compleat Account, besides that his Relation goes no further than 1714, since which time many remarkable Occurrences have happened; I have at length at the desire of several Persons of Note and Friends, overcome my natural Averseness for appearing in Print, and resolved faithfully to communicate to the Reader part of the Observations which I have made in that Country during eleven Years Conversation with the Natives, and in two Journeys I made thither.

As it is not my Design to give the Reader a regular Description of the several Provinces and Towns, nor the History of their Princes, I think it necessary to inform him, that I have only related the abovesaid Changes and Improvements, and represented the State of Russia as it is at this time, together with their Domestick Occurrences, and their Transactions with their
several

The Author's

several Asiatick *Vassals and Neighbours, without observing any other Method than the Order of Time, and that I have passed over all publick Negotiations and Transactions with foreign Powers relating to War and Peace.*

I have inserted the Journal of M. Lange's *Travels to* China, *forasmuch as it shews what Intercourse the Czar has with that Empire, and how much he has the Trade with that Country at Heart.*

I have also inserted an Account of the Ostiacks, *a Nation hitherto little known, who about* 10 *Years ago, began to be converted from Paganism; The same has indeed appeared in Print before in* Germany, *but without the Dedication and Preface, and so full of Faults, that the Author's Meaning was often quite perverted. I have given it here from his own Manuscript, which was communicated to me at* Petersbourg, *as a Proof of the Care which the Czar takes to polish those savage Nations under his Obedience, and by the Principles of Christianity and Maxims of Government to reclaim them from their irregular Life, and to render them such Subjects as may in time be useful to him in carrying on his Designs.*

The Advices interspersed in several Places relating to the Calmucks *and other* Tartarian *Nations, will give the Reader an Idea how far these People owe* Obedience *to the Czar.*

After

PREFACE.

After my Return to Germany, *I met with M.* Le Brun's Travels *newly come out in* French, *which Book being very dear on account of the many Prints it contains, I was defired to give an Extract of that Gentleman's Obfervations on thofe parts of* Ruffia, *where I had not been, which I have done accordingly, and added a few of my own Remarks to it.*

Some Years ago, a Book appeared in the World under the Title of Memoires amufans & fatyriques, *in which feveral things are impofed upon the Publick for Truths and Facts, which are without any Foundation. There are indeed fome Particulars in the Book, againft which no Objections can be made, as for inftance the Campaign of the* Ruffians *againft the* Turks, *and the like. But the Author who never was at* Petersbourg, *has inferted many ill grounded Stories and grofs Falfhoods (fuggefted to him by his Wife, who had been difgufted at fome ill ufage fhe had met with at* Petersbourg*) on which he has commented with particular Reflexions of his own. But confidering how eafy it is for a Man who has no regard to Truth, Charity and the Refpect due to Perfons of Rank, to invent Tales of remote Countries, and flander and libel his Neighbours among Strangers; the whole Book was quickly fufpected of forgery, and confequently detefted by all honeft Minds.*

The AUTHOR's PREFACE.

To conclude, I muſt acquaint the Reader, that the following Account was not printed at the ſame Place where it was written, that I ſent it to the Preſs Sheet by Sheet, and that conſequently I had no Opportunity of taking care of its Correction, which Circumſtance I hope will excuſe ſome ſmall Miſtakes that may have crept into it.

THE

AN EXPLANATION OF SOME Difficult WORDS.

ALBERTUS DALER, see *Daler*, and *Rubel*.
ALTIN, see *Rubel*.
AMBARE, a Magazin or Warehouse.
ARCHIERE, an Archbishop, from ἀρχιερεύς.
ARCHIMANDRITA, the Prior of a Monastry. Gr. Ἀρχιμανδρείτης.

BADOG or BATTOCKS, a Punishment used in *Russia* like the *Bastinado* in *Turky*, inflicted for lesser Crimes than the *Knout*; described at large in Capt. *Perry*'s Account of *Russia*, pag. 217. See also *Le Brun*, pag. (403.)
BANCO DALER, see *Daler*, and *Rubel*.
BOG, signifies *God* in *Russian*. *Bogdan*, a Christian Name used among them, signifies *a-Deo-datus*, *Dieu-donné*.
BOYAR, is a Privy-Councellor or Senator. Their Number is not limited, but the Czar chuses as many as he pleases from among the chief Nobility.

CAN,

An Explanation of

CAN, a Title of Honour given by the *Tartars* and other Eastern Nations to their Sovereigns. It signifies *King*.

COPECK, see *Rubel*.

CZAR, is said to signify *King* in the *Slavonian* Language, though some derive it from *Cæsar*, and explain it *Emperor*. The *Tartars* call their Sovereigns also by the Name of Czar.

CZAREWITZ, the Title given to the reigning Czar's eldest Son and Heir Apparent.

CZARITZA, (commonly *Czarina*) the Czar's Consort. CZARENNA or CZAREWNA, the Czar's Daughter. See pag. 134. 203.

DALER, a *German* Coin. There are two sorts of it: *Rix Dalers*, an imaginary Coin, each of 24 Grosch; and *Specie-Dalers*, worth 32 Grosch each, which are also sometimes called *Banco-Dalers*. But there are other sorts of *Specie-Dalers*, the intrinsick Value of which is less than 32 Grosch; of that sort are the *Albertus Dalers*, *Lewen Dalers*, &c. A *Specie* or *Banco-Daler* is worth something less than Five Shillings Sterling.

DENING, see *Rubel*.

DIAK, a Clerk or Secretary. The *Russian* Secretaries of State are called *Dumenoi Diaki*.

DUCAT, is a Gold Coin, current in *Germany*, *Holland*, and the Northern Countries, intrinsically worth two *Specie-Dalers*, or two *Rix-Dalers* and 16 Grosch, which makes 9 Shillings 6 Pence Sterling.

FATHOM

some difficult Words.

FATHOM in *Russia*, is 7 *English* Feet, and about the tenth part of an Inch   See Capt. *Perry*'s Account of *Russia*, p. 33.

GAMA, see *Jam*.
GOROD, the Termination of the Names of several Places in *Russia*. It signifies *City*, or a Place that is walled in.
GRIVE, see *Rubel*.
GROSCH, see *Daler*.

HEERMEISTER, *i. e.* Master or Commander of the Army. The *Livonian* Knights (*Ensiferi*, or *the Friars of the short Sword*,) before they submitted to the Great Master of the Teutonick Order in *Prussia*, had a Head or Sovereign of their own, who was thus called.
HETMAN. Commonly called the General of the *Cosacks* in the *Ukraina*, who is elected by them, not only to command their Forces, but also to govern them in civil Affairs, under the Czar's Protection.
HORDA. A number of *Tartars*, marching or encamping together under the command of a Head or Leader.
HOSPODAR. From δεσπότης, *Despota*. The Title given to the Princes of *Walachia* and *Moldavia*, otherwise also called *Woywodes*. The *Russians* use to call their Czar by a Name like this, *Gossudar*, i. e. *Dominus absolutè*.

JAM or GAMA. A Station on the Post-Roads, where Travellers are furnished with fresh Horses.

IGUMENOS,

An Explanation of

IGUMENOS, IGUMENA. An Abbot or Abbess of a *Russian* Monastery; from the Greek ἡγέομαι.

KABACK. A publick House in *Russia*, where they sell Beer and strong Liquors for the Czar's Account.

KITAY. By this Name not only the *Russians*, but also the *Tartars* and *Persians* denote *China*. The Error of former Geographers, who took this *Kitay* or *Cathay* to be a Country different from *China*, and situate North of it, has been sufficiently refuted since, and it has been made out by incontestable Proofs that the Name of *Cathay* was already several Ages ago given to the Northern Part of *China*; the Southern Provinces having been called *Mangi*.

KNEES, signifies a *Prince*, and is the highest Dignity among *Russian* Subjects, out of whose number the Czar chuses Vice-Roys, and *Woywodes*, or Governors. The *Russians* speaking of their Sovereign, use to call him *Weliki Knees*, Great Prince.

KNOUT. The severe Punishment used in *Russia*, which Capt. *Perry* describes at large, pag. 218. See also *Le Brun*, p. 403.

LEWEN DALER, see *Daler*.

METROPOLITAN, is an Ecclesiastical Dignity, a Degree above an Archbishop.

MORE, in Russian signifies *Sea*.

MURZA, among the *Tartars* denotes a *Prince*.

NISI, occurs in the name of a City called *Nisi*
Novo-

some difficult Words.

NOVOGROD, or *Nisi gorod*, and signifies *Novogrod* of the lower Country.

NOS, signifies in the *Russian* a Promontory or Cape. As for Instance: *Candenos, Svetoinos*, &c. In *England, Scotland* and *Norway* it is *Ness*.

NOVA, signifies *New* in *Russian*; it occurs in the Geography of *Russia*, as for instance: *Nova Russa*, i. e. New *Russa* in opposition to *Stara Russa*, Old *Russa*; *Nova Zemla*, i. e. New Land.

OKOLNITZEY. An inferior Degree of Privy-Councellors or Senators, who upon Vacancies are advanced to that of *Boyars*.

OSTROFF, or OSTROW. This Word frequently occurs in the Maps of *Russia*, and signifies an Island.

OZERA or OSERO, is likewise often to be met with in the Maps, and means a *Lake*; it is therefore a Tautology to say the Lake *Ivan Ozero, Bialozero*.

PATRIARCH. The chief Dignity in the Church of *Russia*, at present suspended. The *Russian* Clergy at first depended on the Patriach of *Constantinople* till the year 1588, when they set up a Patriarch of their own, upon the pretended Resignation of one *Hieronymus* Patriarch of *Constantinople*, or *Chio*, expelled by the *Turks*, who himself consecrated *Job* the first Patriarch of *Moskow*.

PODWODDEN, is an Order from the Czar to all his Subjects, injoyning them to furnish Passengers on the Road with Horses and other Necessaries.

POGOST, signifies the same with what the *Swedes*

An Explanation of

Swedes call *Karspel, i. e.* a District making one Parish.

POPE, signifies a *Priest* in *Russian*.

PROTOPOPE, is an *Arch-Priest*.

PRECASE. A publick Office in *Russia*, where all Affairs of Government, Civil, Ecclesiastical and Military are examined and determined by Chancellors thereto appointed; there were formerly 33 such *Precases* at *Moskow*.

PRISTAFF. A Gentleman appointed by the *Russian* Court to meet and receive foreign Ambassadors on the Frontiers, to attend them and see them provided with all Necessaries.

PUDDE, is 40 Pound Weight.

REKA, the *Russian* Word for *River*, often made use of in Maps.

RUBEL, was formerly an imaginary Coin in *Russia*, when Payments were made in Sacks full of *Copecks*, 100 of which in one Sack were called a Rubel; but of late the Czar has caused Pieces of them to be coined in Specie. The Value of a Rubel cannot be exactly determined because of the frequent Variations the Standard and Allay of it undergoes in *Russia*. It was formerly reckoned to be worth about two Specie-Dalers *German* Money, or nine Shillings Sterling *English* Money. But Capt. *Perry* says, pag. 7. that at his time a Rubel was worth full 100 *English* Pence, or 8 Shillings 4 Pence, after which, by recoining the Money, it was reduced to little more than half the former Value.

One RUBEL contains 100 *Copecks*.

some difficult Words.

A DENIN is half a *Copeck.*
An ALTIN is 3 *Copecks.*
A GRIVE is 10 *Copecks.*
A POLTIN or JASIMKE is 50 *Copecks.*
As to the foreign Species carried to *Russia*, the Merchants complain that the *Russians* will not take them unless under their intrinsick Value, in order to recoin them into a greater number of *Copecks* than they took them for, and so to pay them back with great Advantage. At the Author's Time an *Albertus-Daler* went for 80 *Copecks*, a *Banco-Daler* for 90, and a *Ducat* (two *Banco-Dalers*) for 180.

SLABODA, seems to signify any Place not walled in, either a Town, Suburbs, or Borrough.
STARA, signifies *old*. See *Nova*.
STEP, a *Russian* Word frequently to be met with in the Maps of *Russia* and *Siberia*, as also in *Isbrand Ides*'s Travels to *China*. It means a *Desart* or *Wilderness*.
STRELITZES, a sort of Foot Soldiery distinguish'd from common Soldiers by their Pay and Marks of Honour, like the *Janizaries* among the *Turks*: They formerly were the Czar's Foot-Guards, and lay in Garrison at *Moskow*, being sometimes to the number of 12000, sometimes 24000. Their frequent Rebellions have obliged the present Czar to break and disperse them into the most remote Garrisons in *Astracan*, *Siberia*, &c. where the remainder of them still go by the Name of *Strelitzes*.

VLADIKO

An Explanation of

VLADIKO, signifies a *Bishop*. It is derived from the *Russian* Word *Wlodars*, i. e. *Oeconomus*, *Dispensator*.

WELIKI, signifies *Great*, for instance, in *Weliki Permia*, Great *Permia*; *Weliki Novogrod*, Great *Novogrod*; *Weliki Knees*, Great Prince.

WERST, contains 3504 *English* Feet, or about two thirds of an *English* Mile, according to Capt. *Perry*'s Computation, pag. 3. Supposing, pursuant to the usual way of Computation in *Geography*, that one Degree contains 80 *Wersts*, 60 *English* and *Italian* Miles, 20 *French* and *Dutch* Leagues, and 15 *German* Miles,

One *German* Mile is reckoned to contain about 6 *Wersts*,

One League 4 *Wersts*,

Two *English* Miles are equal to three *Wersts*.

WOYWODE, a *Slavonian* Word variously applied: The Princes of *Walachia*, *Moldavia*, and *Transylvania*, are sometimes called *Hospodars*, sometimes *Woywodes*. In *Poland* that Name is given to the *Palatines*, or Governors of Palatinates. In *Russia* it seems to signify a Governor of a Province.

ZEMLA, signifies *Land* in the *Russian* Tongue. It occurs in the Name of *Nova Zemla*, which is as much as to say *New Land*. See pag. (56.)

The Termination of WITZ in proper Names, is a Mark of Nobility. For Instance, one *Alexander*, a Man of common Extraction, whose

some difficult Words.

whose Father's Name was *John*, calls himself *Alexander Ivanow*, (*Alexander*, *John*'s Son); but if he is of noble Birth, or ennobled, he will style himself *Alexander Ivanowitz*. This will serve to explain what is said, pag. 231. *viz.* That the Czar when in the Fleet, will not be called otherwise than *Peter Michailow*, to shew that in the Capacity of a Seaman he does not pretend to be better than any of his Subjects.

Several of the Christian Names among the *Russians* are used to be written according to their own way: Thus *Ivan* is written for *John*, *Wassili* for *Basilius*, *Fedor* for *Theodore*, *Afonassief* for *Athanasius*, *Stepan* for *Stephen*, &c. And here I must take notice from whence the Variation proceeds, that is observed in the Orthography of their Names in divers Authors of different Nations. *TH* is pronounced and written by the *Russians* as an *F*, in *Fedor* or *Feodor*, *Afonassief*; for *Theodore*, *Athanasius*. *B*, *V*, *W* and *F*, are often indifferently used for each other, by reason of the Affinity of the sound in the Pronunciation; for instance *Ivan* and *Iwan*; *Boinow* and *Voinoff*; *Basili*, *Vassili* and *Wassili*; *Kiow* and *Kiof*; *Rostow* and *Rostof*; *Ostrow* and *Ostrof*. *CZ* and *TZ* being pronounced like *TCH*, some write *Czar* and *Tzar*; *Czarewitz* and *Czarewitch*; *Czeremetow*, *Scheremetoff*, and *Tscheremetof*; *Czornogar*, and *Tschornogar*, *Menchicoff* and *Mentzikow*, &c.

THE
INDEX
OF
The Principal Matters contained in both Volumes.

NB. The Numbers between thefe two Crotchets ( ) refer to the fecond Volume.

A.

Academy *of the Marine*	180
Adrian, *the Patriarch of* Mofkow	66. 132 (404)
Atrofini, *See* Euphrofyne	
Ajuga, *a* Tartarian *Prince*	14. 20. (45. 86)
Alabafter Mountains	(431)
Alexander *the Great paſſes the* Tanais	(411. 412)
Alexei Petrowitz, *fee* Czarewitz	
Alexius Michalowitz, *the Czar's Father*	27. 133
Alliance between the Emperor Maximilian I. *and the Czar* Bafilius	257
Alonitz	204. 251
Anne, *the Czar's Niece, Dutcheſs Dowager of* Courland	45. (399)
Antiquities, near Samarcand	112. 185

——— *in*

The INDEX.

——— *in* Siberia	166. (14)
——— *about the* Wolga	(415)
Apraxin, *Grand Admiral*	4. 270
——— *accused of Male administration*	58. 245
——— *punished*	248
April-Mirth	263
Archangel, *Description of it*	(387)
——— *its Trade*	(393)
——— *its Trade to be removed to* Petersbourg	102. (392)
Areskin, *the Czar's first Physician*	104. 186. (328)
——— *dies*	246
Assemblies at Petersbourg	186
Astracan *described*	(418)
——— *suffers by Fire*	234
——— *the Country about it*	109. 157
——— *Roman Catholicks there*	253. 269
Astracan *Tartars*	161. (422)
Aurora Borealis	(432)
Azoff, *besieged by the* Don-Cosacks	88
——— *Wine to be planted there*	157
——— *restored to the* Turks	157. (315)

B.

Bagnios *or Bathing in* Russia	31
——— *how taxed*	65, 67
Bahadır, *a* Tartarian *Prince*	14, 20, 24
Barabinsky Tartars	274. (12)
Bathing, *see Bagnios*.	
Battus *or* Bathii, *a* Tartarian *King*	(212. 426)
Beards *in great Veneration in* Russia	142. (406)
——— *cut off by the Czar's Orders*	(405)
——— *are still wore by the Peasants and the Clergy*	87. 120. 142. 180
Bekewitz, *a* Circassian *Prince*	161. 198
——— *is killed*	198. 234
Bell, *a large one at* Moskow	130
——— *the sound of Bells is thought to be of a particular Virtue*	127
Birds *carried to* Petersbourg	142
Boards *or Colleges established for the Administration of publick Affairs*	183. 240. 241
Bratsky *Tartars*	(16)
Brimstone-Works	42. (416)
Bucharia, *See* Usbeck	194. 223
Bucharia *in the* Calmucks *Country*	(45. 86)

Bustucan,

The INDEX.

Buſtucan, *a* Calmuckiſh *Prince* 270
Butter, *Stone-Butter, a Mineral.* (52)
Butterweek, *the Carnival of the* Ruſſians. 121. 128

C.

Calmuck *Tartars.* 51. 83. 154. 159. 160. 270. 273. ſeqq (427)
Canals *for making Communications between ſeveral Rivers and Seas* 110. 177. 289. (409. 416)
Cantacuzeno, *Hoſpodar of* Walachia 91. 249
Cantimir, *Hoſpodar of* Moldavia 8. 91. 249
Caravans, *going from* Ruſſia *to* China *every Year,* 21. 168. 195
——— *of the* Calmucks 159
Carnival *of the* Ruſſians 121
Caſan *deſcribed* (414)
——— *conquered by the* Ruſſians 203
Caſpian Sea, *Expedition thither* 101. 154. 197.
——— *a Draught of it taken by the Czar's Orders* 154
Catharine Alexevna, *one of the Czar's Siſters* 27. 138
——— ——— *dies* 225
Catharine Jwanoffna, *one of the Czar's Nieces married to the Duke of* Mecklenbourg 45. 133. (399.)
Cedar Trees *in* Siberia *and* Ruſſia (46. 430)
Chancery *at* Petersbourg 45. 315
Changes *introduced in* Ruſſia 37. 111. 119. 121. (405)
Chimes, *at* Moſkow 127. 323
——— *at* Petersbourg 185. 304, 323
China. Ruſſian *Affairs with* China 13
——— *ſeveral Journeys thither* 101. 168. (3 385)
——— *a Caravan goes thither from* Ruſſia *every Year,* 21. 168. 195
——— *the* Ruſſians *are not allowed to ſtay there long,* 170. 172. 179
——— *the great Wall of* China 169
——— The *Emperor of* China, *ſee* Kamhi.
Chriſtenings *of the* Ruſſians 8. 33. (425)
Chriſtian Religion *propagated in* Ruſſia 173. (5. 7. 8. 40. 42. 61. 85. 89. 92.)
——— ——— *the State of it in* Perſia 253
——— ——— ——— *in* China 171. 172. 206. (35.)

Church

The INDEX

Church Service in Ruſſia   136
Circaſſia *deſcribed*   155
——— *a Prince of that Country, ſee* Bekewitz.
Civility, ſtrange ſorts of it.   137. 163. (386)
Clergy in Ruſſia, *their preſent State* 66. 86. 141. 173.
       221. 238. 280. 281. 324. (163. 179. 185)
Cloth made in Ruſſia   181 (429.)
Coach, how made uſe of by a Can of the Calmucks 83
Colonies, in Livonia   44, 45
——— *in* Ruſſia   191. (429)
——— *a* Finlandiſh *one in* Ruſſia   123
Colleges founded by the Czar   128
Colmogrod   (394. 431)
Conſecration of the Water in Ruſſia   85. (397)
——— ——— *of Houſes*   (407)
Contouche, *ſee* Kontaſch.
Coſacks *in* Ukraina *have great Privileges*   50
——— *are of two ſorts, viz.* Zaporowſky *and* Don-
   Coſacks   50. 68 88. (417)
——— *Freebooters, in other parts of the Czar's Domi-*
   nions   12. (10. 49. 428.)
Courland, *the State of it*   2
——— *the Duke of it*   ibid.
——— *the Dutcheſs Dowager of it*   191. (399)
Coin, the State of it in Ruſſia   73. 240. 252
Crim Tartars   87
Cronſlot *deſcribed*   345
Cryſtal in Siberia   (14. 50)
Cuban Tartars   113. 160. 196
Czar
——— *his Family and Relations*   27
——— *his Education*   38
——— *part of his Character*   19, 38. 189. 209
——— *makes Speeches*   15. 209
——— *is diſtinguiſhed in the Fleet only by the Name of*
   Peter Michailof, *and his Employment* 35, 153. 224.
       231. 270
——— *is Rear-Admiral*   26. 35
——— *is made Vice-Admiral*   36
——— *takes his Pay as General and Vice-Admiral* 60. 61
——— *skilful in Turner's Work*   205. 251
——— *is Patriarch himſelf, and Head of the Church and*
   officiates as ſuch   84. 85. 282
——— *undaunted in danger at Sea*   41
                                     ——— *his*

The INDEX.

―― *his Daughters* 45. 92
*A Mock-*Czar *of* Moſkow 90
*A Vice-*Czar, *ſee* Romadonoffky.
Czarewitz, *is but a Sergeant in the Army* 44
―――― *his Flight* 192
―――― *his Criminal Proceſs* 201. 228. (93. ſeqq.)
―――― *is ſentenced to Death* 228. (117. 200)
―――― *dies* 229
Czarewitz's *Conſort* 7
―――― *brought to Bed of a Princeſs* 33
―――――――――― *of a Prince* 104
―――― *dies* 105
Czarewitz *of* Siberia 203
Czar, Czarewitz, Czaritza, Czarewna, *the ſignification of theſe Words* 134. 203
Czarina, *the divorced* 208. 216. 244
―――― *her Brother executed* 243
Czarina *Dowager, ſee* Marvea, *and* Proſcovia.
Czercaſſes *in* Ukraina 50
Czeremetoff, *a General* 253. (402)
Czeremiſſes Tartars. (414)

D.

Dalai Lama, *High-Prieſt or Pope of the* Tartars 273. (20. 86)
Dangerous Voyage 22
―――― *Journey* 224
Daria, *a River that carries Gold Sand* 101. 154. 200
Days, long ones in Ruſſia 179. 334. (430)
Demetrius, *a Prince of the* Czariſh *Family aſſaſſinated,* 133. (249)
Diſcovery on the Eaſtern Ocean 178
―――― *of a new Iſland* (387)
―――― *of the Country of* Camſhatky (45)
Diſpenſary, at Moſkow 142. (428)
―――― *at* Peterſburg 305
Dogs that draw ſleds 13. (66)
Dolgoruki *diſgraced* 34. 204. 211. 233
―――― *another of that Name* 34. 245, 248
Dôrpt, *deſtroyed and the Inhabitants carried to* Ruſſia (429)
―――― *to be repeopled by the former Inhabitants* 45. 96
Drink in Ruſſia 179
Drinking-bout 92
Dwarfs 83. 285

E. Eaſter-

The INDEX.

E.
Easter-day, *how solemnized in* Russia   9
Elephant, at Petersbourg   10. 309
Elephants Teeth found not far from Veronitz   (411)
Emperor, this Title given to the Czar Basilius   257
────── *of* China, *see* Kamhi.
Entertainments in Russia   4, 26. 148
Esthonia *the State of it*   97
Euphrosyne *the Czarewitz's* Mistress   225. (160)
Executions   82. 153. 219. 243. (429)

F.
Fasts, how rigorously kept in Russia   54. 237. 333. 344
Fedor, *see* Theodore.
Finland, *the State of that Country*   46. 278
Fire, good Regulations against it   238. 315
Fleet, the State of the Czar's Fleet   231. 313. 346
Forces, the State of the Czar's Land-Forces 37. 40. 283
France, *Manufacturers and Artificers sent for from thence*   43. 184
Funerals   83. 111. 230. 246. 248. 256. 266

G.
Gagarin. *Prince, Governor of* Siberia   13. (89)
────── *his Care in propagating the Christian Religion* (8. 89)
────── *accused of Male-administration*   79
────── *his Magnificence*   151
────── *his Generosity towards the* Swedish *Prisoners* 12, 166
────── *loses the Government of* Siberia   246
────── *is hanged*   79
────── *his Daughter retires into a Monastery*   44
Genghiz-Can, *Emperor of the* Tartars, *a great Conqueror* (425)
Glass-house at Moskow   (429)
Globe of Gottorp   83. 186. 253. 309
────── *at* Moskow   142
Golden Fleece, a Conjecture relating to it   143
Gold Sand and Oar   11. 199. (14)
Government of Russia *is absolute*   48. 221. 282. (162. 164. 179. 195)
Guns and Gunfounderies   182. 206. 311. (395)

The INDEX.

H.

Harbour, at Reval	177. 346
——— at Dageroe	232
——— at Rogerwick	280
——— at Cronflot	346
Healths, how drunk at Court	7
Heathens, in the Russian Dominions converted,	173
(5. 7. 8. 40. 42. 61. 85. 89 92)	
Heats, excessive at Petersbourg	179, 332. 333
Hermits in Russia	(401)
Hermitage of a Patriarch	140
History of Russia imperfect	222
——————— part of it related (210. seqq. 241. seqq.)	
——— of their intestine Troubles	(249. seqq.)
——— of Siberia	(47)
——— of the Turks written by Cantimir	250
Holydays of the Russians, viz.	
——— New Year's-day	84
——— Twelfth-day	85
——— Radetili Sabbot	122
——— Butter-week	121. 128
Houses in Russia described 118. 126. 302 307. 337. (389)	
Huzza, the English Acclamation introduced in Russia	231

I.

Japan is believed to join with the Continent of Great Tartary	178
Jesuits, among the Chineze Embassy	14
——— in China	171. (22. 33.)
——————— are in distress	206
——— banished out of Russia	267
——— readmitted	278
Images in great Veneration among the Russians 82. 129.	
130. 152. 236. (400)	
——— are not bought or sold in Russia, but exchanged for Money	125
Impostor punished	235
Ingria, superstitious Peasants in that Country	96
Inhumanity, an Instance of it	233
Inquisition into the Mismanagement of the Revenue	47. 58
——— into Male-administration	192. 245. 247
——— against the Czarewitz and the late Czarina	
201. 208. 226. (93, seqq.)	
Iron Works	183. 205. 311. (50)

Ivan

The INDEX.

Ivan Alexiewitz, *the Czar's Brother*   27. 37. 45, 133. (398)
Justice how administred in Ruffia   152

K.

Kabacks, *or publick Houses belong to the Czar* 74. 179. 318
—— —— *built along the Roads*   (408)
Kamhi, *the present Emperor of* China, *his Character*   170. (31)
—— *favours the Christians*   171. 172 (35, 36)
Kamfky Tartars   (16)
Kardis, *a Peace concluded there between* Ruffia *and* Sweden   (226)
Kibick Tartars   199
Kitai, *signifies* China *with the* Ruffians. 125. (68. 413)
Kontafch, *a* Tartarian *Prince*   (12. 13. 45. 86)
Kuine, *see* Genghiz-Can.
Kutuchta, *High-Priest or Pope of the* Tartars.   (20. 86)

L.

Lange *sent Ambassador to* China   101. (3. feqq.)
—— *returns from thence*   206
Language, *those of* Livonia *and* Efthonia *differ*   100
—— —— *that of* Efthonia *has a relation with that of the* Oftiacks   (62)
Lapponia, *the State of that Country*   46
Learning *encouraged by the Czar*   128. 180. 183. 282. 318. 324. (274.)
Le Brun's *Travels through* Ruffia   (369. feqq)
Liberty, *whether it suits with the Temper of the* Ruffians   49
Library *at* Peterfbourg   177. 185. 253
—— *at* Mofkow   131
Linen, *incombuftible*   (413)
Linen *Manufacture*   181
Livonia, *State of that Country*   283
Livonians *tranflated into* Ruffia   45. (429)
—— *return home*   96

M.

Mahometan Tartars *in the Czar's Dominions*   161. (11)
Mamant *Bones found in* Siberia   12. 78. (15. 50)
Mammon, *a King of the ancient* Tartars   (415)
Mangafea, *a Town in* Siberia   (51. 55)
—— —— *Gulf of* Mangafea *or* Taffarfkoja   (47. 54)
Manifefto *of the Czarewitz's Procefs*   228. (93. feqq.)

Manu-

The INDEX.

Manufactures of Cloth   181
———— *of Linen*   ibid.
———— *of Silk*   157. 184. 193
———— *of Stockings*   43
Marble near Petersbourg   (431)
Marriages, humorous ones   89. 267. 285
Marvea, Czarina Dowager, dies   110
Mary, the Czar's Sister 27.138.211.244.(122.145.160.)
Masquerade   89
Maximilian I. *Emperor, concludes a League with the Czar* Basilius, *and gives him the Title of Emperor of* Russia   257
Mazeppa, *Hetman or General of the* Cosacks (299. seqq. 402.)
Menzikoff, *Prince*   322
———— *falls under the Inquisition*   58 245
———— *punished*   247
———— *assaulted by all the Inhabitants of a Village*   153
Michael Fedrowitz Romanoff, *the Czar's Grand-father elected*   (219. 263.)
Miletetzki, *Father and Son, Princes of* Georgia, *under the Czar's Protection*   91
Mineral Waters at Alonitz   204
———— *in* Astracan   250
Mines, discovered and opened in the Russian *Dominions* 10. 11. 155. 183. 200. 240. 269. (14.)
Mints in Russia   73
Mock-Czar of Moskow   90
Mock-Patriarch, see Sotoff.
Monasteries described   134. 137. 138. 139.(396)
———— *Places of Refuge for married and unmarried People*   44. 136
Money, scarcity of it in Russia   48. 80. 252
Mongal Tartars   223. 273. (18. 20. 86. 426)
Mordwa Tartars   (413)
Moskow *described*   124, seqq. (402. 428)
———— *decays by the Increase of* Petersbourg   126. 151
Mummies in Esthonia   98
Musick in Russia   188. (400)
———— *Method of teaching it*   189
Musk-cats in Siberia   (53)

N.

Narva, *the State of it*   45. 96. (429)
Nariskin, *a Family related to the Czar*   27. 225
Nassau *Streights*   (56)
Natalia *the Czar's Sister*   26. 27. 189
  — *dies*

The INDEX.

―― *dies* 27. 177
Natalia *the Czarewitz's Daughter* 33. 108
Navigation, a Method of teaching it 9 290. 327
New Year's Day how celebrated in Ruſſia 84
―――――――――― *in* China (29)
Nicon, *Patriarch of* Moſkow 132. 139. 140. (404)
Nien ſchantz, *demoliſhed* 42 298. 306
Niſi-Novogrod (413)
Nobility in Ruſſia, *the preſent State thereof* 48. 49.
 193. 221
―――― *at* Moſkow 150
Notebourg, *ſee* Sleutelbourg.
Northern Nations in Siberia (385)
Nova Dwinka, *a Fort near* Archangel (371. 431)
Nova Zemla (56)
Novogrod *the Great, deſcribed* 117
―――― *how brought under the* Ruſſian *Dominion*
 (215. 219)
―――― *the Governor of it uſed to treat with* Sweden
 (241. 245)
Nuns, how they take the Habit 145
―― *their way of Life* 135. 136

O.

Oak planted at Peterſbourg 31. 308
―― *for the building of Ships, fetched from* Caſan 290. 340
Oby *River* (10. 54)
Offices or Boards eſtabliſhed 183. 240. 241. 252. 315
Oranjenbaum, *Prince* Menzicoff's *Country Houſe* 350
Order of St. Andrew 80. 242. (402)
―― *of the Czarina* 81
Oſtiacks 13. 168. (13)
―――― *a Deſcription of that Nation* 173. (37, ſeqq.)

P.

Paddon, *Rear Admiral dies* 248
Patches, extravagant ones 149
Patriarch, his Houſe and Pontificalia at Moſkow 131, 132
―――― *a Liſt of the Patriarchs of* Moſkow (404)
―――― *the laſt of them, ſee* Adrian.
―――― *that Dignity ſuppreſſed* 66. 280
―――― *a Mock-Patriarch, ſee* Sotoff.
Pearls found in Ruſſia (394)
Peaſants, their Condition in Ruſſia 48. 118. ſeqq. 192.
 335. ſeqq.
Perſia, *the State of Affairs there* 251
―――――― *of the Chriſtian Religion in that King-*
 dom 253
 ― *the*

The INDEX.

————— *the King of* Perſia's *Character* 92
————— Ruſſian *Embaſſy ſent thither* 100. 195. 250
————— *an Ambaſſador ſent from thence to* Sweden (422)
Peter Alexewitz, *ſee* Czar.
————————— *the Czar's Grandſon, born* 104
————————— *is of a hopeful Genius* 108. 193. 265
Peter Petrowitz, *the Czar's ſecond Son, born* 108 (102)
————————— *declared preſumtive Heir to the Crown* 206
————————— *dies* 265
Peterhof, *the Czar's Pleaſure Houſe* 42. 350
Petersbourg, *deſcribed* 293. ſeqq.
————— *the irregular ſituation of it* 4. 306
————— *Number of Houſes there* 9. 177. 302
————— *whether like to be reſorted to by Travellers* 190
————— *is the Ruin of many People* 56. 191. 242. 300
————— *exceſſive Dearneſs there* 102. 151. 190
————— *liable to Inundations* 302. 319. 326. 328
Philaretus Romanoff, *Patriarch of* Moſkow, *the Czar's Great Grandfather* (260. 404)
Philotheus, *Archbiſhop of* Tobolſky, *converts the Oſtiacks to Chriſtianity* (40. 86)
Piper, *Count, the* Swediſh *Prime Miniſter, Priſoner in* Ruſſia 87. 103. (303)
Plays *to be introduced in* Ruſſia 188
Police, *eſtabliſhed at* Petersbourg 184. 188. 277
Pope, Knees Pope *or Mock Patriarch, ſee* Sotoff.
————— Tartarian *Popes, ſee* Dalai-Lama, *and* Kutuchta.
Poſts *how regulated in* Ruſſia 115
Preaching, *introduced in* Ruſſia 280. 324
Printing-Houſe *at* Petersbourg 183. 318.
Privileges *taken from the Nobility* 221
Product *of* Ruſſia 102. 119. (393)
Proſcovia, *Czarina Dowager of* Ivan Alexewitz, 45. 112. (398)
————— *her Daughters* (399)
Pruth, *the Action with the* Turks *on that River* 81. (315)
Pultava, *the* Swedes *defeated there* 163. 285. (303)
Puniſhment *of a backward Scholar* 242
Puniſhments *uſed in* Ruſſia 82. 153. (397. 402)

R.

Raindeer *deſcribed* 28. (378)
Rebellion *at* Aſtracan (424)
Religion, *the State of it in the* Ruſſian *Dominions* 70. 82. 84. 86. 120. 124. 173, ſeqq. 235. 236. 280. ſeqq. 324. 348. (8. 92.)

——— *of*

The INDEX.

|——— *of the* Samoieds | 29. (383) |
|——— *of the* Oſtiacks | (75. feqq.) |

Reval, *the State of that Town*   98. 283
——— *the Harbour there damaged*   177
Revenue, *the State thereof in* Ruſſia   47. feqq.
——— *a new Board for the Adminiſtration of it* 80. 241
Rhubarb, *a Product of* Ruſſia   305
Riga, *the State of that Town*   2. 283
Road, *a ſtreight one from* Peterſbourg *to* Moſkow 116
——— *planted with Trees, and provided with Inns* (408)
Romadonoffſky, *Vice-Czar of* Moſkow   5. 34. 36. 137.
                                                                                  152. 153
——————— *his Son*   200. 224. 231
Roman *Catholicks in* Ruſſia   253. 267. 268. 278. 309.
Romanoff, *the Czar's Family Name*   (249. 260)
Roſkolnicks, *a Sect in* Ruſſia   70. 82. 238
Ruſſians, *their Character*   17
——— *their way of Life and Cuſtoms* 118, feqq. (400)
——— *their Superſtition*   236
——— *their Buryings*   111. 121
——— *their manner of Sleeping*   118. 338
——— *their Remedies*   32. 205. (53)

S.

Sables   143. (9. 46. 64)
Samoieds *deſcribed*   27. (373. feqq.)
——— *their preſent Kings*   30. 43. 256
Saltpeter *in* Ruſſia   (422)
Salt *in* Ruſſia   53. 77. 155. 274. (6. 418. 431)
Schafiroff, *Baron, Vice-Chancellor* 8. 34. 43. 81. 82. 257
Schulimſky *Tartars*   (14)
Sea-Dogs   (380)
Seamen *how raiſed in* Ruſſia   53
Senators *and Councellors of State at the* Ruſſian *Court*,
                                                                                    34. (404)
Ships *built*   8. 14. 92. 225. 230. 267. 313. (410. 411.
                                                                                                                412. 414)
Siberia, *deſcribed*   12. feqq. (44. feqq.)
——— *of its former Czars or Kings*   203
Silk-worms *and Silk-Manufactures*   157. 184. 193
Silver Oar *in* Siberia   11. (50)
Sled, *Deſcription of a* Ruſſian *one*   114
——— *of a* Samoied *one*   (378)
Sleutelbourg, *formerly* Nôtebourg, Londs-crona, *or*
   Oreſchek   103. 298. (213. 244)
Soothſayers *among the* Oſtiacks   77
——— *among the* Samoieds   (384)

Sophia,

The INDEX.

Sophia, *the Czar's Sister*   27. 37. 137. 138
Sorbone, *the Project of some Doctors of the* Sorbone *for uniting the Churches of* Russia *and* Rome **281**. (353. seqq.)
Sotoff, Knees Pope, *or Mock Patriarch and Senator* 34 89 (399)
Spain, *Commerce with that Kingdom projected* 100
Step, *or great Desart in the Country of the* Calmucks   197. 199
——— ——— ——— *in the Country of the* Mungals (20)
Stephen *Bishop of* Permia *converts several Heathen Nations* (7. 61)
Sterlet, *a delicious Fish*   343. (15. 420)
Stolbowa, *a Peace concluded there between* Sweden *and* Russia (221. 269)
Streets *in the* Russian *Towns how paved,* 127. (389)
——— *at* Moskow *unsafe at Night* 128
——— *at* Petersbourg *have no Names* 310
Strelitzes, *often rebellious* 39. 144. (424)
Strelna-muise, *the Czar's Pleasure House* 42. 351
Strength, *a Man of extraordinary Strength* 264
Stroganoff, *a Family of rich Farmers in* Russia 77. 203. 235. (414)
Stumpf, *a Jesuit in* China 171. 208. (22.)
Swedish *Prisoners, their State in the* Russian *Dominions* 12. 163. 267. 277. 285. (339. 340)
——— ——— *sold for Slaves* 167. (340. 407)
Syrenia *a Country* (5)

T.

Tamerlan the Great   112. 273. (415)
Tartars,
— *of* Astracan ⎫
— Barabinsky |
— Bratsky |
— Calmucks |
— Crim |
— Cuban |
— Czeremisses   ⎬ *see under the respective Letters.*
— Kamsky |
— Kibicks |
— *Mahometan* Tartars |
— Mongals |
— Mordwa |
— Schulimsky ⎭
——— *their ancient Glory* (425)
——— *conquer* Russia (212)

Teeth,

The INDEX.

Teeth, black ones an Ornament with the Russian *Women* 27
Theodore, *or* Fedor Alexiewitz, *the Czar's Brother,* 37.
110. 133. 221
Tobacco Trade in Russia 75
Tobolsky, *the Capital of* Siberia (10)
———— *its Latitude* (59)
Tombs of the Czarish Family at Moskow 132. 134
——————————— *at* Petersbourg 108. 111. 230
Trade in Russia *suffers* 240. 252
Triumphant Entry of the Czar at Petersbourg 35
Trooyts, *a Monastery, described* (396)
Turks, *Affairs between them and* Russia 8. 43. 81. 82. 88. 196. 225. (315 317)
Turkish *History written by* Cantimir 250
Turnips, fine ones near Archangel (375)
Tweer, *a Town in* Russia 117

V. U.

Veronitz *described* (409)
Vice-Czar, see Romadonoffky.
Visits not usual in Russia 6
Ukraina, *the County of the* Cosacks, *its Privileges* 50. 68. 74
Vogulitzes, *a Nation in* Siberia (8. 46. 54)

W.

Waigats *Streights* (56)
Wagulitzes, *see* Vogulitzes.
War, Preparations of War against Sweden 255. 269
———— *against* Sweden, *Writings relating to it* 104. 256. (209. seqq. 235. seqq.)
Wine at Astracan 157. (421)
Wolga *River* 158
Wologda, *a Town in* Russia 102. (395. 430)
————— *a River* (430)
Women, their Condition in Russia 136. 147. seqq.
————— *whether they judge of the Love of their Husbands by being beaten* 149
————— *a design of sending them abroad to travel* 148
————— *of* Circassia 156
————— *of the* Calmucks (427)

AD-

ADVERTISEMENT.

WHILE thefe Sheets were printing, the publick Advices from *Ruffia* informed us, " That in the lateſt Letters from *Aſtracan*, the River which carries Gold-Sand, is called *Korr*, inſtead of *Daria*, which latter is the Name of a Lake ". This confirms in part the Conjecture in the Tranſlator's Preface, and determines the ſituation of the ſaid River, which is accordingly ſet down in the Map belonging to this Account, from M. *Reland*'s Map of *Perſia*, where he marks the River by the Name of *Cur*, anciently *Cyrus*, and the Lake by that of *Darja Schirin*, or *Lacus Irivan*.

Errata.

In the firſt Volume.

Page 25. l. 23. *dele* the Words: *Killed without Mercy.*
p. 43. in the Margin, for *p.* 27. read *p.* 30.
p. 45. l. 5. ſeq. there is a Miſtake in the Original as well as the Tranſlation. The Dutcheſs of *Mecklenbourg* is the elder Siſter, and the Dutcheſs Dowager of *Courland* the younger. See p. 113. and p. (399)
p. 61. in the Margin, l. 4. *dele, either.*
p. 67. l. penult. *& ultima, dele* the two Crotchets [ ]
p. 91. l. 38. after *Moſkow*, read, *The fourth of thoſe Princes was the latter's only Son, who being,* &c.
p. 120. in the Margin, l. 3. read *Villages.*
p. 145. l. 10. dele *any more.*
p. 234. lin. penult. read *deſtroyed by Fire.*
p. 340. l. 34. for *ſpurns*, read *ſpurs.*

In the ſecond Volume.

p. 26. l. 3. for *Parennius*, read *Parrenim.*
p. 32. l. 13. for *by*, read *with.*
p. 42. l. 32. for *we*, read *he.*
p. 193. l. 33. for *eſtabliſhed*, read *appointed.*
p. 260. l. 18. read *Philaretus.*
p. 265. l. 7. read *Fedrowitz.*
p. 384. l. 16. read *Sticks.*
 ibid. l. ult. for *p.* 19. read *p.* 29.

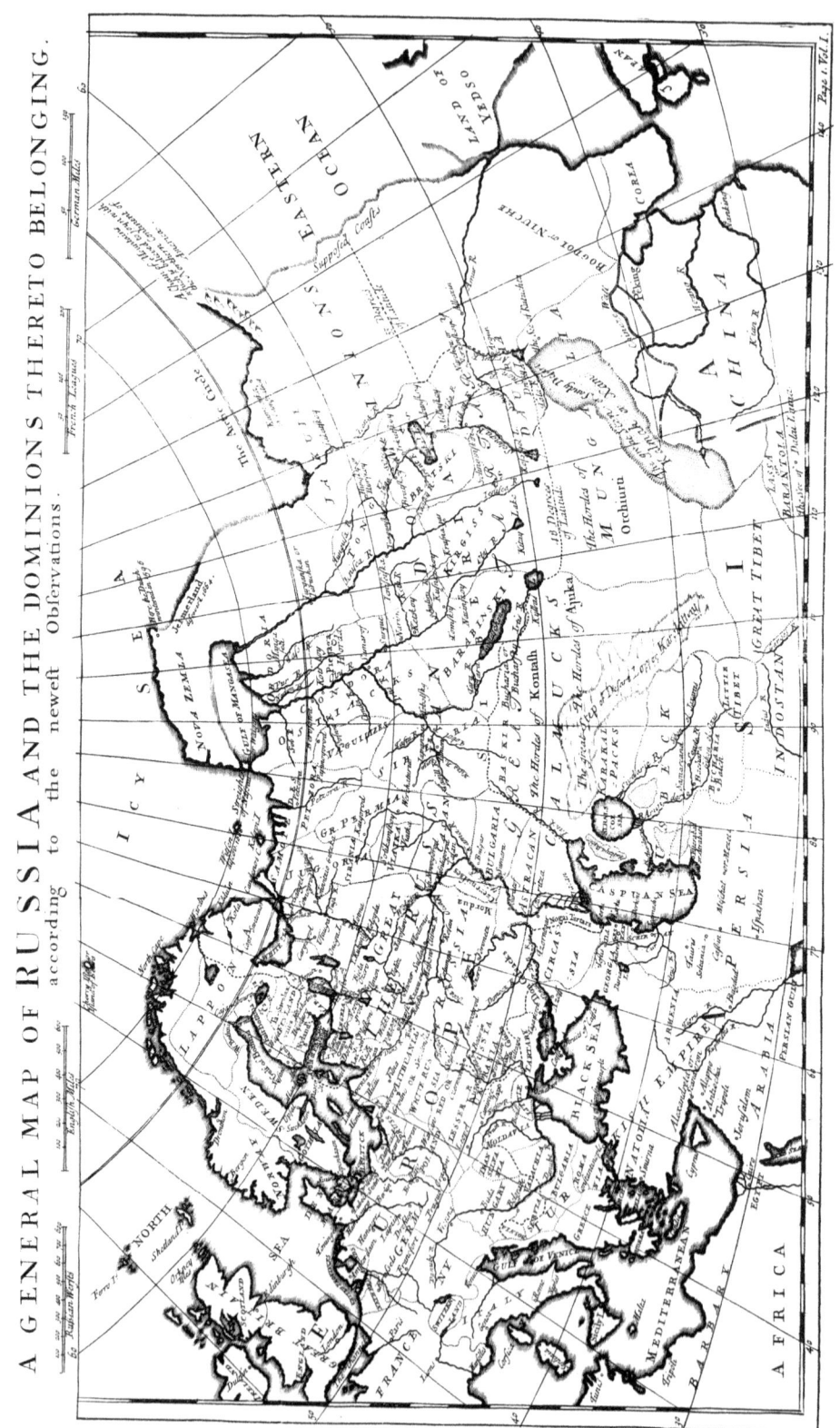

THE

PRESENT STATE

OF

RUSSIA, &c.

HE Campaign in *Holstein* being *January* brought to a Period in the Year 1713, upon the Surrender of the *Swedish* Army commanded by General *Steenbock*, some Months before which Event the Czar was returned to *Petersbourg*, I follow'd him thither, and on the 22^d of *February* 1714 arrived at *Dantzick*, where I found nothing new, except Duke *Ferdinand* of *Courland*'s being there.

January 1714. My Departure for Petersbourg.

He

He leads a very retired Life in that City where he is constantly residing to avoid being any longer exposed to the Vexations proceeding from the Misunderstanding between him and the Nobility of *Courland*, which still continues.

The State of Courland. From *Memel* to *Mitau* I found almost an universal Desolation; the Road being without Houses, Inhabitants, or Cattle. For the said Duchy has been visited with all sort of Calamities to such a Degree, that pursuant to a Computation that has been made, not the eighth Part of the former Inhabitants were then remaining.

Courland is divided into four Lieutenancies, and is governed by so many Land-raths or provincial Commissioners, who are the chief of the Country. Duke *Ferdinand* has declared void all the Regulations and Alterations made in the Government by his Nephew and Predecessor, because he had not attained full Age: Besides that he had no Right to do any thing of his own Authority without the Consent and Concurrence of the King and the Republick of *Poland*, his Lords Paramount, of whom he held the Duchy in Fief. For these Reasons he refuses to make good the Marriage Contract concluded between his Predecessor and the second Princess of the late Czar *Ivan*, and to pay the Dowry stipulated for her, amounting to forty thousand Rubels a Year, a Sum far beyond what the Country can afford; notwithstanding which he cannot hinder its being extorted from the Subjects.

Feb. 1714. *The State of Riga.* At *Riga* I found things still in a worse Condition; the Plague had carried off sixty thousand

The Present State of Russia. 3

sand Persons, and the Houses there bore a melancholy Aspect, by reason there had been eight thousand Bombs thrown into the Town by the *Russians* during the Siege. Many Families had withdrawn from thence before the Siege, and those that stayed behind complained particularly of the little Hopes they had of ever being paid some Millions which the *Poles* owe them, considering the Interest did already exceed the principal Sum.

On my Arrival at *Riga* I was informed, that his Czarish Majesty was expected there in a few Days, to take a View of the Fortifications. The Inhabitants were very busy in making extraordinary Preparations and embellishing their Houses, in order to go and meet the Czar in a splendid manner, and to receive him with all imaginable Demonstrations of Honour. The Czar upon his Arrival was well pleased with their Zeal, assuring the Magistrates of his constant Favour, and that it was his Intention to let the City enjoy their ancient Privileges without Disturbance. However the Oppression the Inhabitants laboured under, sufficiently shewed, that the Czar had no true Information of the Misery in *Livonia*. I observed on this Occasion, that the Nobility were for continuing under the *Russian* Government, as they entertained Hopes of being restored to their former Estates which they lost by the late *Resumption* during the *Swedish* Administration; but the Burghers and Country People wished to return to their former Allegiance. *The Czar arrives there.*

On the 23^d of *February* the Czar set out on his Return to *Petersbourg*. When I arrived *The Czar returns to Petersbourg.*

rived there, I was surprized to find instead of a regular City, as I expected, a Heap of Villages linked together, like some Plantation in the *West Indies*. However at present *Petersbourg* may with Reason be looked upon as a Wonder of the World, considering its magnificent Palaces, sixty odd thousand Houses, and the short time that was employed in the building of it.

An Entertainment given by Admiral Apraxin.

I was hardly arrived in this new Residence when Admiral *Apraxin* gave a magnificent Entertainment to the whole Court, and by his Czarish Majesty's Order, caused me also to be invited. This was the Day on which I entered upon my Apprenticeship, and paid pretty dear for my first Instructions. Being come to the Door of the Hall, I acquainted the commanding Officer who I was, but instead of being admitted, I had foul Language returned to me, and they kept me out by putting their Halbards across the Door. I alledged the abovesaid Invitation and my Character, but this had so little Effect that with the greatest Rudeness they turned me down Stairs. I forthwith applied to a Friend, who acquainted the Court with the rude Usage I had met with; soon after which the said Officer came to me to conduct me in, begging my Excuse for what had passed. On this Occasion a certain Minister gave me the following Lesson, that seeing the *Russians* knew nothing as yet from whence I came, I ran a great Hazard of exposing my self to the like Treatment for the future, unless I changed my plain though clean Dress, and appeared all trimmed over with Gold and Silver, and with a Couple of Footmen walking

The Present State of Russia.

ing before me, and bawling out, *Clear the Way*. I had no time to conn over this important Lesson, and to reflect on that rude Method of teaching People; for I was soon made sensible that I had a great many things more to learn. After having gulped down at Dinner a Dozen of Bumpers of *Hungary* Wine, I received from the Hands of the Vice-Czar *Romadonoffsky* (who is since dead) a full Quart of Brandy, and being forced to empty it in two Draughts, I soon lost my Senses, though I had the Comfort to observe that the rest of the Guests lying already asleep on the Floor, were in no Condition to make Reflexions on my little Skill in drinking.

The following Morning I had the Honour to meet an Ambassador of a Can of the *Calmucks* at the Chancery Office for foreign Affairs, a Man of a frightful and fierce Aspect; his Head was shaved all over, except a Lock of Hair which hung from the Crown down to the Neck, according to the Custom of that Nation. He delivered to the Great Chancellor on the Part of his Master, who is the Czar's Vassal, a Roll of Paper, throwing himself down to the Ground, and muttering for a long while something between his Teeth, which Complement being interpreted to the Great Chancellor by a *Jew*, he had this short Answer, that it was very well. This Ceremony being over the Ambassador resumed his fierce Air, and made but short Replies to the Questions we took the Liberty to ask him. However we learnt so much from some *Russians*, that he had brought from the Can for the Czar, a Saddle made

March. 1714. *An Ambassador of the Cal-mucks.*

all

6   *The Present State of* Russia.

all of Iron and very artificially wrought, and from the Can's Wife for the Czarina several Pieces of Silk with Figs and other Fruits of their Country.

Visits not usual in Russia.   Having left this dirty Company, I went according to the Custom in all polite Countries to pay my Respects to the chief Nobility of the *Russian* Court, in order to get acquainted with them. It is to be observed that it is not the Custom in *Russia* to send in word of one's coming, and that for this Reason it is very difficult to see their great Men. This was more than I knew, and therefore being gone to pay a Visit to a certain Boyar, none of his Servants would acquaint his Master with it, so that I was obliged to wait in the Court Yard half starved with Cold, till his Lordship came out. Having made my Complements to him, he asked me whether I had any thing else to say; upon my answering in the Negative, he dismissed me with this Reply: *I have nothing to say to you neither.* Though this Behaviour would not easily go down with me, yet I ventured to go a second time to visit another *Russian*. But as soon as he heard me mentioning my own Country, he cut me short and flatly told me; *I know nothing of that Country, you may go and apply to those to whom you are directed.* This put an End to my Desire of making Visits, and I firmly resolved never to go any more to any *Russian* without being desired, except to the Ministers with whom I had Business, who indeed shewed me all imaginable Civility. A Week after I met those impolite Courtiers at Court, and as they had observed his Czarish Majesty discoursing

discoursing with me for a considerable while, and treating me with a great deal of Favour, besides that he had given particular Orders to Admiral *Apraxin* to see me well entertained, they now both came up to me, and in a very mean and abject manner asked my Pardon for their Fault, almost falling down to the Ground, and very liberally offering me all their Brandy to oblige me.

But I now had done meddling with them, and turned my Eyes upon the *Czarewitz's* Consort of the Family of *Brunswick-Wolfenbuttel*, who was then just entering the Room. I was charmed with the Behaviour of that admirable Princess. For besides that she shewed all imaginable Submission to their Czarish Majesties, and an uncommon Humanity to all sorts of People, which gained her a general Love, her majestick Presence commanded also a particular Veneration from Persons of all Ranks and Degrees. However if one reflects how unfortunate she was as to her Marriage, that the old *Russians* were her Enemies, and that her Houshold was in the greatest Disorder, it is easy to imagine what inward Torments she had to smother. I shall mention more Particulars of her unhappy Fate, when I come to speak of her Death. *Of the Czarewitz's Consort.*

On the 14th of *March* there was a great Entertainment, occasioned by the publick Rejoycing appointed for the Victory obtained over the *Swedes* in *Finland* by Prince *Gallitzin*. On this Occasion I took notice for the first time of the Order observed in the drinking of Healths. The first was of *Bosche Milusti*, or the Mercy of God, the second *The drinking of Healths.*

to all brave Sailors, the third to all faithful Allies, next to all brave Soldiers, and so on.

Of the Hospodar of Moldavia. Demetrius Cantimir, the Hospodar of Moldavia, was newly arrived from Moskow, and was present at this Festival. He is a learned Prince, and of a very agreeable Conversation. In the late War he sided with the Czar, but soon after was obliged to fly; whereupon the Czar gave him several considerable Lordships in the Ukraina, which yield above twenty thousand Rubels a Year. His Consort was then already dead, she had borne him two Princes and two Princesses: The eldest of the Princes made a congratulatory Harangue in Greek to the Czar, who gave him a Present for it.

Prince Menzicoff's Son christen'd. Prince Menzicoff's new born Prince, now his only Son, was christen'd on the 23^d of March. The Mother, who is one of the most agreeable Ladies in Russia, was treated after the Custom of the Country on this occasion, according to which the Relations and others who are Wellwishers to the Family go to the Christening, and pay a Visit to the Woman in Childbed, kissing her and laying divers Presents on the Bed.

New Gallies built. During this Month sixty half Gallies were finished in the Docks, which afterwards with the rest were so advantagiously employed in the Skaren, or between the Islands on the rocky Coast of Finland, that Sweden felt it grievously enough.

Advice from Constantinople. The Czar received a Courier from Baron Schafiroff at Constantinople, with Advice that he was on the Point of taking his leave of the Port, so soon as the settling of the Limits was brought to a Conclusion, for which

The Present State of Russia.

which End two Commissaries had been sent on each Side to *Azoph*.

In *April* the Czar caused an exact List to be taken of all the Houses at *Petersbourg*, the Number of which were found to be 34,550, reckoning greater and less together.

April 1714. *Number of Houses at Petersbourg.*

An Express came from *Moskow* with Advice that the Ambassador of the *Tartar Can* of *Usbeck* was arrived there, and might be expected at *Petersbourg* in a few Days.

An Ambassador from Usbeck on the Road.

The Czar issued an Order forbidding on a severe Penalty of great Fines and corporal Punishment, the using of Oars on the River *Neva*, and enjoyning the constant Use of Sails after the Ice should be gone off: Notwithstanding the frequent Misfortunes that have happened to People on the crossing of that River, and that it was proposed to the Czar to make a Bridge on Pontons over it, the Duty on which would bring in a great Revenue, yet it prevailed nothing, he being resolved to force his *Russians* to learn Navigation, which forcible Method has actually made many an able Sailor.

A forcible Method of teaching Navigation.

The Festival of *Easter* was celebrated with particular Pomp, when large Amends were made for the severe and pinching Abstinence, to which the *Russians* are kept during the preceding *Lent*. Their Mirth, or rather Madness in those Days, is inexpressible, it being their Opinion, that he who has not been drunk at least a dozen times, has shewn but little of *Easter* Devotion. Their Singers in Churches are as extravagant as any of them, and it was no little Surprize to me to see two Parties of them, who fell out among themselves at a publick House, come to Blows,

The Easter Festival of the Russians.

Blows, and beat each other with great Poles so furiously, that several of them were carry'd off for dead. The most remarkable Ceremony in the said Holidays, is, that the *Russians* of both Sexes present each other with painted Eggs, giving the Kiss of Peace, the one saying, *Christos woskres*, Christ is risen, and the other answering, *Waistino woskres*, verily he is risen; whereupon they exchange their Eggs, and so part. For this Reason many Persons, particularly Foreigners, who delight in that Way of kissing the Women, are seen rambling up and down with their Eggs the whole Day long. The Clergy put a spiritual Interpretation upon this Custom, as if done in Remembrance of *Christ*'s Resurrection, which, they say, is like Chickens coming forth out of Eggs.

The Persian Elephant. The Elephant sent as a Present to the Czar by the King of *Persia*, was also produced in his rich Trappings, to make a low Bow before the Palace. The *Armenians*, his Leaders, told us, that when they arrived at *Astracan*, the Russians of that Place paid almost divine Honours to that Beast, and even some hundreds of them took their Knapsacks, and accompany'd him like an Idol above forty German Miles. This Beast not being able to bear the cold Air, notwithstanding a House was purposely built for him, and heated in the Winter time, dy'd three Years ago, and his Skin was stuffed. He stood the Czar every Day in fifteen Rubels for Brandy, Currants, Rice, and Attendance.

Advices from Siberia. Some Years ago the Czar desired of the King of *Poland* a Man experienced in Mineral

The Present State of Russia.

ral Works, to give Directions about the Mines already discovered in *Russia*, and to find out where others might be opened. Upon this one M. *Blüher* went thither, and was sent by the Czar farther into *Russia* and *Siberia*. After having been on this Journey eighteen Months, he returned to *Petersbourg* in company of Prince *Gagarin*, Governor of *Siberia*, and gave me the following Account.

From *Mosko* he went directly to *Tobolsky*, the Metropolis of *Siberia*, from thence turning sometimes to the left, and sometimes to the right, he proceeded some thousands of *Werfts* farther into *Siberia*, meeting with several Places where Copper and Silver Works might be established. The Boyars and Sub-Governours have set People to work in several Parts up and down the Country, but things are so ill managed, that the Profit is not like to defray the Expences. Of this he made Report to the Czar, representing that if he was to go again and take the Work in Hand, he ought to be provided with a good Number of Men, and a considerable Sum of Money to dispose of as he should think fit; but the Senate who were not sensible of the Profit, and pretended that the Expences should be refunded out of the Produce of one Year, opposed his Design. However the Czar assured him that as soon as he had Peace, he would set about it in good earnest. Prince *Gagarin* brought Gold Dust with him, of which the said *Blüher* made an Essay in the Czar's Presence, when one Pound Weight of it was found to yield fourteen Ounces of pure Gold. The Prince acquainted

ed only his Czarish Majesty with the Secret where the *Russians* had found the said Gold Dust. *Siberia,* according to *Blüher*'s Report, is a plentiful Country, where there is Store of Cattle, Corn, and Fruits. The Governour has only four Companies of regular Forces, but the Inhabitants are a sort of *Cosacks* or Free-booters, who upon his Orders are immediately mounted. There are in *Siberia* about nine thousand *Swedish* Prisoners, Officers and Subalterns included, who indeed are not put to hard Labour and the hunting of Sables, in which none but *Russian* Prisoners are employed, however they lead a miserable Life. There are only at *Tobolsky* upwards of eight hundred Officers who are poorly dressed like Peasants, wearing nothing but Frocks; they receive nothing for their Subsistence neither from their King nor from their Relations, so that they are obliged to do Day-Labourer's Work for the *Russians.* Some of them make Cards, (some Packs of which Prince *Gagarin* brought to the Czar) others turn Snuff-Boxes out of an unknown sort of huge Bones which they dig out of the Earth. Prince *Gagarin,* whom they almost adore in *Siberia* on account of his Liberality and good Nature, has distributed near fifteen thousand Crowns among the Prisoners during the three Years of his Government. They have built a *Swedish* Church with their own Hands, and have a Minister, who was formerly of the *Lutheran* Church at *Petersbourg,* but by speaking some unguarded Words incurred the Czar's Displeasure, and was banished into *Siberia.* A certain *Swedish* Lieutenant Colonel, who was likewise

likewise for some Reasons exiled beyond *Siberia* among the *Oſtiacks*, lives very well there: He has so far insinuated himself into the Affection of the Inhabitants, that they let him want for nothing, and consult him about all their Affairs. He told M. *Blüher*, that he willingly would end his Days there, were he allowed to send for his Family. The Engineer M. *La Val*, who came into *Ruſſia* with the famous M. *Le Fort*, and likewise fell into Disgrace and was sent to the Frontiers of *China*, lately dy'd there: He had so well settled himself in those Parts, that when the Czar forgave him and recalled him, he excused himself, and offered to his Majesty to build a Fortress on the Frontiers of *China*, with which Proposal the Czar was pleased, and ordered to give him all possible Encouragement; but the *Chineſe* opposing the said Work in the Beginning, and M. *La Val* dying afterwards, the whole Design was left unfinished. Prince *Gagarin*'s Government extends as far as the Dominions of *China*, and he appoints Sub-Governors in the Parts lying beyond the Rivers *Jeniſea* and *Lena*, with whom he keeps Correspondence after a particular manner. The Courier gets into a Sled, which is twenty Foot long, and two and a half broad, and is drawn with a surprizing Swiftness either by four Dogs or two Men furnished with large Scates like those of the *Lapponians*. At *Tobolsky* M. *Blüher* saw the Embassy that was then come from *China*; Prince *Gagarin* caused them to be received on the Frontiers of *Siberia*, and all their Expences to be defrayed: When they went to pay him a Visit

at

at *Tobolsky*, he sent his own Coaches and Servants to meet them with great Pomp. In the Coaches they smoaked Tobacco and did not quit their Pipes till they alighted. During Dinner they called again for Tobacco, but the Prince excused himself, alledging that this was not the Custom in *Russia*; but after Dinner he caused a Pipe to be presented to one of them who appeared to distinguish himself from the rest, but he refused it, saying: *They were seven Ambassadors who had dined with him, and as they were all equal in Rank, they ought to be equally used.* They afterwards delivered their credential Letters, it being the Custom of the Emperours of *China* on ordinary Occasions, to send their Ambassadors only to the Czar's Governour, or Vice-Roy of *Siberia*. The said Letters were written in the *Latin*, *Chinese*, and *Mongalian* Languages. The Ambassadors told the Prince, that there was like to be a War between their Master and *Bahadir* a powerful *Tartarian* Prince, and that they were sent to Cham *Ajuga*, whose Dominions are situate between those of Cham *Bahadir* and *China*, to persuade him to a Rupture with *Bahadir*, or at least to a Neutrality. M. *Blüher* added to this Account, that the said Ambassadors had already been two Years on the Road, and that he was told there were three Jesuits privately among them, who upon their Return were to give an Account to the Emperour of what they had observed in their Travels.

May 1714
The Czar's new Ships.

Three Men of War bought in *England* arrived at *Riga*, and another was launched at *Petersbourg*, on which Occasion the Czar appeared

The Present State of Russia.

peared in a very good Humour, and discoursed with great Judgment on the prosperous Success of his Ship-building. Among many other notable and ingenious Discourses which I heard held by his Czarish Majesty on the like Occurrences, there is one very remarkable, which he directed to his old *Russians* sitting round about him, on Board that new launched Man of War, reproving them for not following the Example of other *Russian* Ministers and Generals, and taking Encouragement from their Experience.

"Brethren, *said he*, who is that Man a- *His Speech.*
"mong you, who thirty Years ago could
"have had only the Thought of being em-
"ployed with me in Ship Carpenter's Work
"here in the *Baltick*; of coming hither in
"a *German* Dress to settle in these Countries
"conquered by our Fatigues and Bravery;
"of living to see so many brave and victo-
"rious Soldiers and Seamen sprung from
"*Russian* Blood; to see our Sons coming
"home able Men from foreign Countries;
"to see so many outlandish Artificers and
"Handicrafts Men settling in our Domini-
"ons, and to see the remotest Potentates
"express so great an Esteem for us? The
"Historians place the ancient Seat of all
"Sciences in *Greece*, from whence being
"expelled by the Fatality of the Times,
"they spread in *Italy*, and afterwards dis-
"persed themselves all over *Europe*, but by
"the Perverseness of our Ancestors were hin-
"dered from penetrating any farther than in-
"to *Poland*, though the *Polanders* as well
"as the *Germans* formerly groped in the
"same

"same Darkness in which we have lived hitherto, but the indefatigable Care of their Governours opened their Eyes at length that they made themselves Masters of those Arts, Sciences, and Improvements of Life that formerly *Greece* boasted of. It is now our Turn, if you will seriously second my Designs, and add to your blind Obedience a voluntary Knowledge, and apply your selves to the Enquiry of Good and Evil. I can compare this Transmigration of Sciences with nothing better than the Circulation of the Blood in the human Body, and my Mind almost gives me they will some time or other quit their Abode in *England*, *France*, and *Germany*, and come to settle for some Centuries among us, and perhaps afterwards return again to their original Home into *Greece*. In the mean time I earnestly recommend to your Practice the *Latin* Saying, Ora & labora, pray and work, and in that Case be persuaded, you may happen even in our Life-time to put other civilized Nations to the Blush, and to carry the Glory of the *Russian* Name to the highest Pitch."

Character of the Russians. The old *Russians* listened with a profound Silence to their haranguing Monarch, applauding him afterwards with a loud *Je je prawda* ('tis very true) and offering a ready Obedience. But immediately after they fell again with great Eagerness to the Center of their Happiness, I mean the Brandy-Bowl, leaving the Czar, who appeared very thoughtful, to study how to work about their Conversion, and compass the great Ends he had proposed to himself. The Untowardness of those

The Present State of Russia.

these People made me astonished as well as some *Russian* Ministers: The many Instances of their Character, which I had occasion farther to observe in Process of Time, convinced me of the Truth of the Picture, which a certain *French* Gentleman has drawn of that Nation in a Letter, which for its Likeness I think deserves being inserted here. " The " *Russians*, says he, are the most conceited " and proudest of all Mankind; formerly " they looked upon all other Nations to be " *Barbarians*, and fansied themselves the on- " ly polite, sensible and ingenious People in " the World. Since the time that his Czar- " ish Majesty has perceived the Ridiculous- " ness of this Conceit, and that he has forc'd " his Subjects to take Instructions from Fo- " reigners, they obey, but with such inve- " terate Pride that it hinders them from pe- " netrating into what they are taught, and " makes them upon the first Tincture of " Knowledge fansy themselves more learned " and more able than their Masters, whom " they hate and vex; it being impossible that " Presumption should yield to the Obliga- " tions they owe them. What is called " Glory, Honour, and Disinterestedness, is " but a Chimera with them. They cannot " conceive any other Object of the Soul but " what terminates in the Senses; nor can " they comprehend that a Foreigner of Di- " stinction who comes to serve them, should " be guided by a Principle different from " that of getting Money; hence it is that " they are continually railing among them- " selves at Foreigners, for selling their Lives " for a little Money." Every Man will be
convinced

convinced by the Sequel of this Journal, that though this Gentleman knew the *Ruffians* perfectly well, yet he did not mention all their Qualities: But the Czar himself by his excellent Judgement soon thoroughly discovered the Faults of his Subjects whom he used to call a Herd of Brutes whom he put into the Shape of Man, but despaired of ever breaking their Obstinacy or rooting up the Perverseness of their Hearts. This is the Reason that the Travels of so many of the young *Ruffian* Nobility, which they undertake well stored with Money, but without any Instruction or Manuduction, produce no other Effect than their picking out what is vicious in *Germany* and other Countries, with a Neglect of that which is good, and upon their Return into *Ruffia* making such a Compound of *Ruffian* Vices with it as proves destructive both to the Body and the Soul, and will hardly ever leave Room for true Virtue and sincere Piety in *Ruffia*. There were some *Ruffians* indeed who in their Travels by their Politeness and the good Behaviour they had acquired, had gained the Affection and Esteem of some Persons in *Germany*, who by their Example were induced to believe that it was possible for a *Ruffian* to become an honest and civilized Man, and consequently that the Czar might at length be able to model his Subjects into true Humanity: But should one of those *Germans* go into *Ruffia* to search for such Travellers of whom there are some thousands, and meet one or other he was formerly acquainted with, it would be hard for him to know them again after that Metamorphosis which the greater part of them (I do not say all

The Present State of Russia.

all) have undergone: For they have not only thrown off again that Politeness they had acquired in foreign Parts, and shew an intolerable Pride on account of what they may have learned there of bodily Exercises (for to cultivate the Mind was not their Design;) but also are returned again to their former Way of Life. However I must make this Exception, that a good Genius of some Russian or other, if he stays in foreign Parts, may be cultivated and improved, and it can be made out by several Instances that it is possible for a young Russian, by reason of that Sagacity and Cunning which is natural to almost the whole Nation, to attain by the means of a good Education and Instruction abroad, to the same Degree of Perfection as Children of other civilized Nations. Those Russians of Distinction, who partly are still in *Germany*, partly are returned Home, and have distinguished themselves by their Capacity, Prudence and polite Conduct, are Instances of this Assertion to the Reproach of their Countrymen. As for that Notion which the World entertains of the Czar's extensive Knowledge, the same is entirely agreeable to Truth; and there is no Man who rightly knows the Czar that can question his being the chief and most judicious Minister, the most experienced General, Officer and Soldier of his Empire, the most learned of all Russian Divines and Philosophers, well versed in History and Mechanicks, an able Shipwright, and still a better Sailor; in all which Sciences though he has but dull and resty Disciples, yet he has put the State of War upon an admirable foot, and brought his Soldiery,

diery, particularly the Infantry, to that Reputation that they yield to none in the World, though they are still in great want of good Officers. In short, as far as Fear and blind Obedience rather than Wisdom of Government can carry things, the Russians surpass all other Nations, and should the Czar enjoy the Scepter but twenty Years longer, he will do more in his Dominions by this Obedience than ever any other Monarch did.

The Arrival of the Ambassador of Usbeck, and his Audience and Commission.

On the 17th of *May* arrived at *Petersbourg* the Ambassador of the Can of *Usbeck* with sixteen Persons of his Retinue coming from *Moskow* where he had left his Wife, his Son, and above thirty of his Servants. The following Day he had Audience of the Czar. According to a certain Ceremonial that had been agreed upon, the Ambassador ought to have made his Speech kneeling, but the Czar was pleased to wave that Ceremony for that time, and therefore admitted him only at Prince *Dolgorucki*'s House. The Ambassador upon his entering the Room put his Hands on his Knees and made three very low Bows, then he made his Speech, which being interpreted, the Czar caused a short Answer to be made to it only by a Secretary (whereas *Persian* Ambassadors are answered by the Great Chancellor) and assured him of his Favour by laying his own Hand on his Head. His Commission consisted of three Articles. First, that his Prince and Master *Hadgi Mahomet Bahadir Cham* rejoyced at his Czarish Majesty's Success in War and the Increase of his Power, and recommended himself to his Favour and Protection. Secondly, he desired the Czar to enjoin his Vassal the *Tartarian* Can *Ajuga*,

to keep good Neighbourhood and Peace with him, he seeming inclined to join with the *Tartars* subject to *China*, and to stir up others of his Neighbours against him: For which the Can of *Usbeck* offer'd in Acknowledgment fifty thousand Soldiers to the Czar, who should be always ready to march upon his Command. Thirdly, for a farther Testimony of the Can's Friendship he offer'd a Passage through his Dominions for the Czar's yearly Caravans to *China*, and even proposed to enter into a Treaty of Commerce with *Russia*, by which an incredible Advantage was to accrue to his Czarish Majesty, considering the Caravans were at that time obliged to make their Journey to *Peking* with great Inconveniency and in a Year's time, through the whole Extent of *Siberia*, following the Windings and Turnings of the Rivers, there being no beaten Road; whereas they might go thither through his Master's Dominions on a good Road in four Months. He afterwards laid many Silks and other *Chinese* and *Persian* Goods together with rare Furrs at the Czar's Feet as a Present from his Master; telling withal that he left some *Persian* Horses and Beasts behind at *Moskow*, and expressing his Concern that a fine Leopard and an Ape died on the Road. In this Speech he never styled the Czar otherwise than the wise Emperor, which with them is the highest Title of Honour. His Name was *Atscherbi*, being about fifty Years of Age, of a lively and venerable Aspect, he wore a long Beard, his Habit was according to the Fashion of the Eastern Nations, and on his Turbant he wore an Ostriche's Feather, which, as he reported,
only

only Princes and Lords of the first Rank are allowed to wear in his Country.

Our dangerous Voyage to Cronflot.
The Czar afterwards sent him Word, to go with the Great-Chancellor, Count *Golofkin*, on Board a *Snow*, called the *Rake*, and to follow his Majesty to *Cronflot*. On the 20th, two Hundred Half-Gallies put to Sea from *Petersbourg* in the finest Order, and under continual Firing of their Guns, for Diversion sake, and arrived the next Day at *Cronflot*. On the 21st, about Dinner time, which was the Hour appointed, we repaired on Board our *Snow*, where we found the Ambassador of *Usbeck*, and seven Senators. The Weather was sultry when we sailed, and we had a gentle Breeze. Two Leagues off of *Petersbourg*, by the Unskilfulness of our *Russian* Captain, we got among the Flats, which extend two Leagues into that Sea, as far as *Cronflot*, till at length our Ship stuck on the Sand. The Sailors and Marines worked till seven in the Evening, when we got off; and the Captain, who was not apprehensive of any Storm, gave plainly enough to understand, that he had Orders to exercise the Patience of the Ambassador of *Usbeck*, and of the rest of the Company, for some Days on the Water; but at nine in the Evening, there arose such a violent and dreadful Storm, that the like was not remember'd at *Petersbourg* for the last four Years. What made our Condition the more dangerous, was the little Experience of the Captain, and his Mate, both *Russians*, the old and leaky Ship in which we were, the Flats lying round about us, and the Storm more and more increasing; upon our asking the Mate, what was to be done, and
whe-

whether there was any Hope of our escaping, he folded his Hands together, and answered, *Bog snait,* God knows. After twelve at Night the Boats ty'd to our Vessel were beat to pieces, and we lost our best Anchor, and with it all Courage, thinking of nothing but Death. The Ambassador of *Usbeck,* who never had been on such a Sea before, looked as pale as Death, and at last wrapt himself up in a Silk Quilt, and caused his Priest to sit down on his Knees before him, and read something out of a Book of the Prophet *Aly,* they being of the *Persian* Religion. Towards Morning the Storm began to abate, when we saw the Vessels that were driven from their Anchors, floating in the Sea. About ten the same Morning, a Captain arrived in a *Boyer* from *Cronslot,* being sent by the Czar to look out for us, and to enquire how we fared. He was obliged, by reason of the Flats, to step into a Boat, and told us of the great Concern his Czarish Majesty had expressed all Night on our account, and desired us to endeavour to come away; whereupon he left as, and we were forc'd to continue there the whole Day. On the 23^d about Noon, the same Captain came to us again in a Half-Galley, which towed us, but slowly, out of the Flats, so that in the Evening we got within four Leagues of *Cronslot.* On the 24th we had a gentle Side Wind, which carried us to *Cronslot,* where we at length arrived at three in the Afternoon. The whole *Russian* Fleet was ranged in a Line without the Harbour, and saluted our *Snow* with all their Guns by the Czar's Order, that Honour being designed for the Vice-Czar *Romadonoffsky,*

donoffsky, who was on board with us. His Czarish Majesty, with his Court, was on board the *Catharine*, to see us come up to the Shoar, and as soon as we had cast Anchor, sent us Orders to stay on board till he came to us. After having congratulated us on our safe Arrival, he bantered us for being so brave Seamen, went into our Cabin, and stay'd there above two Hours. The Ambassador of *Usbeck* caused divers Fruits of his Country to be served up, and sent for his Singers and Musicians. The Czar was most pleased with the two Singers, and their odd Tunes, which they accompanied with the clapping of their Hands, whistling with their Mouths, and strange Gestures.

The Usbeck's Ambassador's Accounts.

The Czar asked the Ambassador several Questions relating to his Country and its Neighbours. He gave the following Account, which the Czar was graciously pleased to repeat to us in *High-Dutch*. That as to himself, he was his Master's first Servant, and had been formerly his Governor; the Can was upwards of twenty Years of Age, and married a Year ago the King of *Persia*'s eldest Daughter, with whom he had a rich Dowry; his Country was called *Usbeck*, and the Residence *Chiva*, which only consisted of Tents and Huts, and was never fixed on a certain Place; the Can was a Sovereign Prince, but his Authority was limited by a sort of a Senate; the Country of *Usbeck* bordered upon *China*, *Indostan*, and *Persia*, with which Nations they had hitherto lived in Amity; but their Wars had generally been with the neighbouring *Tartars* on this side *Russia*; his Master was able to raise an Army of two hundred thousand Men, all on Horseback; (which his Czarish Majesty judged to be understood of all his Male-Subjects, reckoning old and young;) hitherto they had no Cannon, nor made use of them till of late, when they took some from their Enemies, which, however, were neither of the same Size, nor gave such a Report, as those of the Russians; the strangest of their Neighbours was the Great *Mogul*, on Account of his Government, and the odd Way of obtaining it; for if the reigning Emperor had several Sons, certain Governments were assigned to each of them; but they gave their Orders out of a Prison, to which they remained constantly confined during their Father's Life-time; but upon his Death they were set at Liberty, and every one of them gathered as many Forces in his Government as he could raise, with which they were fighting among themselves, till one overcame the rest, who caused the others to be put to Death, killed without Mercy, which was the Case of the present Emperor, who has now five Sons himself. The Czar took this Opportunity of reasoning on Cruelty and Tyranny, and commended the *Turks* for having this thirty or forty Years past changed their Maxims of State, as to this Point, to which he added something more in Praise of the great *Chineze* Empire, and then retired to his House. Upon our parting, the Ambassador told us, he was informed that we also came from a remote Empire, and that our Masters formerly beat the *Turks*, and raised the Siege of *Vienna*; he wished to us as well as to himself, that our long Journies might be recompensed penfed by good Succefs in our refpective Commiffions; defiring us at the fame time to give him this Mark of Friendfhip on our Return to *Petersbourg*, as to come to dine with him, which Honour he would not forget to remember to his Mafter.

The Czar goes on an Expedition in Finland.
On the 31ſt of *May* the Czar, in Quality of Rear-Admiral, failed with his Fleet of Men of War and Gallies from *Cronflot* to the Height of *Helfingfors*; during which Abfence of the Czar from *Petersbourg*, there happened but few things, of which I fhall take notice.

July, 1714. Ruffian Entertainments.
Princefs *Natalia*, the Czar's own Sifter, gave a noble Entertainment at *Petersbourg*, which was an Opportunity for me to obferve the Ruffian Cuftoms in Feafting. Before they fit down to eat, the Mafter and Miftrefs of the Houfe, even the Czar and Czarina, as well as the chief Nobility, prefent to their Guefts with their own Hands a fmall Cup of Brandy on a Plate, and among particular Friends the Miftrefs falutes her Guefts with a Kifs. After fitting down the firft Courfe is ferved up, confifting of cold Meat, Hams, Saufages, Jelly-broth, and divers forts of Meat dreffed with Oil of Olives, Onions and Garlick, which is left on the Table above an Hour; then come the Soups, roaft Meat, and other hot Victuals, which make up the fecond Courfe, and laft of all the Deffert. The Healths are begun at the very Beginning of the Meal, in large Cups and Glaffes in the Form of Bells. At the Entertainments of People of Diftinction, no other Wine is to be feen but that of *Hungary*, the Ruffians affecting a particular Profufenefs that way,

The Present State of Russia. 27

way, to shew their Magnificence. All the Beauties of *Petersbourg* appeared at this Entertainment, they were already at that time in the *French* Dress, but it seemed to sit very uneasy upon them, particularly the Hoop-Petticoats, and their black Teeth were a sufficient Proof, that they had not yet weaned themselves from that Notion so fast riveted in the Minds of the old *Russians*, that white Teeth only became Blackmoors and Monkeys: However, the like Prepossessions have since been so far removed, that a Stranger, who comes into a polite Assembly at *Petersbourg*, will hardly believe he is in *Russia*, but rather, as long as he enters into no Discourse, think himself in the midst of *London* or *Paris*.

The Czar's Brothers and Sisters.

The Princess *Natalia* died four Years ago (1716.) she was the Czar's only Sister by his Mother. The Czar *Alexius Michaelowitz* was twice married, first to *Mary Ilgenisa* by whom he had the two Czars, *Fedor* and *Ivan*, and the Princesses *Sophia*, *Mary* and *Catharine*, of whose respective Fates I shall have an opportunity to speak hereafter. The Czar *Alexius* again married *Natalia Kirilowna* the Daughter of his Prime Minister *Kirili Poluchrowitz Nariskin*, of whom was born the present Czar *(June* 11th, 1672.) and the foresaid Princess *Natalia*. *Kirili Poluchrowitz Nariskin* had also a Son *Leo Kirilowitz Nariskin* the Father of the Chamberlain *Nariskin*, who in the Year 1714. was the Czar's Envoy in *Poland*.

Samoieds with their Rain-deer near Petersbourg.

Having heard of some *Samoieds* living on the Island *Petri-ostrow*, I went thither in company of some Friends. The Czar has caused two Pleasure-Houses to be built there,

one

one of which lies hard by the Shore, and has but fix narrow Apartments, adorned with abundance of Peacock Feathers, all the Furniture confifting only of fome Chairs and Tables. There is conftantly a Guard of two *Ruffians* in that Houfe. A Musket-fhot further, in the thick Wood, lies the Houfe of the *Ruffian* Overfeer, and near to it the Hut of the *Samoieds*, as alfo a fmall Farm, in which there were then upwards of twenty Cows, which feed on the Grafs of the Ifland, and give the beft Milk in thofe Parts; for which reafon the Butter made of it, is kept for the Czar and his Family. Upon our entring thofe Huts, the *Samoieds* came creeping out from under their Hurdles, ftaring upon us. They were feven in number all of a hideous Countenance, with flat tawny Faces, little Eyes, fhort flat Nofes, and little or no Beard. The firft of them who was their Commander, ftept before the others, laying his Arms acrofs and fhaking his Head with a four Look, in which Pofture he continued for fome time; the Women who were of our Company coming in afterwards, he grinned at them, fet up a loud Laugh, and fhaking his Head again crept in under his Hurdle, but foon came out again to us; then he went to his Rain-deer, made them rife from the Ground, and led them by their Horns up to us, offering to take the Women by the Hand and make them fit down upon the Skins of Rain-deer, which Civility we prevented by giving him fome Money, and fo we left him. There were but four Rain-deer, two old ones, and two young, the reft were dead, the Horns and Skins of which were hung up in the Hut round

round about the Walls. From thence we went to the Farm in which lived two *Finland* Peasants who had the care of the Cows and twelve Peacocks. Towards Evening the *Russian* Overseer came home from *Petersbourg*; he welcomed us, invited us to his House, kissed us after the *Russian* Custom, and sent for a great Pot of Butter-milk, which he took to himself, leaving us to make shift as well as we could to come at it. We desired him to send for the chief of the *Samoieds*, and to talk with him, which he did and ordered at the same time another of the *Samoieds* to be brought along him, who having been nine Years in *Russia* and learned a little of the Language, was to serve for an Interpreter. He obliged the chief *Samoied* to make a Bow after the *Russian* way, and to talk with his Comrade in their own Language. He obeyed but with an ill Will, and the *Russian* Overseer told us, that he was such a wild and ill natured Fellow that several times he fell upon Strangers, who came to see the Island in the Overseer's absence, bit them in the Face and Ears, and used them very barbarously. For which being lately chastised with the *Batogs*, he grew so furious that he bit a Morsel of Flesh out of his own Hand, (the Scar of which he forced him to shew to the Company) but that he was resolved to repeat the *Batogs* often enough till he had tamed him. He was at length brought to answer those Questions which we asked him by the means of the Overseer and the Interpreter, to this Effect. That in their Countrey they knew nothing of Religion, Churches, Priests, or Prayers, nor had they any Towns or Villages, but their Habitations were such Hurdles as we had seen in their Hut, which by the help of their Rain-deer they carried over the deep Snow from Place to Place, and fixed their Abode where they liked best; their chief Delight was in scating; they had no other Magistrates than a Boyar, but he lived at a great distance from them, and a *King* the Czar lately put over them. On this Occasion the Overseer acquainted us that the said *King of the Samoieds* was a *Polander*, who had an Allowance of ten Rubels a Month, besides eating and drinking, and that he constantly lived at *Petersbourg* being at the same time the Jester of the Court. The *Samoied* further said that he liked his native Countrey *Sambtjidi* (as they pronounce it) better than *Petersbourg*, and that he longed soon to return to his Wife and four Sons, who (said he) can all scate. The Overseer ordering him to count, he lifted up his Fingers and by them counted till ten, and being desired to go on, he always began at one and left off at ten, saying, they had no other Numbers than those which sufficiently served their Purpose. Being asked how far he was advanced in Years, he answered he had lived a great many, to which the Interpreter added that they knew nothing of Years and Times any further than the Sun's rising and setting. We guessed him to be about fifty Years of Age. He being very cross in making his Answers, we let him go, but before he left us, he bid the Interpreter with a disdainful Air, tell our Ladies, that the Women of his Country were very near as handsome as they. After this he was ordered to bring forth the Rain-deer and to

let

The Present State of Russia.

let them run. The Overseer shewed us a little Grove, or Nursery of Oaks, as a very great Rarity about *Petersbourg*, and so we took our leave of him.

The next Day we went to see the *Russian* way of bathing, which they make use of for an universal Medicine against any Indisposition. There are four different sorts of Baths, out of which they chuse one which they think to be the most proper against their Distemper. Some sit naked in a Boat, and having brought themselves by violent rowing into a great Sweat, suddenly throw themselves into the River, and after having swum for some time, they get out and dry themselves either by the Sun, or with their Shirts. Others leap cold into the River, and afterwards lie close to a Fire which they make on the Shore, rubbing themselves over the whole Body with Oil or Grease, and turn themselves so long about the Fire till it is chafed in; which in their Opinion renders their Limbs supple and nimble. The third sort is the most common: Behind the *Finlandish Slaboda* in the Forest along a little River are built upwards of thirty Bagnios, one half for Men, and the other half for Women; on the tops of the Houses are placed Children who cry that their Bagnios are thoroughly heated. Those who have a mind to bath, undress under the open Sky, and run into the Bagnio; after having sufficiently sweated and got cold Water poured upon them, they go to bask and air themselves, and run up and down through the Bushes sporting with one another. It is astonishing to see not only the Men, but also the Women unmarried as well as married in their

Different Bathing of the Russians.

their several Districts, running about, to the number of forty or fifty, and more together, stark naked without any sort of Shame or Decency, so far from shunning the Strangers who are walking thereabouts, that they even laugh at them. The *Russians* in general both Men and Women use this sort of bathing Winter and Summer twice a Week 'at least; they pay one Copeck a Head, the Bagnios belonging to the Czar. Those that have Bagnios in their Houses, pay yearly something for it; which universal Bathing throughout *Russia* brings a considerable Revenue into the Czar's Coffers. There is a fourth sort of Bathing which is their most powerful Remedy in the greatest Distempers: They cause an Oven to be heated as usual, and when the Heat is somewhat abated (yet still so hot that I was not able to hold my Hand on the Bottom above a quarter of a Minute) five or six *Russians*, more or less, creep into it, and having stretched themselves out at their full length, their Companion who waits without, shuts the Hole so fast, that they can hardly breath within: When they can endure it no longer they call, upon which he that is upon the Watch lets the Sick come out again, who after having breathed some fresh Air, creep into the Oven again, and repeat this Operation till they are almost roasted, and coming out, their Bodies being ruddy like a Piece of red Cloth, throw themselves, in the Summer time into the Water, or in Winter which they love best, into the Snow, with which they are covered all over, leaving only the Nose and Eyes open, and so they lie buried for two or three Hours according

cording to the State of their Distemper; this they count an excellent method for the recovery of their Health. The last time that the Czar returned from *Riga*, passing thro' a Place called *Duderhof*, he was informed that the *Russian* Commissary there never would drink *Hungary* Wine because it did not agree with him, he gave Orders to ply him so hard with Bumpers of it, that he soon was knocked down. The Czar being gone, the Commissary's Servants seeing their Master sick to Death and having almost no Life in him, they stript him naked, carried him into the Yard and buried him under the Snow to take a Nap for twenty four Hours, after which time he rose again, and went briskly about his Business.

On the 23d of *July* the Czarewitz's Consort was brought to Bed of a Princess, who was baptized on the 29th by a *Russian* Priest, and named *Natalia Alexevna* after the Godmother Princess *Natalia*. The Czarewitz was then at *Carlsbad* in *Germany*, and some were of Opinion that under the Pretext of an Indisposition he was designedly gone so far off, that he might not be present at his Consort's Delivery. The Princess begged it as a Favour to be dispensed with the *Russian* Ceremonies of making Presents, kissing and the like usually made on Christnings. By the Laws of the *Grecian* or *Russian* Church no Woman with Child, nor a Man and his Wife, or two Persons contracted, may stand Godfathers and Godmothers together, nor are two single Persons, who once stood Godfathers and Godmothers together, allowed to marry each other, no more than a Godfather or

The Czarewitz's Consort brought to Bed of a Princess.

or Godmother to marry their God-child; however by the Czar's Orders thefe Cuftoms are now no longer fo ftrictly obferved.

Names of the Ruffian Senators. All the Senators were prefent at this Solemnity, of whofe Names I had the following Lift given me. (1.) *Knees James Fedorowitz Dolgoruky* (*Longimanus* or Long-Arms) an aged Man, who twenty odd Years ago was Ambaffador in *France*, and afterwards ten Years a Prifoner at *Stockholm*, where he made his Efcape by a particular Stratagem with forty other *Ruffians* from on board a *Swedifh* Ship. He died 1720. (2.) *Michael Wladimirowitz Dolgoruky*, the former's Nephew. He fell into Difgrace on occafion of the Inquifition againft the Czarewitz, in the Year 1718. (3.) Count *Ivan Alexewitz Mufchin Puskin*, well verfed in the Affairs of the Finances, who was Governor of *Aftracan* for feveral Years, and Prefident of the forefaid Inquifition. (4.) *Tichon Nikititz Strafnoff*, was formerly in great Favour having been the Czar's Preceptor. He died 1719. (5.) *Mikiti Mofeitz Sotoff*, the nominal *Knees Pape*, or Prince Pope. He died two Years ago. (6.) *Knees Fedor Jurgowitz Romadonoffsky*, Vice-Czar of *Moskow*, alfo died two Years ago: He was fucceeded in that Dignity by his Son. (7.) *Andrewitz Opuchtow. M. Matueof*, late Ambaffador in *England*, after his return was alfo made a Senator, and Prefident of the Court of Juftice. The four actual Privy-Counfellors, Count *Golofkin*, Great Chancelllor; Baron *Schafiroff*, Vice-Chancellor; Prince *Dolgoruky*, at prefent Ambaffador in *Poland*; and M. *Tolftoy* formerly Ambaffador at the *Porte*, are alfo Members of the Senate.

The Present State of Russia. 35

On the 20th of *August* a Courier brought Advice of the first Victory at Sea obtained by the Czar over a *Swedish* Squadron off *Hango* on the Coast of *Finland*. On which Occasion the Czar made his triumphant Entry at *Petersbourg*, through an Arch erected for that Purpose; the Particulars of which are as follow. On the 15th of *September* the Czar arrived at *Cronslot*, where he stayed two Days, till the Czarina was brought to Bed of a Princess, whereupon on the 20th he approached the Fortress with the *Russian* and *Swedish* Ships, and was saluted with 150 Guns. First, came three *Russian* Gallies. Secondly, Three *Swedish Scher-boats* of four Guns each. Thirdly, Six *Swedish* Gallies of fourteen Guns each. Fourthly, The *Swedish* Fregat with the Rear-Admiral *Oehrenschield*. Fifthly, A *Scampavie* with the *Russian Rear-Admiral* (viz. the *Czar*, who will not suffer himself in the Fleet to be called or distinguished otherwise than by his Employment.) Sixthly, Three *Russian Scampavies* full of *Russian* Soldiers. Those Ships having cast Anchor, and the Men being landed, they marched through the Triumphal Arch in the following Order. 1. Major General *Gollowin* leading a Company of the *Preobrazinsky* Guards. 2. Ten Pieces of Canon, sixty Colours and three Standards, taken by General *Knees Gallizin* in the Engagement near *Wasa* in *Finland* against the *Swedish* Major General *Arenfeld*. 3 Two Companies of the Regiment of *Astracan*. 4. Two hundred *Swedish* Subaltern Sea-Officers, Soldiers and Sailors. 5. Two Companies of the Regiment *Preobrazinsky*. 6. Fourteen *Swedish* Sea-Officers. 7. The Flag of the

Swedish

August and Sept. 1714. The Czar's triumphant Entry at Petersbourg.

Swedish Rear-Admiral, carried by four Subalterns. 8. The *Swedish* Rear-Admiral *Oehrenschield*, in new Clothes, laced with Silver, of which the Czar had made him a Present. 9. The Czar as *Rear-Admiral* in a green Suit laced with Gold. 10. The remaining Companies of the Regiment of *Preobrazinsky* closed the Procession. The Triumphal Arch was most magnificently adorned, and represented divers Emblems: Among others was to be seen the *Russian* Eagle seizing an Elephant, with this Inscription: *The Russian Eagle catches no Flies.* (Aquila non capit muscas.) The Name of the *Swedish* Fregat the *Elephant*, gave the Explanation. In this Order the victorious and vanquished proceeded to the Fortress, where the Vice-Czar *Romadonofsky* sitting on a Throne surrounded by the whole Senate, caused the *Czar* as *Rear-Admiral* to be called before the Assembly, and received at his Hands a Relation in writing of the Victory obtained. The same being read by *Romadonofsky* and the Senators, they took it under Deliberation and proposed several Questions to the *Russian* Rear-Admiral; after which they unanimously declared him *Vice-Admiral* of *Russia* in consideration of the faithful Service he had done to his native Country, of which Proclamation being made, the whole Room resounded with *Sdrastwi Vice-Admiral*, Health to the Vice-Admiral (which is the *Russian Vivat*.) The Czar having returned Thanks, went on board his Sloop, on which he hoisted the Flag of Vice-Admiral, and having received ours and other Foreigners Compliments or Congratulation, he went to Prince *Menzikof*'s Palace where a noble

The Present State of Ruſſia.

noble Entertainment was prepared. After being riſen from Table he ſhewed particular Marks of Eſteem to M. *Oehrenſchield,* and ſaid to all the noble Ruſſians ſtanding about him; *Here you ſee a brave and faithful Servant of his Maſter, who has made himſelf worthy of the higheſt Reward at his Hands, and who ſhall always have my Favour as long as he is with me, though he killed me many a brave Ruſſian: I forgive it you* (ſaid he, turning to him with a Smile) *and you may depend on my good Will.* M. *Oehrenſchield* having thanked the Czar, anſwered; *However honourably I may have acted with regard to my Maſter, I did but my Duty: I ſought Death* (he had received ſeven Wounds) *but did not meet it, and it is no ſmall Comfort to me in my Misfortune to be a Priſoner of your Majeſty, and to be uſed ſo favourably and with ſo much Diſtinction by ſo great a Sea-Officer, and now worthily Vice-Admiral.* M. *Oehrenſchield* aſſured us that the Ruſſians fought like Lyons, and that nothing but his own Experience could have convinced him, that the Czar had made ſo good Soldiers of his ſtupid Subjects. Such is the Effect of ſevere Diſcipline, Time and Prudence.

It is hoped the Reader will be pleaſed to hear on what occaſion and by what means the Czar put his military Affairs in that good Poſture, which has ſince ſo deſervedly been the Admiration of all the World. It is well known, that the preſent Czar after the Death of *Fedor* his eldeſt Brother by the Father's Side, at firſt held the Adminiſtration jointly with *Ivan* the ſecond Brother likewiſe by the Father's Side, and that the Princeſs *Sophia,* *How the preſent State of military Affairs in Ruſſia was eſtabliſhed.*

Siſter

Sister of the whole Blood to *Fedor* and *Ivan*, did either out of Love to *Ivan*, or out of a boundless Desire of governing, try all Methods imaginable to remove out of the Way the *present Czar* her Brother by the Father's second Marriage, or at least to get him some way or other excluded from the Succession. To compass which End she judged it the surest Method to deprive the young Czar *Peter* of all Education by letting him carelessly grow up among a Company of raw Youths, in Hopes that by an unbecoming Conduct he would in time render himself odious to the People, and that his promising Genius and the good Sense, of which he gave early Proofs, would be stifled by Debauches and Licentiousness, and consequently he be rendered unfit for Government and great Enterprizes. But all these Devices proved ineffectual, for the young Czar's admirable natural Parts growing with his Age broke through all Difficulties; the Rebellion raised by *Sophia* in the Year 1683, and the Exhortations of his faithful Russians at length opened his Eyes, and filled him with Discontent against many of the chief Nobility, and raised in him a Desire of being revenged on his Adversaries in proper time. The continual Apprehensions from his Sister's Party put him under a Necessity of ruining it, and made him resolve to establish himself on the Throne by the Help of Foreigners, and to this End insensibly to draw them into his Service from all Countries of the World, more than any Czar had done before him; He well judged, that such a Flock of Strangers would be persecuted by his Subjects, and consequently have no
other

The Present State of Russia.

other Support but himself, whose Interest they would absolutely espouse in case any Rebellion should break out and share his good or bad Fortune with him. The frequent Attempts and Conspiracies against the Czar's Person, which he escaped in a wonderful manner, hastened the engaging of foreign Officers into his Service, and as there were many able Men among them, especially the famous M. *Le Fort*, who gained the Czar's Favour and had his ear, it naturally followed that by their Relations of the State of other Countries, and their Projects for extending the Power of *Russia* by putting it upon the Foot of *Germany*, and reducing the disaffected Russians to Obedience, they increased the Czar's Desire of making an Alteration in the Form of Government. And so he firmly resolved to counterbalance the Russian Perverseness by a German Force, and by the Help of the latter to conquer their inveterate Malice. His first Care was to ruin the Corps of the *Strelitzes*, who were entirely in his Sister's Interest, and amounted to upwards of forty thousand Men; but they being veteran Soldiers who were both too obstinate and too powerful so easily to suffer themselves to be modelled and tutored by German Officers, it was very necessary to manage this Affair with such Circumspection as not to exasperate the Russians by letting them see through the Design, nor to frighten the Foreigners by the Danger into a Resolution of quitting the Service. The Czar therefore first raised a Company of fifty Men independent of the *Strelitzes*, cloathed and exercised after the German manner, setting foreign Officers

ficers over them, and himself for the greater Encouragement of the new raised Men served among them first as Drummer, then Serjeant, Corporal, and so on, till he was made Captain, and appeared at their Head to review and exercise them. The Russians in general looked upon this small Body as being only kept for the Czar's Diversion, and the *Strelitzes* themselves took Delight in the Novelty of seeing them perform those strange Exercises. And so this Project took wonderfully, that little Company was augmented from time to time till it grew into a Batallion, and at last into several Regiments, so that this pretended Mock-Shew proved in good earnest the Nursery of a new Army, which was able to cope with the *Strelitzes* when they rebelled again, broke the Neck of that veteran Corps, established the Czar's Throne, procured him Safety at home and Reputation abroad. For which Reason he caresses and maintains this Guard, which now consists of ten thousand Men, as the Support of his Government, above any other of his Forces. Now if one adds to these ten thousand Men the great Armies on foot in *Finland* and *Ukraina*, the Garrisons of *Petersbourg*, *Narva*, *Riga*, *Reval*, and the Frontier Places in *Ukraina*, it may safely be asserted, that the Czar's Forces actually consist of one hundred thousand Soldiers, all well exercised, cloathed and armed, without reckoning the *Cossacks*, *Tartars* and *Calmucks* his Vassals, nor the *Black Regiments* (as they are called) who are a sort of Militia. These Forces are kept in the strictest Discipline, and are regularly recruited; however,

consi-

The Present State of Russia.

considering the small Pay of the Russian Officers, they do not stand the Czar in so much as Armies do in other Countries. Their Infantry yields to none, their Cavalry it is true, consists all of stout Men, yet there are still several things wanting to make it completely good, the chief of which are that *Russia* produces no large Horses, and that a Russian is not to be brought to use and keep his Horse well.

At the abovementioned Entertainment, I was told by the Officers who had been with the Czar in that Expedition at Sea, that his Majesty was in such Danger with his Ship in a dreadful Storm that happened in *July*, that he was given over for lost by all that understood the Sea, but he chose the least of two Evils, and ventured on board a strong Sloop, notwithstanding the Dissuasions and Intreaties the Russians made to him on their Knees, to whom he answered, *You Gentlemen believe no Predestination*, and sailed four Leagues along the Coast in the midst of the Storm, and in a very dark Night; immediately after his landing he caused a Fire to be made on the Shore, according to Agreement, to give the Fleet a Signal of his being in Safety. *The Czar in imminent Danger at Sea.*

The two Months of *October* and *November* were spent in divers useful Regulations, especially about the Fortress and other publick Edifices, as also the building of Ships, in which several Works the Czar caused more than forty thousand Men to be employed, which Number not being sufficient, the *Finlandish* Peasants and *Swedish* Prisoners were obliged to help. Six hundred of the latter were sent for *October and November* 1714. *Numbers of Men employed in carrying on the Works at Petersbourg.*

for from *Samara* a Town lying on the *Wolga* beyond *Cafan*, where they had been working for some Years in the Brimstone Mines, and had buried the greater Part of their Companions who died in that unwholsome Employment. When they arrived at *Petersbourg*, they were furnished with Cloathing for the Winter and some Money by the Czarina, the Benefactress and Protectress of all distressed People.

Ruins of Nienschantz.
In *November* I went to view the Ruins of *Nienschantz*, a Town demolished by the Russians the Beginning of the present War, lying two short Leagues from *Petersbourg* up the River near its Banks. I only found there some Ruins, the deep Ditch, Wells, and Cellars, all the Materials of the Houses having been removed to *Petersbourg*, and employed in the building of that City. The Inhabitants, who carried on a good Trade in the *Baltick*, are for the greater Part Prisoners, and the single Women were taken into the Service of the Czarina, Princess *Menzicoff*, and other Ladies of Quality, and afterwards married.

The Pleasure Houses at Petershoff and Strelnamuse.
About the same time I went to see the Pleasure House *Petershoff*, situate on the Mouth of the River. I shall content my self with mentioning only that the ablest Architects and some thousands of Workmen have been employed about it for these ten Years past, and forced Nature, which will give a sufficient Idea of the Magnificence of that Work, as also of another at *Strelnamuse*, where I saw last Year ten thousand Men daily employed, who are like to make another *Versailles* of that Place.

The Present State of Russia. 43

On the first of December died the above-mentioned * *King of the Samoieds*, and was buried with a great deal of Ceremony in the Roman Catholick Church, which Religion he professed. Some Years ago he had been crowned at *Moskow*, and received Homage of twenty four *Samoieds*, and as many Rain-Deer, who had been sent for to this end from *Samoiedia*.

December 1714. King of Samoiedia dies.
* p. 27.

The Beginning of December a Courier arrived from *Constantinople* with Letters from Vice-Chancellor *Schaffiroff*, bringing Advice to the Czar, that the said Minister, after having endured a great deal of Uneasiness and Vexation, had received favourable Dispatches from the *Porte*, and was departed from *Constantinople* in a perfect good Understanding with them, having dispatched the Courier before him six Leagues from *Constantinople*. The Czar greatly rejoiced at the Return of that Minister, who has deserved so well of all the Russian Empire.

Vice-chancellor Schaffiroff's Departure from Constantinople.

The Czar gave Orders to write to *France*, and give Commission to his Agents there, to look out for a good Number of able Handicraftsmen, and to dispose them to come into *Russia*, by offering them good Terms, among others, free Habitation and Exemption for ten Years from all Imposts.

Handicraftsmen looked out for in France.

A French-man arrived from *Berlin*, and undertook to establish a Stocking Manufacture, to which end they began to build a great Stone-House at *Petersbourg*.

A Manufacture of Stockings.

Strict Orders were issued to all the Inhabitants of *Petersbourg*, who had Houses but one Story high, to put another Story upon them. As for the rest, a late Mandate was confirmed,

Regulation concerning Houses.

ed, by Virtue of which the great number of Wooden Houses were permitted to stand; but it was forbid to build any more, otherwise than with Roofs of Tiles and Walls of Stone-work.

Orders sent to the Czarewitz to return.
The Czar sent Orders to the *Czarewitz* at *Carlsbad*, to return to *Petersbourg* as soon as he had done using the medicinal Waters. It was said, he shewed but little Inclination upon the Receipt of the Letter, and in his Answer; and that he resented his being still continued *Serjeant*.

Prince Gagarin's Daughter retires to a Monastery.
Prince *Gagarin*, the rich Governor of *Siberia*, pretending to oblige his only Daughter, a beautiful and sensible young Lady, to marry the Senator, *Muschin Puskin*'s eldest Son, lately returned from *France*; in order to avoid a forced Marriage, she fled from *Moskow* into a Russian Monastery, and got her Head shaved. It is frequent in those Parts for Wives to leave their Husbands, and for Daughters to run away from their Parents, and to take Refuge in *Convents*; and if they be shaved, it is in no Person's Power to get them out again.

New Colonies in Ingria.
The Czar made a Journey to *Duderhoff*, and other Places in *Ingria*, to view the State of the *Colonies* planted there out of *Russia*. He had caused Numbers of rich Peasants in *Russia*, to be translated with their Wives and Children into *Ingria*, and profitable Lands to be assigned to them in that Country, which by the War and Plague was reduced to a Desart; and had appropriated those Possessions which the new Planters were obliged to leave, to poor People in *Russia*.

Profcovia, the late Czar *Ivan*'s Dowager, received Orders to repair to *Petersbourg* from *Ifmailoff*, her Jointure and Pleafure-houfe fix Leagues from *Moskow*, with the three Princeffes her Daughters, the eldeft of whom, *Anna*, was at that time Dutchefs Dowager of *Courland*, and the fecond was afterwards married to the Duke of *Mecklenbourg*.

 The Czar's own *Daughters* were well educated at *Petersbourg*, and carefully inftructed in all that was neceffary. They already fpoke good *High-Dutch*, but had not yet learnt *French*. The Czar had asked a certain Perfon, whether the *German* Language was not copious enough for one to exprefs one's felf in it, and being anfwered in the Affirmative, he fhewed himfelf furprized at the *Germans* being fo fond of the *French* Tongue.

 People were hard at Work upon the large Building of the new *Chancery*, which is at prefent finifhed. There is hardly any publick Office of State in the World, befides this in *Ruffia*, where Difpatches are iffued in fo many Languages. They have above fixteen Interpreters and Secretaries, *viz.* in the *Ruffian*, *Polifh*, *Latin*, *High-Dutch*, *Englifh*, *Low-Dutch*, *Danifh*, *French*, *Italian*, *Spanifh*, *Greek*, *Turkifh*, *Chineze*, *Tartarian*, *Calmuckifh*, and *Mongalian* Languages.

 Search having been made the Summer before in *Cafan*, *Aftracan*, *Siberia*, and *Moskow*, after the former Inhabitants of *Derpt* and *Narva*, who, to the number of One thoufand fix hundred and ten Perfons, were, after the taking of thofe Places, carried away Prifoners into the Ruffian Dominions. Notice having been given to them, to prepare for their return home;

Profcovia the Czarine Dowager, fent for from Moskow.

Education of the Czar's Daughters.

Of the new Chancery at Peterfbourg.

Derpt and Narva to be repeopled.

home; about two hundred of the moſt ſubſtantial of theſe People had already repaired to *Narva*, in purſuance of that Order, ſome Months ago, but the reſt lay at *Moskow*, and repreſented to the Czar, by very moving Letters, that having ſpent all they were worth on their March, they were unable to proceed further. Upon this the Czar ordered two hundred Waggons to be raiſed, in order to bring them to *Petersbourg*. At preſent they are ſettling their Affairs at *Narva*; but Trade will not revive, and the greater part of theſe Priſoners preferred to ſtay in their Captivity where they could ſubſiſt better, and to keep their acquired Habitations and Lands.

State inland Lappia. I was informed by an Officer coming from *Finland*, that *Caianebourg*, ſituate on a great Lake, was the only Place in which was a *Swediſh* Garriſon, though that alſo is ſince fallen into the Czar's Hands. It is remarkable, that the *Swediſh* Governor of that Town has lived, during all the War, in good Friendſhip with the neighbouring Ruſſians and Lapponians, and that with Approbation on the Swediſh, as well as the Ruſſian ſide, there being no Benefit to be reaped from Hoſtility, by reaſon of the Poorneſs of the Country, and the Miſery of the Inhabitants. It is the ſame Caſe (as I heard from the Czar himſelf) with relation to *Kola*, the Capital of *Lapponia*, where the Borders of the Swediſh, Daniſh, and Ruſſian Lapponians join; for thoſe different Subjects, who ſubſiſt but poorly on Bread made of Fiſhes, lived during all this War in perfect Concord, and carried on their little Trade without Interruption. The foreſaid Officer further told me, me, that the State of *Finland* was extreamly miserable, the Peasants in some Parts having had for some Time past no Bread, but lived upon the Barks of Trees; there were no Villages in the Country, but the Houses lay single and dispersed, and to a Tract of Land of eight or ten Leagues belonged but one Clergyman; the Soil of almost all *Finland* was barren, and the Country full of Rocks, Lakes, Bogs, and Bushes, which the Swedish Freebooters, by the Help of the Peasants, knew how to make use of.

This Month disclosed at length the Reason of the Czar's having for several Weeks appeared extremely pensive. He had searched to the Bottom of the Disorders crept into Administration since the Year 1706, and found out whence it proceeded that the Army had been so ill paid, and suffered so much for Want; that the German Officers had quitted the Service; that so many thousands of Workmen had most miserably perished; that such a Dearth had overspread all the Country, that the Inland-trade had decayed; in short, that the Finances were in such Confusion; and he had taken a firm Resolution to remedy all those Evils, if not thoroughly, yet at least as far as possible, to which end he established towards the End of the Year a Grand Inquisition. *The Czar discovers great Disorders in the Administration of his Revenue, and establishes an Inquisition.*

The Experience of twenty Years and upwards has shewn, that notwithstanding the great Expences which the Czar has been at in maintaining his Armies and Fleet, and carrying on so many vast Buildings, yet he was not obliged to contract Debts, but always found new Supplies in his Dominions to support *The State of the Finances in Russia.*

port his Undertakings. *Ruſſia* abounds in Merchandize, but not in ready Money, and conſidering the vaſt Extent of its Empire, it is juſtly matter of Surprize, that there is ſuch a Diſproportion between its Extent and Revenues, there being many Provinces, which yield to none in the World in Fruitfulneſs and the plentiful Produce of all that is neceſſary for human Life. The Czar has indeed diſcovered great part of the Cauſes of this Defect, and in ſome meaſure redreſſed ſeveral of them; but it is impoſſible for him as yet to remove the Difficulties ſtill remaining; and as for the reſt, he has had neither Time nor Opportunity to get a true Information about them. It cannot be denied that there are but few Towns, and many Foreſts and Deſarts in *Ruſſia*, and that the greater Part of the Land is barren, or rather lies untilled; but one of the chief Reaſons of this is, that the War has deprived the Country of abundance of Inhabitants, and thoſe who are left, labour under the Oppreſſion of the Czar's Officers, and of the Nobility, to ſuch a Degree, that they are quite diſheartened from Induſtry, and content themſelves with making a poor Shift of living from Hand to Mouth. For in the ſame manner as the Czars have exerciſed, time out of Mind, the Power of ſeizing the Eſtates of their Boyars, on any pretences they think ſufficient; ſo the latter are of Opinion, that, by Parity of Reaſon, they may exerciſe the ſame Power over their Peaſants, from whence it proceeds, that all manner of Induſtry and Deſire of Gain is extinguiſhed among the Boors, and if by chance one happens privately to get a ſmall Sum,

The Present State of Russia. 49

Sum, he hides it out of Fear of his Lord under a Dunghil, where it lies dead to him. The Nobility, on the other Hand, having thus by Violence and Cunning drained the Peasants of their very Blood, and being afraid of making themselves obnoxious to the Court, by the Shew of their ill-gotten Wealth, commonly lock it, either up in their Coffers to moulder there, or others, who are since grown wiser, convey it into the Banks of *London, Venice,* and *Amsterdam.* Consequently all the Money being thus concealed, both by the Nobility and Peasants, it has no Circulation, and the Country reaps no Benefit from it. The Czar was once advised to abolish *Slavery,* and to introduce a moderate Liberty, which would both encourage his Subjects, and promote his own Interest at the same time; but the wild Temper of the Russians, who are not to be governed without Constraint, was a sufficient Reason for rejecting that Proposition at that Time.

I took great Pains ever since my being in *Russia,* though long in vain, to get an exact Calculation of the Czar's Revenues, till at length, by the Assistance of some Friends, I was let into the Secret. I am now going faithfully to communicate to the Reader, as something unknown before, the several Observations, which I partly had from the said Friends, partly gathered my self at different Times, and on different Occasions, relating to the State of the Czar's Revenue, as it stood from 1714 to 1717. which will give an exact Idea of the present State of his powerful Empire. The Profits accruing every Year to the Czar's Treasury out of those far extended

The Czar's Revenue consists of three sorts.

ed Provinces, of which the Russian Empire is composed, are of three Sorts, consisting either of *Personal Service, Provisions,* or *Money.*

I. The Profits arising from the personal Service of his Subjects.

1. The Cosacks.

Among the *Persons* whose *Service* turns to the Czar's Account, are to be reckoned, (1.) The *Cosacks,* or *Czercasses,* who inhabit the Country called *Ukraina,* situate between the Rivers *Don* and *Dnieper,* above its Cataracts, from whence they call themselves *Zaporowsky, Za* in the Russian Tongue signifying *above,* and *Poroga,* a *Water-fall.* In former Times they were subject to *Poland,* but being oppressed by that Nation, they submitted first to the Turks and (probably not finding their Account in their Subjection to those Infidels) afterwards to the Czar *Alexius,* his present Majesty's Father. That Submission was advised by *Dorossenka* their General or *Hetman,* whose Posterity are to this Day counted one of their noblest Families: He had the Address to obtain such advantageous Terms in the Treaty of Submission, that, had not some Alteration been made since, the Cosacks would hardly have known what Subjection implies: Besides the Czar's Protection, he stipulated for *Ukraina* an Exemption from all Imposts and Taxes; that the Inhabitants should be governed by their own Magistrates according to their own Laws, which are those of the City of *Magdebourg,* formerly received in the *Ukraina,* and still obtaining in that Country; that no Russians or Foreigners should be obtruded upon them; that they should enjoy full Liberty of Trade, particularly of brewing, preparing and selling Brandy, Beer; and Mead; in exchange whereof he obliged himself to furnish the Czar upon the first Summons

The Present State of Russia.

mons with a Body of sixty thousand Horse. This was indeed a great Advantage to *Russia*, at a Time when they knew nothing of regular Forces, and when the Cossacks were looked upon by them and the Polanders to be the best sort of Troops; but now that the Czar having put his own Forces upon so good a Foot, can do without them, he would willingly remit them that Service, the rather because they are at present hardly able to raise thirty thousand Men, and he would be glad to treat them on the same Foot as the Russians, were it not to be apprehended that they may withdraw over the *Dnieper* to the Polish Frontiers, or even over the *Don* to the Tartars, whom they use to call their Brethren; in which Case not only that fertile Country would become desolate, but also the Danger of the Tartarian Invasions would increase by such a Reinforcement from the Cosacks, who would serve the Tartars for Guides. The Russians therefore being convinced of the Danger of openly attempting it, are endeavouring to subdue them in another manner, and by silent Steps, towards which they have already made a good Beginning; for since the War with the Turks they have forced the Cosacks to quarter the Russian Horse, which continue there to this Day; besides, they have ruined the Inhabitants by obliging them every Moment to furnish Post-Horses, without ever being paid, so that the *Ukraina* at present is but the Shadow of what it was before.

(2.) The *Calmucks* are likewise obliged to raise their *Hordes* for his Czarish Majesty's military Service. But they are seldom employed,

2. The Calmucks.

ployed, because they are to be furnished with certain Subsidies, which, by the Accounts of the Russian Ministers, amount to more than their Assistance is worth.

3. The Tartars. (3.) The *Tartars* under the Czar's Dominion, who are likewise obliged to mount upon his Orders, are somewhat more serviceable. In former Times they only attended in Warlike Expeditions, but at present they are forced to do all other sort of Work.

4. Recruits (4.) The greatest Profit of all arises from the *Recruits*, with which the Country is obliged to furnish to the Czar, in such Numbers as he pleases, and without the least Disbursement on his Part. In former Times, before the Regiments were formed, Recruits were raised after a very confused manner. A little before the Campaign was to be begun, Lists were sent from the War-Office to the Colonels, containing the Names of the Villages out of which they were to take their Men, which Method brought the very Refuse of Mankind into the Field; for the Officers having their private Interest more at Heart than that of the Czar, they made use of that natural Aversion to War among the common People of *Russia*, to extort Money from them, by frightening them with the Service, and there was no body to observe their Mismanagement, much less to punish it. But since the State of War in *Russia* has been otherwise modelled, those Abuses have been mostly redressed, and seeing it is hard to find a voluntary Soldier among the common sort, the following Regulation was made relating to the raising of Recruits. The Senate shares that Service out among the several Governments,

ments, ordering how many Men each Governor is to raise in Proportion of his Jurisdiction. Each Governor makes Repartitions according to the Number of Farms in his Government, so that commonly forty or fifty, or sometimes even twenty Farms are obliged to find one Man, and send him to *Moskow*, or any other Rendezvous, from whence they are afterwards carried two and two tied together to *Petersbourg*, or to the Army. It is computed, that there are regularly raised every Year about twenty thousand Recruits, which seems the less incredible, because of the vast Extent of the Countries in the Czar's Possession, particularly if one considers, that these People are but poorly maintained according to the common Russian Fare, and that more of them perish with Hunger and Cold, during the first Years of the Service, than fall before the Enemy. The Beginning of this present War, when the Russians suffered such Overthrows at *Narva*, and on other Occasions, the Levies extended even to the Housholds of the Nobility, who, according to the old Russian Fashion, maintained four or five hundred Footmen, the fourth or fifth of whom was draughted out to carry Arms; but now that the Armies have no such great Want of Recruits, that Method is laid aside, though not forbid by any Edict or Declaration.

(5.) The Case is much the same with regard to *Seamen*. At first they were only drawn out of the Provinces lying on great Rivers, as are, for Instance, the Governments of *Archangel-Gorod* and *Casan*. Afterwards they were taken out of the *Salt-works* on the Coast of the frozen Sea, where the Russians
used

5. *Seamen.*

used to make abundance of Salt of Sea-water by the Help of Fire, for which they have Plenty of Wood. Those People being used to swim in Leather-Boats sewed together, it was thought they would soon learn to use Ships made of Timber, and so they were all brought to *Petersbourg*, to the Ruin of the Salt-Works, which afterwards obliged the Czar to get foreign Salt imported at a great yearly Expence. At present the Want of Hands having increased with the Number of Ships in the Czar's Fleet, the most remote Governments are also obliged to furnish Recruits for manning them, so that they even take the People out of the Mines where they worked from their Youth, who coming on the Water, and being not used to that Element, Numbers of them are swept away by Distempers, and the more, because their Superstition will not allow them to break their long Fasts. The Fleet being that which the Czar has most at Heart, preferably to all other warlike Affairs, he takes an extraordinary Care that all things necessary for equipping it, be furnished in the most expeditious manner. Hence it is, that whereas the raising of Recruits for Land Forces is commonly left to the Governors, the Czar in case of raising Seamen, almost always sends some Officers of the Regiments of Guards, called *Preobrazinsky* and *Simonoffsky*, into the Governments, with an Order under his own Hand, by which they are impowered to proceed as they think fit, even contrary to the Intentions of the Governors.

6. Handi-craftsmen. (6.) The Subjects of *Russia* are likewise obliged to furnish their Sovereign with divers Handi-

The Present State of Russia.

Handicraftsmen, as Bricklayers, Masons, Carpenters, and Smiths. Such Sort of Men, who have learned their Trade after the Russian way, almost without Instruction, being found in most of the Villages, and of great Service in a new Place as *Petersbourg*, they are demanded of the Peasants by the Governor, as well as Recruits, saving only that four or five hundred Farms deliver but one Man, who is maintained and provided on his Journey, by the Contribution of the Owners, till he arrives at the Place appointed, and then his Wages commence, which the Czar pays him at the Rate of one Rubel a Month, and are usually continued to him till his Death, sometimes with an Augmentation, on account of his good Behaviour or Skill in Trade. Artists, and other Handicraftsmen, whose Trade requires greater Ingenuity, as for Instance, Watchmakers, Gold and Silver Smiths, Lock-Smiths, Braziers, Shoemakers, Tailors, Book-binders, &c. are not demanded from the Country; but if any such Man is known to live at a Place, he is fetched away, without Consideration of his being settled there, and carried to *Petersbourg*.

(7.) The Fortifications which were raised chiefly during the Reign of the present Czar at *Petersbourg, Kioff, Moskow, Azoff, Taganerok, Czernichoff, Nizyn, Perejeslaff*, and other Places, and the great Edifices that have been erected, have made it necessary to demand of the Country *Day-Labourers*, by Right of *Villenage*. Such of these as are employed at *Petersbourg*, are raised in any of the Provinces, by reason of the many Works that are carrying on there; but those who are to work

7. *Labourers.*

work at the other Places, are gathered only in the refpective Governments where the Fortifications are to be raifed, *viz.* thefe for *Kioff*, *Nizyn*, *Perejeſlaff*, and *Czernichoff*, are taken out of the Government of *Kioff*, and thefe for *Azoff*, *Taganerok*, *Czerka*, are drawn out of the Government of *Weronetz* or *Azoff*. They are furniſhed with travelling Charges and Subfiftence for fix Months, after which Term they return home, and their Places are fupplied by others. And this is, as it were, the bottomlefs Pit in which innumerable Ruffian Subjects perifh and are deftroyed. It is affured by Perfons, who pretend to have well examined it, that in the building of the Fortrefs of *Taganerok* on the *Black Sea*, more than three hundred thoufand Peafants periſhed with Hunger, and Difeafes contracted in that marfhy Ground, and ftill a greater Number were deftroyed in the Works of *Petersbourg* and *Cronflot*. So much may fuffice, as to the Profit accruing to the Czar, by the *Perfonal Service* of his Subjects.

II. The Revenue of Provifions, the Mifmanagement of which gives Occafion to the grand Inquifition.

Provifions for the Czar's Armies make up another confiderable part of his Revenue. The Affefsments of which are not alike at all times, but are either raifed or lowered according to the Circumftances of Time, and the Occafion of the Army. Formerly, when the Countrey provided for the Garrifons who were to guard the Frontier Towns againft the *Turks*, againft the *Crim* and other *Tartars*, the *Poles*, the *Swedes* and other Neighbours, as alfo for the Army when quartered in their own Dominions, that Contribution was raifed on the Villages, each Farm being taxed a certain Meafure of Corn, Grout and Oatmeal, which

which amounted to no small Quantity, considering their numerous Armies and Garrisons. But when the Limits of the *Russian* Empire were extended to the North-side, this Method of raising Provisions was not only continued, but the Peasants were even forced to deliver them at *Petersbourg* and other Places of the new Conquests, which, considering the distance through which those Provisions were to be carried, fell heavier on the Farmers than the Impost it self. Great Complaints therefore arising, it was resolved to remedy this Grievance by letting out the said Delivery of Provisions to Undertakers, and to assess the Country for the value of it. This might have proved a great ease to the Country, had it been honestly executed: But innumerable Frauds being committed, and the great Men who were commissioned to agree with the Undertakers, taking the Delivery upon themselves under borrowed Names, and stipulating for themselves in the Contracts such Rates as they thought fit, it was found that each Tun of Meal stood the Czar in more than the Market-price, and this Expedient which was calculated for the Relief of the Subjects, proved such an insupportable Burthen on them, that numbers of them ran away from their Possessions. And this Oppression continued a considerable time, the Czar being mostly absent from his Dominions, and no body daring to do that ill Office to the chief Nobility who were all concerned in it, as to break the Matter to him. At length one Man was found, with whom the Misery of his native Country was of greater Weight than his own Danger, who
ventured

ventured on acquainting the Czar with thofe Mifmanagements, however in fuch a manner as to fave his own Neck by remaining undifcovered in cafe no Ear was given to his Reprefentations. He difperfed Papers containing the Grievances of the Nation, and good Fortune ordered it fo that the Czar himfelf read one and reflected upon it; upon which, Protection and a Reward being offered to the Author if he would make himfelf known and make good what he alledged, he appeared, and fo well fupported the Contents of thofe Papers, as to convince the Czar of the palpable Breach of Truft his Servants were guilty of. This gave occafion to the Grand Inquifition above mentioned, which was eftablifhed the beginning of the Year 1715. All the great Men of *Ruffia* were involved in it, *viz.* Admiral General *Apraxin*, Prince *Menzicoff*, M. *Korfakoff* Vice-Governor of *Petersbourg*, M. *Kikin* firft Lord of the Admiralty, M. *Sinavin* firft Commiffioner of the Admiralty, Mr. *Bruce* Great Mafter of the Artillery, Prince *Wolchonsky* and M. *Apouchtin*, both Senators, and an incredible number of others of the Czar's Servants of inferior Ranks. *Apraxin*, *Menzicoff* and *Bruce* alledged for their Excufe, that they had feldom been at *Petersbourg*, but for the greater part of that Time in the Field or in Foreign Parts, fo that they had been fo far from being able to find out the ill Practices of their unfaithful Servants, or to prevent them, that they were even unacquainted with what was done during that time in their own Houfes; which Excufe, partly on account of its Probability, partly in Favour of them, was allowed

lowed, with this Proviso however, that their Purses were to smart severely for it. But the others who could not justify their Conduct, underwent greater Punishments; *Korsakoff* publickly suffered the *Knout*; *Apouchtin* and *Wolchonsky* were punished after the same manner, and had besides red hot Irons drawn over their Tongues; some of an inferior Degree were chastised with *Batogs*, and others sent into *Siberia* and other remote Places, and all their Estates confiscated. The Inquisition being ended, a proper Regulation was made to prevent the like Frauds of Commissaries for the future, and to make the Burthen lie a great deal easier on the People, at least for some time. But what eased the Subjects far more, was, that after the Battel of *Pultava*, it was thought proper to quarter the greater part of the Troops in *Poland*, and a good Body of Horse among the Cosacks on pretence of being apprehensive of Incursions from the Tartars: But when the Russian Army, in pursuance of the Peace made with the Turks on the River *Pruth* was obliged to evacuate the Polish Territories, and that it was not designed to employ all those Forces in *Pomerania*, there was a Necessity of quartering some Regiments in *Russia* which fell particularly on the Government of *Petersbourg*, that the Troops might be the nearer at hand, and not too much harassed by long Marches: They were afterwards joined by some Regiments of Horse which were recalled from *Ukrania* (seemingly in consideration of the continual Complaints of the Cosacks) which Regiments for the greater part were cantonned in the Neighbourhoods of *Smolensko* and *Riga*. Besides this, the Town of *Dorpt* is bound by Capitulation

tulation conftantly to provide for two Regiments in their Territory, which proves of great Advantage for thofe Forces the Czar has occafion for to keep near *Petersbourg.* The Territory of *Novogrod* is alfo obliged to furnifh Quarters for the Guards of *Preobrazinsky* and *Simonofsky,* together with the Regiments of *Aftracan* and *Ingria,* at all times when they are not in the Field, which Quarters however are not near fo defirable as thofe they were formerly ufed to in *Poland.* The Garrifons which in old Times were kept in moft Places of *Ruffia,* are for the greater part withdrawn, and only a moderate number of Militia kept in tenable Towns and Caftles, who are maintained out of the Territories affigned to each Place. In the fame manner the Officers appointed in the Towns, as Commanders, Provincial Commiffioners, Commiffaries, *Fifcals* or Sergeants at Law, Chancellors, Secretaries, Clerks, and other Officers, receive from the Territories of the Towns Rye and Oats, being part of their Allowance, purfuant to a Regulation publifhed by the Czar.

III. *The Money-Revenue arifing out of the Czar's Demefne'.*

The Revenue of the Czar's Treafury confifting of *ready Money* levied on the Subjects, is of two forts, either *conftant* or *variable.* In which Diftinction are not comprehended the *Demefnes,* or Revenues arifing from publick Funds which are the Czar's own both as to Propriety and Perception, and are appropriated folely to the Support of his Houfhold. For it was never heard, at leaft during the Reign of the prefent Czar, that he applied any Money levied on the Subjects for the Support of his Houfhold or for his Diverfions, except the Salaries of General and Vice-Admiral

The Present State of Ruffia.

miral, which he caufes to be paid to him out of the Pay-Office of War as doing Service for them. There are fome who determine the Sum which thofe Funds yield, to amount to four hundred thoufand Rubels a Year; but befides that it is a difficult matter to penetrate into fuch Things, which can not be learned in any Ruffian *Pricaffe* or Office, nor altogether at one Place, but muft be gathered from all Provinces where thofe Funds arife; there is ftill another Reafon why it is impoffible to attain to any Certainty as to their Produce, which is, that thofe Funds are liable to Variations every Year; for fome times part thereof are difpofed of by way of Grant to fome deferving Officer or Favourite of the Czar, fometimes they increafe more or lefs, according to the Times, by Confifcation of the Eftates belonging to Rebels, or Families that are fallen under the Czar's Difpleafure.

The *conftant* Revenue chiefly arifes from ordinary Taxes. A Ruffian Peafant pays for his Houfe and Land as follows:

From Taxes which are either conftant and fixed, raifed on all Subjects in general.

	Copecks.
To the War-Office	25
To the Admiralty	10
For Recruits	6
Contribution Money for Horfes kept for Travellers in the feveral Governments	11
Towards Brick-kilns	3
Towards Lime-kilns	3
For Materials for the Fortifications of *Petersbourg*	4
Towards Poft-horfes	5
For the Support of *Pricaffes* or Offices	1
For Extraordinary Expences	$\frac{1}{2}$

Copecks $68\frac{1}{2}$

This Tax is raised on every Village according to the number of its Farms or Houses as determined in the *Visitation Inventory*. Till the Year 1710. they made use of the Registers drawn up in the Year 1679. during the Reign of *Fedor Alexewitz*; but upon Consideration that since that time the number of Inhabitants must have remarkably increased, *Commissioners* were appointed in the said Year 1710. for a new *Visitation* through the whole Country, who were to set down the number of Houses in each Village, with the Names not only of the Masters, but also of their whole Families. In the Year 1715, new Orders were given to the Provincial Commissioners to perambulate the Countrey, and to view all the Houses in order to their being exactly registered, which was done accordingly in the Government of *Moskow*, but deferred in the other Governments, for what Reason is not known. However all these Dispositions are not sufficient for putting a stop to the Corruptions and Artifices made use of by the Nobility to render the Czar's salutary Intentions ineffectual. The only Riches of the greater part of them consisting in Villages and landed Estates, all their Thoughts are bent upon making the best Advantage of them, and skreening as much as possible their Peasants from publick Taxes, to obtain which End they think no Means unlawful; and if there is one or other among the Commissioners of so honest a Mind as to be proof against Corruption (which is a very rare thing in that Nation) yet the Nobility know how to find Expedients for imposing on the very Senses of the said Officers, which they can

do

The Present State of Russia.

do the more easily, seeing the Houses of the Peasants are wholly made of Timber notched in on the four Corners, which they can unjoint in a few Hours and remove whither they please. This Trick is well enough known, but as there is no Remedy against it, the Senate has judged proper to gather in the Contributions according to the old Visitation-Registers of 1679. except only in the Government of *Kioff*, where the number of Houses specified in the said old Visitation, having increased too much, especially by new Settlements made there since *Ukrania* submitted to the Obedience of *Russia*, the Deficiency was thought too gross and palpable to be passed over; and therefore the Taxes are levied in the said Government according to the Visitation of 1710. Besides these ordinary Taxes the Country People pay yearly a certain *Impost* to the Czar on Mills, Ponds, Fishing, Bee-hives, Meadows, Gardens, Bagnios, and other the like Possessions. The Mills are assessed in proportion to the Quantity that may yearly be ground in them, the Owner paying to the Czar the value of the fourth part of what he clears. This Proportion is observed as to the Mills belonging to ordinary People and the Clergy, but those that are above them have found Means in this Article as well as others, to persuade the Commissioners that their Mills yield much less than they really do, and to prevail with them to be very favourably used. The Bagnios of the Peasants pay no more than five *Altins* a Year, which though a small matter in Appearance, yields a great Revenue, considering their great number, and that a Russian can be without a Church sooner than without a Bagnio. As for the Taxes on Fishing, Ponds, Meadows, Gardens and the like, they bear no just Proportion to the Property of the Owner, but are subject to the Impost which was laid on them in ancient Times, be it high or low, according as Circumstances went then. The Province of *Dorpt* pays according to Capitulation 25000 Rubels, *Riga* 600, *Oesel* 9000, and *Reval* 15000.

In particular on Townsmen.

The Inhabitants of the Towns and Market Towns in *Russia* not only pay the abovesaid ordinary Taxes in common with the Peasants, but also over and above some other Imposts. Two of which are general, *viz. Ground-Rents,* and a *Tax on Estates real and personal.* Ground-Rents are levied on all Burghers Houses that do not stand on *White Ground,* at the Rate of five *Copecks* a Year on every fathom Square. *White Ground* signifies in *Russia* such Parcels of Land as in former times were assigned to great Men or the Nobility, as also to Soldiers for their Habitation, by which they were exempted from that sort of Contribution. The rest are called *black Ground* and are liable to the abovesaid Rent, by whomsoever inhabited, even the greatest Men not excepted if they build on such Ground. However this Tax is very easy in Comparison to *that on Estates real and personal,* which is only laid on such Persons as exercise Trade, Handicrafts, or the like. This is reputed a constant Revenue, though it varies almost every Year. For considering that in the way of Trade one Man decays in his Circumstances, while another rises, some Years ago they began to introduce

duce the choice of Burghermasters among them: who are to see an Equality observed in Contributions, and in case one of the Inhabitants is so reduced as not to be able to pay his Quota, to free him from that Burthen and to lay it on another who is in better Circumstances. They divide all the Inhabitants as to their Possessions into certain Classes, rating some at half a Copeck, others at two, three, and so on to one Rubel: But notwithstanding the Townsmen or Burghers find much Ease by this Method, yet the Tax itself is still an heavy Burthen upon them, for they find, that what the Collectors softly term being rated at one Altin or three Copecks, amounts upon the upshot to twenty or thirty Rubels, and those of the first Classes even yearly pay five or six hundred Rubels reckoning one Year with another, besides the usual Customs which they pay in their respective Ways of Trade. There are two particular Imposts more which Townsmen pay; the one is for their *Bagnios*; an ordinary Burgher pays one Rubel, but rich Merchants trading by wholesale and Boyars pay three, and this is almost the sole Duty the Nobility pay for their Houses which are free from all other Imposts besides. All Possessors of Houses of what Condition soever, are obliged to contribute towards repairing the *Pavement*, or rather the flooring of the Streets, (for they are laid over with Timber like a Bridge) paying every fifth Year five Copecks for each Fathom the House holds in front; this Tax however yields little or no Profit to the Treasury, but is given to the

Undertakers who have the care of mending the Streets.

On the Clergy. The *Clergy* of the Land enjoy no Exemption from publick Taxes, but pay as well as the Laity. The Archbishops and Bishops are possessed of great Estates, but are compelled to pay Taxes with as much Rigour as any other Subject. Ten Years ago, and upwards, when the unfortunate War against *Sweden* required vast Sums of Money, all the Church-Lands were taken from the Bishops and Monasteries by the Advice of the Privy-Counsellor Count *Muffin Puschkin*, and united to the Czar's Demesnes: But in the Year 1711. the Bishops had theirs restored, which the Court did either to get rid of their Importunities and Complaints, or to remove all occasion of intestine Commotions at a time when a War was breaking out with the *Turks*. However this Restoration was clogged with a Salvo, that after having let those Prelates hoard up for two or three Years, a free Gift of about twenty or thirty thousand Rubels should be asked of them every third or fourth Year in proportion to their Dioceses, the Income of which the Court had had in the mean while an opportunity of knowing. The Czar also reserved to himself the Patriarchal Lands after having suppressed that Dignity upon the Death of the last Patriarch *Adrian*, and ordered the Archbishop of *Reisan*, or *Riazan*, to exercise the Functions of it as *Exarchus Patriarchalis Sedis*, or Vicegerent of the Patriarchal See. All the Monasteries had not the same good Fortune with the Bishops. The largest indeed observing the good Disposition of the Court, made Application, and got the Villages

Villages that had been taken from them, restored without any Difficulty; but the lesser Monasteries who knew nothing of the Resolutions the Court had taken in their Favour, till the first Heat was again abated, met with great Difficulties in getting their former Possessions restored; and many Monks are to this Day seen haunting the Senate and solliciting with great pains, though perhaps to no purpose, for a thing that at first was willingly offered. The secular Clergy as they are less honoured than any other Persons in Russia, so they labour under greater Imposts in proportion to their Revenue, than other Burghers. He that is Curate of a Place, pays six Copecks for each House lying in his Parish, though it hardly yields so much to himself. Besides this he pays another Tax on account of his Priestly Character, and even another still for his Children. Moreover as it is known that they may not say Mass after Conjugal Embraces till they have first bathed themselves, which makes Bagnios absolutely necessary for them, they are also higher rated than Laymen in this Point; a Peasant pays for his Bagnio but fifteen Copecks, but the Priest is obliged to pay a Rubel for his, how ever indifferent it may be.

These are the Revenues of Russia that may be reckoned certain, though by reason of some Circumstances they are not every Year alike. To determine the true Account of the several Taxes in particular, is a thing very difficult in it self, by reason of their variation, but for a Stranger who is debarred all Access to the supreme Chamber of Accompts [it is almost impossible.] Notwithstanding which there

The State of that Branch of the Revenue.

The *Present State of* Russia.

there have been curious Persons, who at length have prevailed with some Officers of the said Chamber, to communicate to them the following State of the fixed Revenue:

Governments	Towns	Burgher-Houses	Peasant-Houses	Revenue *Rubels*
Moskow	39	17301	236672	1149687
Petersbourg	28	8324	132652	408627
Kioff	56	1864	25816	114857
Archangel	20	4302	92298	374276
Riga	17	1771	42555	83039
Azoff	17	958	40700	154933
Siberia	30	3740	36154	222080
Cazan	54	2545	20571	344064
Nizegorod	10	3694	78562	259581
	271	44499	705980	3111144

There being a seeming Disproportion between the Number of Towns in the Government of *Kioff*, and the Burgher-Houses there, it is necessary to observe, that the said Government comprehends *Ukraina*, or the Country of the *Cosacks*, whose natural Inhabitants are exempt from all Taxes, which is the Reason that in the above Account, such Russian Houses only are reckoned as are subject to Taxes and publick Charges. The same is to be observed with relation to the Government of *Azoff*, where the *Don-Cosacks* inhabiting the Plains on the River *Don*, are also free from all Taxes, for which Privilege they are obliged to keep a watchful Eye against the Inroads of the neighbouring Tartars. *Riga* and *Smolensko*, with the Places belonging to them, are reckoned but one Government, and hence it is that the ordinary Revenue

The Present State of Russia. 69

venue of it is set down eighty three thousand Rubels, whereas all *Livonia* together scarcely yields half that Sum in the present Times.

Among the *variable* Revenues is chiefly to be reckoned the *extraordinary Tax*, called by the Russians *Tschaprosniedengi*, which is a sort of a Free-Gift or Benevolence. The same is raised when extraordinary Occasions demand extraordinary Supplies; as for Instance, in the Year 1711, when the War with the Turks was breaking out, or when there is Occasion for providing the Frontier Places in *Livonia* or *Ingria* with Necessaries, or on any other Emergency when the ordinary Revenue falls short. Which Incidents not being alike every Year, the extraordinary Tax varies accordingly; however it may be said in general, that this does not prove burthensome, at present, when there is no further Apprehension of a War with the Turks. In the Year 1716, the following extraordinary Imposts were levied on each House of Burghers and Peasants. *Variable Taxes.*

	Copecks
For furnishing *Petersbourg* and *Riga* with Provisions	57
For supplying the Admiralty at *Revel* with Materials	$24\frac{3}{4}$
100 Houses were to to furnish one Day-Labourer, for whose Charges each House was rated at	3
500 Houses were to find one Carpenter, and each House to pay towards his Charges	1
For Salaries of *Land Raths* or Provincial Commissioners, Justices, and other Civil Officers, pursuant to a new Order issued the 28th of January 1715	10
In all, *Copecks*	$95\frac{3}{4}$

Great Disorders committed in levying these Taxes.

Excepting the abovementioned Taxes, neither the Townsmen nor Peasants are charged with any Contributions on Account of their Possessions or Trade, so that if they knew how to make the best Advantage of those Blessings which Nature has bestowed upon them, those Imposts would appear easy enough: But the Peasants, on one side, not understanding either how to improve their Land, or to make the best of its Produce; and, on the other side, the Nobility exhausting their very Substance, the Country groans under an insupportable Burthen, and their Minds seem so darkned, and their Senses so stupified by Slavery, that though they are taught the most obvious Improvements in Husbandry, yet they do not care to depart from the old way, thinking that no body can understand it better than their Ancestors did. And it is easy to judge what Account their fruitful Soil might turn to, if one looks out of *Russia* into the Country of the Cosacks, where the Ground is not near so good; for those People being far more industrious and active than the Russians who live among them, and managing their Husbandry much upon the same Foot as in *Poland*, thrive by it, notwithstanding the quartering of Soldiers, and other Oppressions, much better than the Russians, who have the Protection of the Government. The same Unthriftiness is the Reason that many Country Families run away from their Habitations, when they find themselves insolvent, being apprehensive of the Execution, which in these Parts falls little short of Torture. Some of those Fugitives run into the Forrests, and join the Party of *Roskolnikes*, who are a sort of Zealots that

that stickle for the ancient Liturgy, and will not own the present Russian Church to be orthodox, for having made some Alterations in point of Ceremony; others take their Refuge in some Nobleman's House in another Province; however at present hardly any body will harbour them, it being enacted by the Provincial Law, that if one finds his Peasant in another Man's Estate, the latter is bound not only to deliver up the Fugitive, but also to pay to his right Master twenty five Rubels for every Year, during which he shall have entertained him, so that no Body would be a great Gainer by such a Bargain, seeing a Peasant seldom pays half that Sum to his Lord. But they who suffer most by such a Run-away, are his Neighbours, for as they are under an Incapacity of manuring his Land, which, as it is easy to imagine, is commonly quite out of Heart, and yet are forced to make up the full Sum of the Czar's Taxes, as though there was no Deficiency in the Number of Inhabitants; it follows of Course, that being at length quite ruined themselves, they follow the Example of their Brethren, and fly from their Habitations to the Forrests. Yet even these Disorders are not so prejudicial to the Country as the Mismanagement of the Provincial Commissioners, Chancellors, and Clerks, who are intrusted with the Collection of the Taxes. These Cormorants no sooner enter upon their Offices, but they make it their sole Study how to build their Fortunes upon the Ruin of the Country People, and he that came among them having hardly Clothes to his Back, is often known in four or five Years time, to have scraped so much together,

ther, as to be able to build large Stone-Houses, when at the same Time the poor Subjects are forced to run away from their Cottages. It is certain they cannot clear so much by their Salaries, which some time ago hardly amounted to six Rubels a Year, but were lately augmented to fifteen or twenty, by a new Order from the Czar, to the intent, that no Pretext be left for the like Extortions. But as the superior Officers are no less greedy of unlawful Gains than their Inferiors, and consequently connive at their vile Practices, the Country is exhausted to that Degree, that though in the most difficult Times a House is hardly taxed above six or seven Rubels a Year, yet the Inhabitants by the Extortions of those Officers of the Finances, are forced to pay every Year no less than thirteen, or even fifteen; and a certain Russian, who had been conversant in these Affairs, was once heard to say, that of one hundred Rubels collected in the Country, he was positively assured not thirty ever came into the Czar's Coffers, the Remainder being divided among the Officers for the Trouble of gathering them in. The Artifices which they make use of, are innumerable, and though a Stop is put to some by the Czar's Regulations, yet they are surprizingly dexterous in finding out new ones. For Instance, if a superior Officer has a Mind to shew a Kindness to his Clerk, he provides him with a Commission for examining, whether the Peasants of a certain Territory have paid in all their Taxes, and can produce Receipts for it. The Clerk as soon as he enters into a Village, asks with Importunity for the Receipts, and in the mean

mean while quarters himself with his Train upon the Inhabitants. The Peasant, on the other Hand, if unluckily in his Surprize he is not able immediately to produce the Receipt, which often happens, the Dread they have for those Blood-suckers, making them lose their Senses, he is forced to pay the Tax over again upon the Spot, or at least, if he has any Hopes of finding the Receipt, to bribe the Clerk in order to allow him some Respite. The Receipt being at length produced, he is indeed exempt from any further Payment, however he must fee the Clerk for his Trouble, without reckoning his eating and drinking. This Method is frequently made use of, where they know that the Mannor-House is burnt down, where those Papers concerning Lands are usually kept, in which Case the Plea of such a Misfortune bears no Weight with those unmerciful and greedy Executioners.

Besides the Taxes abovementioned, which are levied on the Nation, the Czar has several other *Royalties*, which yearly yield a considerable Revenue, though some may be thought not well becoming the sovereign Dignity. *The Czar's Royalties.*

The Right of *Coinage* belongs only to the Czar, nor is it allowed to any Princes, Lords, or Towns in his Dominions, and though in former Times the Cities of *Novogrod* and *Pleskow* coined Money of their own, yet that Privilege has long since been taken from them. The Mint Offices at those Places were, for some time after, made use of to coin Money in the Czar's Name, and for his Profit; but they were in Process of Time quite removed from thence, and carried to *Moskow*, where there are at present the only 1. *Coinage*.

two

two Mints in *Ruſſia:* One is called *Monetny Dwor,* in which hitherto nothing has been coined but Copper-Money, at the Rate of two Pound Copper for a Rubel; in the other, named *Denezny,* the Silver Species of all Sizes are coined, and an Aſſayer is conſtantly kept there. It is reckoned that both Offices together are worth to the Czar yearly two hundred thouſand Rubels.

2. *Monopoly of ſtrong Liquors.* The Right of keeping *Publick Houſes* is reſerved to the Czar, in all the Provinces and Dependencies of the Ruſſian Empire, except *Ukraina,* as far as it is inhabited by Coſacks, not by Ruſſians, and *Livonia.* This Right only extends to Liquors brewed and prepared within the Country; as for Inſtance, *Beer, Mead,* and *Brandy* made of Corn, which no body throughout all the Ruſſian Dominions is allowed to ſell but the Czar, the Offenders as to Beer and Mead, being liable to a Fine, and as to Brandy, even to corporal Puniſhment. That Nation being more given to ſtrong Liquors than any other, it is eaſy to conclude, that this Revenue is very conſiderable, the rather, becauſe every thing in thoſe publick Houſes is ſold for double the Price of the prime Coſt. By this Method the greateſt Part of the Nation's Money is drawn into the Czar's Treaſury; for Labourers as well as Soldiers receiving one half of their Pay in Proviſions, and the other half in Money, they are not very ſaving of the latter, but immediately upon receiving it, carry a good deal of it to the Tap-Houſe; and though there are ſome of that Nation, who commonly abſtain from ſtrong Liquors, yet in the Eaſter Week, and on other great Holy-

The Present State of Russia.

Holydays, they would be apprehensive of being thought no good Christians, if they passed that Time in Sobriety. Considering those Circumstances it cannot be surprizing to hear, that the Profit which the *Cabacks,* or publick-Houses, throughout the Russian Dominions, yield to the Czar, amounts to near a Million of Rubels yearly. *Moskow* alone yields above one hundred thousand, and the other Towns in proportion, forty, thirty, twenty, ten, and even the smallest of them one or two thousand. The Profit would still be greater, if the Boyars and Nobles were not allowed to carry Brandy for their own Consumption to *Moskow* and *Petersbourg*; for under this Cover all their Servants carry on a Trade with that Commodity, and easily meet with Buyers, because they can sell it a great deal cheaper than the Publick Houses can afford to do, and yet find their Account by it; and I remember that in one Year there was such a Quantity sold in a certain Family that was none of the largest, as was at least nine hundred Rubels Loss to the Czar, by which may be guessed what he loses by the like Practice in greater Houses.

The Sale of *Tobacco* in all *Russia* is also solely reserved to the Czar, which is to be understood of the *English* Tobacco, and that of the Growth of *Ukraina* and *Russia*; for the *Turkish* Tobacco which comes from *Constantinople,* as also *Snuff,* may be freely bought and sold by any body, and the German Merchants even trade with English Tobacco by Connivance of the great Men, who are obliged to apply to them, if they have a Mind to smoak what is good, instead of the rotten Stuff

3. Monopoly of Tobacco.

Stuff that is sold in the Czar's Shops; but Tobacco of the Growth of *Ruſſia*, properly so called, (under which Denomination *Ukraina* and *Livonia* are not comprehended) is prohibited; and those Persons upon whom any is found, are severely fined, or corporally punished, nor does the Excuse avail of laying up for themselves, for that is also prohibited. Yet notwithstanding all these Precautions, there is as much smuggling committed in this Trade, as in that of Brandy; for the Ruſſians, tempted by the great Profit of being able to sell for six or eight Copecks, in their own Country, what they buy in *Ukraina* for one, endeavour to turn the Penny, though at the Hazard of the *Knout*.

4. *Monopoly of Potaſh, Weedaſh, Icingglaſs, and Tar.* The Czar has also the Monopoly of *Pot-Aſhes*, *Weed-Aſhes*, *Icing-glaſs*, (of that sort which is a Glue made of a Fish) and *Tar*, which Commodities being sold at the Czar's own Price, they bring in a great Profit; if they are found by any private Merchant, he is punished, though only with Confiscation of the prohibited Goods.

5. *A new Monopoly of* Ruſſia *Leather, taken off again.* In the Year 1716, when the Czar was upon his Departure for *Holland*, an Order was issued, forbidding all private Persons to buy any *Ruſſia Leather*, and commanding all Leather-Dreſſers to sell it only to certain Commiſſaries appointed for that purpose, at the Rate of four Rubels a *Pudde*, which is forty Pound Weight. The latter had Orders to send the Leather to *Archangel*, and to let the foreign Merchant there have it at the same Price, on Condition, however, that they ſhould make the Payment in *Holland* in a Specie called *Albertus-Dalers*, reckoning each at eighty

eighty Copecks. This was done for two Reasons; first, because the Remittances to be sent for the Czar to *Holland*, could not be made without considerable Loss, the Course of Exchange running then very high in *Holland*; and, secondly, to try whether this new Method would turn to Account. But the first Reason ceasing, and the Leather-Dressers being apprehensive of the Continuance of that Monopoly, and for that Reason working off less Leather than in former Years, the abovesaid Order was recalled, and the Trade opened again, as before.

6. All the *Salt-works* in *Russia* belong to the Czar in Property. There were a great many of them in former Times, but afterwards they were all abandoned except three, *viz.* those of the *Stroganoffs*, at *Bachmut*, and in *Siberia*. The first are situate in the Government of *Casan*, and are named after one *Stroganoff*, a rich Merchant at *Moskow*, whose Family is still in good Repute there; he had purchased the Salt-Pits, and improved them to that Degree, that he was able to persuade the Czar to ruin all the lesser Works, upon his engaging to furnish all his Territories with Salt a good deal cheaper; on these Terms he kept them several Years, but his Riches becoming an Eye-fore to the great Men, the Management of these Works was taken from him; however, the Pits and Works lying on his own Ground, the Czar allowed him for every *Pudde* of Salt made there $1\frac{1}{2}$ *Copeck*, which is said to amount every Year to twenty thousand *Rubels*, so that it is easy to conceive what Profit they yield to the Czar. The Salt-works at *Bachmut* on the River *Don*, belong

6. *Monopoly of Salt.*

to

to the *Tartars* as to the Property, but have hitherto yielded about thirty thousand Rubels to the Czar's Revenue. However, the common Opinion is, that were it not for the great Frauds committed in the Management of them, they might yield double the Sum; and this was the Occasion why Prince *Demetrius Keltzoff Massalsky*, Governor of *Bachmut*, was taken into Custody the Beginning of the Year 1717, and afterwards publickly hanged at *Petersbourg*, and his Corpse, for an Example to others, left two Months on the Gallows, nor was the Grand-Admiral *Apraxin*, whose Brother the Senator was also involved in that Affair, with all his Credit able to save him. The Salt-Works in *Siberia* are kept but indifferently, and the Produce of them is but just enough to answer the Demand of that Province, and the neighbouring Tartars.

7. *Monopoly of Siberian Goods.* The Czar has also the Monopoly of all *Siberian Commodities*, under which Denomination are comprehended, not only those that are of the Growth of *Siberia*, but also all others that are brought from *China* by the way of *Siberia*. The principal are the Skins of Siberian Foxes, Sables, Hyenas, Ermines, Lynxes, and other Furs, as also Chinese Gold Stuffs, Fish-bones, Teeth of a Beast called *Mamant*, &c. These Commodities are neither publickly sold in *Siberia* or *Russia*, nor prohibited to be sold; but on the Roads, by which all Persons coming from *Siberia*, and going to *Moskow*, necessarily must pass, the strictest Search is made, that nothing of the abovementioned Goods be exported for the Account of private Persons, so that the Officers on the Passes, and the *Waiwods* and *Land-Raths*, i. e. the Governors

The Present State of Russia.

vernors and Commissioners in the Provinces and Towns, upon the least Suspicion, even search and take to pieces the Sled and other Carriages of the Passengers, to prevent the many Frauds that are committed in carrying out Gold. But if one can procure a Passport from the Governor of *Siberia*, and has sufficient Means or Credit, one may purchase very cheap in *Siberia* what will sell at a great Rate in *Russia*. For the Governors, who almost bear a sovereign Sway in that Country, notwithstanding those great Precautions, prefer their own private Interest to that of the Czar, and commonly return with vast Riches to *Russia*. Prince *Gagarin*, the present Governor of *Siberia*, being accused of Mismanagements of this kind, was sent for to *Petersbourg* several times, *viz.* in the Years 1715, 1716, and 1719, and upon my last Departure from *Russia* was still under * Confinement.

All other Merchandize, the free Trade of which is permitted, pay a certain Duty for Importation and Exportation. In every Town of *Russia* there are certain *Toll-booths*, where every Merchant enters the Goods he buys or sells; but as to general *Custom Houses*, there are reckoned but five throughout all *Russia*, viz. at *Archangel*, *Petersbourg*, *Astracan*, *Kioff*, and *Moskow*. At *Archangel* and *Petersbourg* are entered the Exports and Imports of *England*, *Holland*, *Denmark*, *France*, *Prussia*, *Hambourg*, and other Sea-Towns; at *Astracan*, those of *Persia*; at *Kioff*, those of *Turky*; the last of all is the Exchange at *Moskow*, where

8. *Tolls or Customs.*

[* *The publick Advices from* Peterfbourg *have since informed us, that he was at last hanged for it on the* 27th *of* March 1721.]

another

another Duty is paid befides thofe above, for all the Trade and Confumption of the whole *Nation* that centers there.

Obfervations on this State of the Revenue. Thefe are the principal Branches of the Revenues arifing out of the vaft Dominions of the Czar, not to mention at prefent others which he has had the Addrefs to procure by his own Induftry; as for Inftance, the divers Materials neceffary for his Docks, and other Buildings. But though thefe Revenues are fo confiderable, that the Czar, during fo long a War, and amidft fo many Changes and Enterprizes, has had no Occafion as yet to contract Debts with Foreign Nations, as is faid above, nor to have Recourfe to Paper-Money, yet he would be ftill able to raife far larger Sums in his Dominions, if he was feconded by a good Number of wife and faithful Minifters, and if his Finances were modelled after a more regular Method, which would prove a Remedy againft that Want of Money which daily increafes. It is true, they are now about eftablifhing a new Chamber of Finances, which is to put the Revenue into a better Method: But, befides that it will be very difficult, if not entirely impoffible, for ten or twelve Foreigners, to bring thofe Affairs of a Country, to which they are Strangers, into a better Regulation; the Czar will always find the Obftinacy of his Subjects, and their natural Bent to Injuftice and Extortion, an infurmountable Obftacle to the wife Ends he has propofed to himfelf.

Feftival of the Order of St. Andrew. On the 11th of *December* was folemnized the Feftival of St. *Andrew* the Patron of the *Ruffian Order*, the Knights of which were at that time, the *Czar*, the Kings of *Denmark* and

The Present State of Ruſſia.

and *Poland,* Prince *Menzikoff,* Admiral *Apraxin,* the Great Chancellor *Golofkin,* M. *Bruce* Maſter of the Ordnance, General Prince *Repnin,* Count *Vitzdom* the Poliſh Miniſter, General *Weide:* to which have ſince been added Vice-Chancellor Baron *Schafiroff,* and Privy Councellor *Tolſtoy.*

The Czarina appeared on that Solemnity with the Collar of her new *Order,* conſiſting of a Croſs hanging on a white Ribbon, with this Motto: *Out of Love and Fidelity to my Countrey.* The occaſion of erecting this Order was as follows: The Czarina out of Love to her Conſort having attended him in the Campaign on the River *Pruth,* where their Majeſties with the whole Army were in the utmoſt Diſtreſs, ſhe diſpatched a Courrier to the Grand Vizier, unknown to the Czar, as ſome ſay, or according to others with his private Conſent, to make him an Offer of a great Sum of Money if he would hearken to a Negociation with the Czar. The Grand Vizier having given Ear to ſo tempting a Propoſal, a Treaty was ſet on foot, and a Peace concluded through the Czar's prudent Conduct. The Grand Vizier having on this occaſion ſent Deputies into the Ruſſian Camp, charged them in particular to deſire to be admitted to the Czarina's Preſence, in order to be convinced ſhe was actually there, he thinking it improbable that a Lady out of Love to her Husband ſhould venture with him on ſo dangerous an Expedition. The Money was paid, and the Czar ſome time after remembering this Accident, was pleaſed that the Czarina ſhould perpetuate the Memory of it, by erecting the ſaid new Order.

The Czarina's new Order.

The Russian Ambassador's return from Constantinople.

A Heretick of the Sect of the Roskolniks burnt.

On the 20th of *December* Baron *Schafiroff* and Privy Councellor *Tolstoy* arrived at *Petersbourg* being returned from their troublesome Embassy in *Turkey*.

A Russian Priest at *Moskow*, whose Name was *Foma*, having had the Boldness publickly to preach against the Invocation of Saints and other Articles of the Russian Religion, the Clergy at first endeavoured to bring him to recant. But he persisted and even proceeded so far as to rush into the publick Congregation on the Festival of St. *Alexius*, and to cut the Image of that Saint and of the Virgin *Mary* to pieces with an Ax, but when he was going to expose to the People the Unreasonableness of the Russian Faith, he was seized and carried to Prison. Sentence being given against him, he was in the beginning of this Month burned alive at *Moskow*, as a Heretick and Violator of Images, after he had first, pursuant to the Sentence, held his Hand with the Ax in the Flames till both were consumed, shewing great Resolution and preaching to the People till the last Moment. He was reported to be of the Sect of the *Roskolniks*, who have entirely separated from the Russian Church, a few Ceremonies excepted. They live in the Forests and other remote Places, refusing to submit to the same Church Authority as other Russians, though they regularly pay their Taxes, and in all other respects lead an irreproachable Life. They have often been persecuted, but could never be extirpated, and it happened but lately that about three hundred of them being pursued, retired to a Church, and refusing to surrender, set the Building on Fire and burned themselves.

themselves. Upon this the Czar gave Orders to leave them undisturbed in the Forests, as long as they did not spread their Tenets among the other Ruſſians.

At the end of this Year there arrived an Ambaſſador of the *Calmucks* with an odd Commiſſion. Prince *Menzikoff* some time before had made a Preſent of a handſome Coach of Engliſh make to the *Can* of the *Calmucks*, but one of the Wheels being broken, this Embaſſy was ſent to deſire the Prince to let him have another Wheel. The Ambaſſador told us that his Maſter gave Audience to the Envoys of his Neighbours in the ſaid Coach, and that on ſolemn Days he dined in it; the Pole he had looked upon as ſuperfluous and cauſed it to be cut off. *An odd Embaſſy from the Can of the Calmucks.*

On the 3d of *January* the Czar ſent a Ruſſian Lieutenant Colonel to *Pillau* near *Koningsberg*, to ſee the famous *Globe of Gottorp* carried over the Snow by the help of Sleds and large Rollers to *Riga*, from whence it was further carried by Sea to *Petersbourg*. The Tranſportation of that Machine which could not be taken to pieces, cauſed a prodigious Expence, whole Foreſts being cut through to make way for it. It is now put up at *Petersbourg* in the Houſe which was the Perſian Elephant's Habitation. *January 1715. The Globe of Gottorp carried to Petersbourg.*

On the 8th of *January* died a *Dwarf* who was in the Czar's Service, and particularly beloved by him, for which reaſon he ordered a humorous Funeral for him. Four Ruſſian Prieſts in a magnificent Eccleſiaſtical Habit began the Proceſſion; then went thirty Singers followed by two Conductors preceding the Corpſe, which lay in a Coffin covered with *The humourous Funeral of a Dwarf.*

with black Velvet, upon a long Sled drawn by fix little black Horſes; behind the Coffin fate the Brother of the deceaſed, being likewiſe a Dwarf of about fifty Years old, graſping the Coffin between his Arms. Behind the Sled marched twelve couple of Dwarfs two and two holding each other by the Hand. But the moſt diverting part of the Shew were the She-dwarfs that followed the Men in the like Order, being ranged according to their ſeveral Sizes like Organ-pipes. The Czar with all his Miniſters and Servants cloſed the Proceſſion.

New-Year's-Day ſolemnized. New-Year's-day, which is one of the greateſt Feſtivals with the Ruſſians, being come about according to the Old Style, the Czar repaired to Church at four in the Morning, and officiated himſelf, beginning the Tunes and reading the Epiſtle before the Altar, a Cuſtom he has obſerved ever ſince he ſuppreſſed the Patriarchal Dignity. Divine Service being ended, the Czar returned to his Reſidence, and all the Canon of the Fortreſs were diſcharged. We went to complement his Majeſty, the Czarina, the Princeſſes their Daughters, and were admitted to kiſs their Hands, having firſt received from the Czar's own Hand each of us a Cup of Brandy. In the Afternoon the Czar with the Ruſſian Nobility began to perform the Ceremony, which they call *Slawen*, that is to ſay, ſolemnizing a Feſtival and giving Thanks to God, which laſted eight Days. This is a Cuſtom which the Czar has not yet thought fit to aboliſh, and is obſerved as follows. The Men walk firſt with a certain Machine of Iron reſembling a Kettle Drum; the Sticks with

with which they beat it, are twisted about with Cloth in order to deaden the Sound; then comes the Czar with the whole Clergy attended by a great number of Kneefes and Boyars, the whole Company sitting on Sleds, and so they go about from Place to Place visiting the principal Men belonging to the Court. When they have entered a House they sing the Russian *Te Deum* and make a new Years Wish, which being ended, the Master of the House presents the Czar, as Head of the Clergy, with a handsome Present in Money, and invites his Guests to his Table where they are well entertained: The Company do not tarry above two Hours in one Place, but remove to another, making about five or six such Visits in a Day, which are very profitable to the Clergy on account of the Czar's being with them.

Another notable and great Holiday with the Russians, is *Twelfth-day*, and the Consecration of the Water, which was celebrated with particular Pomp on the 17th of *January*. At seven in the Morning divine Service began, which lasted till ten; during that time, seven Battalions of the *Preobrazinsky* Guards marched upon the River *Neva*, that was frozen up, and formed a Square. The Czar himself marched at their Head as Colonel, and the Czarewitz appeared in the Ranks as Sergeant. In the midst of the said Square a Hole was cut into the Ice, round which a House was built, made of several Arches which centered in the Top, and surrounded with a Gallery which was hung with red Cloth. Divine Service being ended, the Procession began from the Church towards the Ice, all the Bells

Consecration of the Water on Twelfth Day.

Bells ringing. Four Priests with burning Tapers walked before the *Archi-Reje* or Archbishop, who carried a large Crucifix set with precious Stones, and was supported by two other Priests: He was followed by a great number of *Popes*, or secular Priests, and a multitude of People. The Clergy sung during the Procession, and were richly dressed in their several Ecclesiastical Habits; when they passed before the Czar's Regiment, his Majesty saluted them with his Sword, and so they went to the said House, said Mass, and consecrated the Water, which Ceremony was attended with a general Discharge of all the Artillery, and a triple Volley of small Arms of the Soldiery. Mean while the Priests took some of the consecrated Water out of the Hole, and gave it to those who stood by to drink, as also baptized the Children that were brought to them. The Clergy being returned back in Procession, the Populace with great eagerness crowded to the Hole, filled their Vessels with Water, and joyfully hastned with it home, even Cripples and sick People crept to it and did the same. It is believed this Custom, which has obtained in *Russia* many Ages, is derived from the ancient Grecians, and the Russians religiously stick to this consecrating the Rivers every Year in Thanksgiving to God for the great Blessing they think they receive from the bathing themselves in them, which they count their chief Remedy against Indispositions. The former Czars were obliged on this Occasion, to attend the Patriarch while he was getting upon his Horse and alighting; but the present Czar has since put Church Affairs on another footing,

ing, and pretty well clipped their Wings; their Revenues are reduced to near a third part of what they were before, and it is with great Difficulty that they have hitherto preserved their venerable Beards.

The End of *January* Count *Piper* was brought from *Moskow* to *Petersbourg*, and afterwards closely confined in the Fortress of *Sleutel-Sleutelbourg*. The Reasons of his hard Usage were thus reported: In the Year 1712. the Russians burned five Dutch Merchantships off *Helsingfors*, mistaking them for Swedish; the States-General long insisted upon Reparation, but to no purpose; the Russian Court therefore pretending that the Swedish Ships which lay at the same time near *Helsingfors*, had been the occasion of that Accident, and bearing an ill Will to Count *Piper* for having been the Cause of great Damages and Affronts to them before he was taken Prisoner, would oblige him to make good that Demand; and he was told at *Petersbourg* that he must either resolve to pay fifty thousand Rubels, or expect to be sent to the remotest Parts of *Siberia*. Accordingly the Count drew a Bill upon his Lady in *Sweden* for the said Sum, which she accepted; but the King of *Sweden* forbidding her under severe Penalties to make Payment, Count *Piper* was for that reason used harder than before in his Imprisonment.

Count Piper carried to Sleutelbourg and put under close Confinement.

About that time the Governor of *Kioff* sent Notice to the Czar, that the *Crim Tartars* were in Arms and drawing near the Frontiers. Those Plunderers are commonly stirred up by the *Porte* to make Disturbance. Two Years ago they made a dreadful Inroad into

The Crim Tartars in Motion.

into the Czar's Territories and carried off twelve thousand People and upwards. The Czar having complained of it to the *Porte*, the latter sent Orders to the Tartarian *Murza* or General to restore the Prisoners; but he only sent back two thousand old Men and Women, pretending the rest had disperfed or died. The Czar in order to secure his Frontiers against those Invaders, has already for some Years sent his Army in *Ukrania*, with numbers of Peasants to work on the Fortifications of *Kioff*, *Czernichoff*, *Pultava*, and on a new Fort raised eight Leagues from *Pultava*.

The Don-Cosacks reduced.

An Embassy from the *Don-Cossacks* arrived at *Petersbourg*. Six Years ago when the Czar made so great Levies of Forces in his Dominions, about thirty thousand young Fellows fled the Country and joined with the plundering Gangs of those Cossacks. The Czar reclaimed his Subjects, but was denied, whereupon he sent General *Dolgoruki* and two other Kneefes as Deputies to the Cosacks, to insist on the delivering up his Subjects; but the Cosacks at first used them ill, and at length murthered them with all their Retinue, and went to lay Siege to *Azoff*. The Czar resenting this barbarous Proceeding, sent Lieutenant General *Dolgoruki*, Brother to him that was killed, with twelve thousand Men of well disciplined Troops, to revenge his Brother's Death, and to reduce those Robbers by Force, which he did so effectually, that he twice defeated the Cosacks in the Field, and raised the Siege of *Azoff*, upon which the Cosacks came to Terms and returned to their former Obedience. That Nation

The Present State of Russia.

Nation might be of Service to the Czar, but he does not yet judge proper to let them be instructed in the Military Discipline of *Germany*, but when he has occasion for their Assistance in any Expedition, he furnishes them with Arms, which he takes from them again when the Campaign is ended.

Preparations having been made by the whole Court during three Months for a great Masquerade, the same was at length kept on the 27th and 28th of *January*. I will relate the main Particulars, the World never having heard, for ought I know, of the like before. The occasion of this Masquerade was a Wedding. One *Sotoff*, who had been the Czar's Writing-Master in his Majesty's younger Years, was in the 70th Year of his Age advanced to be his Jester, or merrymaking *Privy-Counsellor*, and afterwards *Mock-Patriarch*. Moreover for Humour fake he was raised to the Dignity of a *Prince*, and at length declared *Pope*. Invested with those imaginary Characters, and being now in the 84th Year of his Age, the Czar married him to a buxom Widow of thirty four, and the Nuptials of this extraordinary Couple were solemnized by the Court in Masks, or Mock-shew. The Company consisted of about four hundred Persons of both Sexes. Every four Persons had their proper Dress and peculiar musical Instruments, so that they represented a hundred different sorts of Habits and Musick, particularly of the Asiatick Nations. The four Persons appointed to invite the Guests, were the greatest Stammerers that could be found in all *Russia*. Old decrepit Men who were not able to walk or stand, had been picked out to serve for Bridesmen,

A great Masquerade.

Bridefmen, Stewards, and Waiters. There were four running Footmen, the moſt unweildy Fellows, who had been troubled with the Gout moſt of their Life-time, and were ſo fat and bulky that they wanted others to lead them. The *Mock-Czar* of *Moskow*, who repreſented King *David* in his Dreſs, inſtead of a Harp had a Lyre covered with a Bearskin, to play upon. He being the Chief of the Company, was carried on a ſort of Pageant placed on a Sled, to the four Corners of which were tied as many Bears, which being prickt with Goads by Fellows purpoſely appointed for it, made ſuch a frightful roaring as well ſuited the confuſed and horrible Dinn raiſed by the diſagreeing Inſtruments of the reſt of the Company. The *Czar* himſelf was dreſſed like a Boor of *Frizeland*, and skilfully beat a Drum in Company with three Generals. In this manner, Bells ringing every-where, the ill-matched Couple were attended by the Masks to the Altar of the great Church, where they were joined in Matrimony by a Prieſt a hundred Years old, who had loſt his Eyeſight and Memory, to ſupply which Defect a pair of Spectacles were put on his Noſe, two Candles held before his Eyes, and the Words ſounded into his Ears, which he was to pronounce. From Church the Proceſſion went to the *Czar's* Palace where the Diverſions laſted ſome Days. Many ſtrange Adventures and comical Accidents happened on their riding on Sleds through the Streets, too long to be related here. Thus much may ſuffice to ſhew, that the Czar among all the heavy Cares of Government knows how to ſet apart ſome Days for the Relaxation of his Mind,

and

and how ingenious he is in the Contrivance of those Diversions.

In *March* Prince *Conto Cantacuzeno* arrived from *Ukraina* at *Petersbourg*. There have been four unfortunate foreign Princes who being driven out of their Dominions, have been taken under the *Czar's* Protection. The first is *Cantimir*, Hospodar of *Moldavia*, who has two Sisters, the eldest of whom was married to *Stefano Cantacuzeno* the late Hospodar of *Walachia*, strangled at *Constantinople*, but she made her Escape with her two Sons out of Prison in *Turkey*; the eldest of whom I saw at *Petersbourg* in the Year 1718. the Czar having taken him into his Guards. *Cantimir* has a Brother who lives concealed at *Constantinople* and keeps Correspondence with him. The second of those exiled Princes is the foresaid *Conto-Cantacuzeno*, married to the younger Sister of the said Hospodar of *Moldavia* with whom he fled from thence to *Russia*, leaving behind him to the value of four hundred thousand Crowns: He is very much beloved by the *Czar* for his extraordinary Merit and Conduct, is Major-General in his Service, and has a Pension of five thousand Rubels. He is at present Governor of a Fortress in *Ukraina*. The third was Prince *Militetzki*, who was divested of his Dominions in *Georgia* by the King of *Persia*, and died at *Moskow*: His only *Son* being General of the Artillery in the Czar's Army, was taken Prisoner in the Battle of *Narva*, and died at *Stockholm*. The *Czar* had promised to his Father to re-establish him in his Dominions by Force of Arms, and to send him thither at the Head of some thousands of Men, as soon as the *Swedish* War

March 1715. Four exiled Princes under the Czar's Protection.

War should be at an End. The *Czar* still persists in this Design of dispossessing the present Usurper from thence, and I was assured by the Hospodar of *Moldavia* that in case the Russians would go in good Earnest about making an Enterprize in *Georgia*, the *Shach* of *Persia* would hardly enter into a War upon that account; to confirm which Assertion he gave the following Character of him: That he is a Prince of forty Years of Age, of a very indolent Temper, giving himself wholly up to Pleasures, adjusting all his Differences with the *Turks, Indians*, and other Neighbours by the Interposition of his Governors and by Dint of Money; that though he called himself *Shani-Shach*, or Emperor of Emperors, yet he dreaded the Turk to that degree, that on all Occasions he bestowed upon him the Title of *Padi-Shach*, or Opposer of Emperors; and notwithstanding the Turks have in the Space of eighty Years conquered from the Persians many great Kingdoms, viz. *Media, Assyria, Babylon* and *Arabia*, yet they always avoided making War against the Porte.

June 1715. Warlike Preparations. Death of a Daughter of the Czar.

The Spring was spent in Preparations for a Sea-Campaign, and several new Men of War were launched. On the 7th of *June* died the Czar's third Daughter lately born.

A hard Drinking-bout and other Diversions, preceding the Czar's putting to Sea with his Fleet.

On the 9th the Czar went to *Cronslot*, whither we followed him in a Galley, in which open Vessel we lay at Anchor two Days and three Nights, by reason of a Storm, without Fire, Beds, or Provisions: Being at last arrived at *Cronslot*, we were invited to the Czar's Pleasure-house *Peterhoff*, situate on the Coast of *Ingria*, where we arrived with a good Wind,

Wind, and were entertained there as usual: For at Dinner we were so plied with *Tockay* Wine, though his Czarish Majesty himself forbore drinking too much, that at our breaking up, we were hardly able to stand, nevertheless we were obliged to empty each a Bowl holding a full Quart, which we received from the Czarina's own Hand, whereupon we quite lost our Senses, and were in that pickle carried off to sleep, some in the Garden, others in the Wood, and the rest here and there on the Ground. At four in the Afternoon we were waked, and brought again to the Pleasure-House, where the Czar gave to each of us an Hatchet, with Orders to follow him. He lead us into a Wood of young Trees, where he marked a Walk of about an hundred Paces in length to the Sea-shore, to be cut out among the Trees. He fell to work foremost, and though we (being seven in Number besides his Majesty) found so unusual a Drudgery very hard for People, who had not half recovered their Senses, yet we followed couragiously, cutting down after him, so that in three Hours we got through, by which Time the Fumes of Wine were pretty well evaporated, nor did we receive any Harm, except a certain Minister, who hacked at the Trees with such Fury, that, by the Fall of one, he was hit, and somewhat bruised. The Czar having thanked us for our Pains by Word of Mouth, the actual Reward followed at Supper, when we received such another Dose of Liquor, as sent us senseless to Bed; but having scarcely slept an Hour and half, a certain Favourite of the Czar's was sent about Midnight to rouse us, and carry us, us, willing or unwilling, to the Prince of *Circaſſia*, who was already a-bed with his Conſort, where we were again by their Bed-ſide peſtered with Wine and Brandy till four in the Morning, that next Day none of us remembered how he got home. About eight we were invited to Court to Breakfaſt, but inſtead of Coffee and Tea, as we expected, we were welcomed with large Cups of Brandy, after which we were ſent to take the Air on a high Hill near the Palace, at the Foot of which we found a Boor attending with eight poor Tits without Saddles or Stirups, which altogether were not worth four Crown Pieces. Thus comically equipped we paſſed the Review before their Czariſh Majeſties, who leaned out at the Window: A certain Ruſſian of Diſtinction led the Vanguard, and by the Help of Switches or Sticks, we made our Jades mount up Hill as well as we could: After having taken a Turn for an Hour in the Wood, and refreſhed our ſelves with hearty Draughts of Water, we had the fourth Drinking-bout at Dinner, and a briſk Gale preſenting, that was like to toſs us well about, we were brought on Board the Czar's *Torrenſchute*: The Czarina and her Ladies took the Cabin; but the Czar ſtayed with us in the open Air, poſitively aſſuring us, notwithſtanding the violent contrary Wind, that we ſhould be at *Cronſlot* in four Hours time. After we had continued tacking about near two Hours, a dreadful Storm aroſe, ſo that the Czar began to lay aſide jeſting, and to put his Hands to the Rudder, ſhewing in that imminent Danger, beſides his great Skill in working a Ship, an uncommon Strength of

Body,

Body, and Undauntedness of Mind. The Czarina was laid on high Benches in the Cabin, which was full of Water, the Waves beating over the Vessel, and violent Rains falling, in which dangerous Condition she shewed a great deal of Resolution; every one of us grew sober through the Thoughts of approaching Death, which made us think on Heaven, and prepare for all Events, having no other Comfort left on Earth, but that of dying in so noble Company. The four *Boyers*, in which were the Czar's Retinue and our Servants, were dispersed and driven ashore, and our Vessel, which was strong built, and provided with good Sailors, was at last, after being tossed about seven Hours, driven into the Port of *Cronslot*, where the Czar left us with these Words: *Good Night t'ye, Gentlemen; this was carrying the Jest too far.* Next Morning he was seized with an Ague. We on our Part being thoroughly soaked, as having for so many Hours sate in Water up to the middle, made haste to get a-shore on the Island; but not being able to get either Clothes or Beds, our own Baggage being gone another Way, we made a Fire, stript stark naked, and wrapt our Bodies up again in the coarse Covers of Sleds, which we had from the Peasants; in which Condition we passed the Night, moralizing and making grave Reflexions on the Miseries and Follies of humane Life. On the 16th of *July* the Czar put to Sea with his Fleet, which we had not the good Fortune to see, being all of us ill of Agues, and other Indispositions; however, in *August* we followed his Majesty by Land to *Reval*, where we found

him

him and the *British* Fleet commanded by Admiral *Norris*.

The State of Narva and Dorpt at that Time.

When I paſſed through *Narva*, I found that Town ſtill in the ſame pitiful State in which I ſaw it laſt Year, except that ſeventy odd Families were ſince returned thither from their Captivity in the Kingdoms of *Caſan* and *Aſtracan*. Thoſe poor People were in the moſt miſerable Circumſtances, ſcarcely had they Bread, much leſs Money, to rebuild their ruinous Houſes, or to fall into ſome way of Trade again. There were alſo Part of the former Inhabitants of *Dorpt*, which Town at preſent lies entirely in Ruins, who were then likewiſe returned from their Exile: But thoſe were not above the ſixth Part of the former Inhabitants of *Narva* and *Dorpt*, as has been already mentioned. When the Town of *Narva* was taken by Storm, and the Ruſſians fell to ſlaughtering all before them, it was not without the greateſt Difficulty that the Czar was able to reſtrain their Cruelty, and we were ſhewn the Table on which he threw down his bloody Sword at that Time, ſaying, *This is no Swediſh, but Ruſſian Blood, which I ſhed to ſave your and your Fellow-Neighbours Lives.* Not far from the Town in the River *Narva*, is a great Cataract formed by Nature, where they catch abundance of Salmons.

Superſtitious Peaſants in Ingria.

Among the Peaſants in *Ingria* there are a certain Sort, who are neither Ruſſians nor Ingrians, but have a mixed Language, a particular Religion, and ſeveral Cuſtoms that have ſome Reſemblance to thoſe of the Jews. They have ſome Lutheran Miniſters; however theſe Peaſants, without minding them, go on
certain

The Present State of Ruſſia. 97

certain Days into the Woods, and confecrate a number of Trees, which they afterwards cut down, and, by the Fire made of them, brue a Quantity of Beer, without ſtirring out of the Wood before it is drunk up; then with the reſt of the Trees they raiſe a Pile, on which they burn a live Cock.

Having paſſed *Narva*, I found the Soil much better, and the Crops in the Fields further advanced than in *Ingria*. The Inhabitants of that Country, which is called *Eſthonia* or *Eaſtland*, in former times carried on a good Trade with their Corn, which the foreign Merchants preferred to that of *Poland*, and all other Countries; becauſe the Peaſants dry it in their Houſes heated by Stoves, ſo that there is no Occaſion of ſtirring or turning it for three or four Years. The War has left but few Villages in *Eſthonia*, and the Houſes in them lie very much diſperſed; they have but every fourth or ſixth League a Church, which are commonly built on ſome Eminence. The Country is ſo diſpeopled, that not the fourth Part of it is inhabited, and the vaſt Number of Ruins of Gentlemens Seats, and other Houſes, ſhew what Ravage the War has made there. The greateſt Calamity which befel that Country, was in the Beginning of the War, when the Czar had but little Likelihood of keeping the Poſſeſſion of it; and therefore in order to terrify the Swedes, ſent the Calmucks and other Tartars thither, who committed horrid Barbarities. The natural Inhabitants remain Slaves; but after the Czar had conquered the whole Principality, he confirmed the Nobility in their ancient Privileges, and took off the *Reſumption* made

The State of Eſthonia in general.

formerly

formerly by the Swedish Government, from which only twenty Estates had remained exempted; so that the Nobility now quietly enjoy their own Estates, and find their Maintenance by them, though they have little ready Money. They turned good Husbands during the time of the said Resumption, when they were reduced to take their own Estates in Farm from the King of *Sweden*. The late King, during the War, drew above fifteen hundred Officers out of *Esthonia*, and there are now only two Noblemen in that Country that did not serve in his Army. *Esthonia* yields to the Czar five and twenty thousand Rubels a Year in Taxes, and the Farmers of the Crown Lands yearly pay forty Rubels to the Czar, for each Piece of Ground containing sixty Acres. It is remarkable that there are *Mummies* to be found in several Places of *Esthonia*: We met with one in our Journey at *Wesenberg*, a Village, where the Corps of a Gentlewoman, of the Family of *Lohe*, lay preserved entire ever since 1604, without being embalmed: When it was taken up, it was like a light Piece of Wood, and there appeared not the least Sign of Corruption in it, just as if it had been buried but a few Days before. When I passed that Road in the Year 1718, I found it still in the same Condition. People reason variously about the natural Cause of this, which is commonly thought to be owing to some Minerals in the Earth. The Town of *Reval* partly lies in a pleasant Plain in a Valley, partly on the Side of a high Hill, on which stand the Cathedral and the Houses of the Country Nobility; the latter are new built, but the rest of the Town

And of Reval in particular.

Town confifts of very old and ruinous Buildings. During the Siege, the Inhabitants of the open Country had retired to the Town, and it appears by the Books that were kept at the Town-Houfe, that the late Plague fwept away in this Place alone fifty five thoufand Perfons. The Inhabitants enjoy their Privileges, and the Exercife of their Religion. The *Ruffians* perform their Worfhip in a Church, which they had here in former times; Though there is a Garrifon of between three and four thoufand Men, yet the Burghers have the Privilege to maintain a Company of Militia at their own Charge, who have their Poft at the Corps-de-Guard in the Market Place. There are three different Jurifdictions in that Town; that of the Magiftrates or Town-Council; the Nobility of the Province, (compofed of twelve *Land-Raths* or Provincial Commiffioners, and a Prefident, who take care of the Concerns of the Country;) and the Governor, in whom is lodged the executive Power. The prefent Governor General of all *Efthonia*, is Admiral *Apraxin*. The Arms of *Denmark*, and Danifh Infcriptions, are frequently feen on the Churches, old Buildings, and other Places of this Town, it having been built by the Kings of *Denmark*, from whom the Inhabitants of this Country derive the greater Part of their Privileges; and it is obferved as fomething worth Notice, that the Defcendants of the Peafants, who in ancient times were brought from *Denmark* to plant this Country, do, to this very Day, diftinguifh themfelves by their Cuftoms from the Natives, particularly by wearing Caps inftead of Hats, which the latter

ter use. It being Harvest-time when I travelled that Way, I met the Reapers every where singing ordinary Tunes during their Work, and was informed by a Clergyman, that they were old Heathen Songs without Rime, which they could not be brought to leave off, though Care was taken to adapt the Esthonian Language by degrees to the Rules of Poetry, and that accordingly many Lutheran Hymns had been actually put into Rhyme. The same has been attempted with the Livonian Language, which entirely differs from that of *Esthonia*.

September 1715. Embassy to Persia. On the 10th of *September* we returned to *Petersbourg*, where I received a Letter from *Moskow*, written to me by *Artemi Wolinski*, who was to go to *Persia* as Russian Ambassador, by which he acquainted me, that he was to set out the said Month of *September*: I learned from the Russian Ministers, that the Czar's View in sending the said *Wolinski* on that Embassy, accompanied by several learned Men, was to get a true Knowledge of the State of the Persian Empire, its Forces, Fortresses, and Limits.

A Commerce with Spain projected. At the same time there was another Design on foot, viz. to send the Czar's great Favourite, and Counsellor of the Admiralty, *Kikin*, to *Spain*, for settling a Treaty of Commerce; there being Reason to believe, that the Russian Commodities, as also Ships built cheap in *Russia*, might be sold to the Spaniards with great Advantage. But the whole Affair came to nothing, and *Kikin* was executed at *Moskow* in the Year 1718, for having been the Adviser of the Czarewitz's Flight.

The Czar received Advice from *Aſtracan*, that rich Minerals and Veins of Gold-Oar had been diſcovered on the Shore of the *Caſpian* Sea, where the River *Dauria* falls into it, which made the Czar reſolve to ſend thither a Prince of the Circaſſian Tartars, *Alexander Beckewitz*, Captain of the Czar's Guard, together with *M. Blüher*, a Man converſant in Mine Affairs, to view thoſe Parts, and previouſly to their ſetting up Works there, they were to clear the Country of the vagrant *Calmucks*, in which they were to be ſupported by the Garriſon of *Aſtracan*, and the auxiliary Forces to be furniſhed by the ſaid Prince's Mother, who is the Czar's Vaſſal.

Expedition on the Caſpian Sea.

The Emperor of *China* had written to Prince *Gagarin*, Governor of *Siberia*, deſiring him to ſend him an able Phyſician, and ſome Medicines provoking to Venery: The Reaſon of his addreſſing himſelf to the ſaid Prince was, becauſe all the Caravans going to *China* were furniſhed with Paſſports by him, and that himſelf carried on a great Trade to *China*, which had rendered his Name famous among the *Chineze*. Hereupon Mr. *Garwin*, an *Engliſh* Chirurgeon at *Petersbourg*, offered his Service for that Journey; and after having been firſt advanced to the Degree of Doctor, ſet out for *China* with the Medicines deſired, in *Auguſt*, (we being then at *Reval*) in Company of *Laurence Lange*, an Engineer, whom the Czar joined with him, and who, among other Commiſſions, was ordered to bring a *Stove* (for heating Rooms) made of Porcelane or China Ware, from thence. Mr. *Lange* being returned in the Year 1718, communicated to me the Journal of his Travels in Manu-

A Phyſician ſent to the Emperor of China.

Manuscript, which, for the Satisfaction of the curious Reader, I have annexed to this Work.

October 1715. Reprefentations againft removing the Trade of Archangel to Petersbourg.

Orders were sent into *Russia*, for twelve thousand Families more to come and settle at *Petersbourg*, whither they were also, with great Pains and Expences, endeavouring to draw the whole Commerce of *Archangel*. The Merchants reprefented againft that Defign; 1. That only at *Wologda*, a Town situate between *Moskow* and *Archangel*, there are three German Merchants, who, at their own Charge, maintain twenty five thousand Persons and upwards, in dressing and preparing Hemp to be sent to *Archangel*, and from thence into foreign Countries: But should they be obliged to keep such a Number of People at *Petersbourg*, where every thing is five times as dear as at *Wologda*, that Trade not only would turn to no Account at all, but they would even be Losers by it. 2. That the greater Part of the Exportation of *Archangel* is of the Growth of the neighbouring Country of *Wologda*, from whence those Commodities are with a great deal of Ease carried by Water to *Archangel*; whereas were they to be transported to *Petersbourg*, it muft be done a great Way over Land, and with far greater Expences to the Merchants. 3. That the Soil at *Petersbourg* is such, that the Hemp cannot be kept there a few Months without growing damp. 4. That the Navigation in the Gulph of *Finland* is very dangerous, and the Insurances on Ships sailing thither moft exorbitant, particularly during the present Northern War.

The Present State of Russia.

On the 20th of *October* we went with the Czar to *Sleutelbourg*, to solemnize there upon the Spot the Anniversary of the taking of that important Fortress. It lies just at that End of the Lake *Ladoga*, which is nearest to *Petersbourg*, in the midst of the *Neva*, both sides of which River it commands with its Cannon. It has high and thick Walls, and six Bastions, and seeing the Place is surrounded on all Sides with the Water of a rapid Stream, it was Matter of Wonder, that the Russians took it with scaling Ladders. It was formerly called *Nôtebourg*; but the Czar changed its Name into that of *Sleutelbourg*, because it opened the Door to the Russian Conquests, *Sleutel* signifying a *Key* in the *Low-Dutch*. It was built four hundred Years ago by a Princess of *Novogrod*, whose Name was *Marfa*. The Czar has provided it with Necessaries for ten Years, and caused it to be strengthened with Out-works, and with Cazerns within, of very durable Work, which may hold above four thousand Men. In the midst of the Fortress stands a Church, to which the Russians have added a Steeple; next to it stands a small wooden House, in which *Count Piper* was confined, leading a melancholy Life, having only one Servant allowed him, and no other Books but the Holy Scriptures and an Ecclesiastical History. We could not obtain Leave to speak with him, or to see him, any further than through the Glass Window. Since his being removed thither from *Petersbourg*, he was seized with a dangerous Indisposition. On the 21st he was visited by Prince *Menzicoff*, and afterwards by Count *Gollofkin* the Great Chancellor.

The Fortress of Sleutelbourg.

Count Piper's Prison.

lor. I was told by the Russians, that, during his Captivity, he shewed great Obstinacy, which still more incensed the Czar against him, but that his fierce Temper was since so much broken, by the severe Usage he had drawn upon himself by his Behaviour, that he declared to Prince *Menzicoff*, that though he found himself in so miserable a Condition, as probably would soon put an End to his Days, yet he felt nothing so insupportable as the Czar's Anger, and that he only wished his Majesty would lay aside his Displeasure against him. Hereupon Mr. *Areskin*, the Czar's own Physician was sent to him, who assured the Czar, that his Life was in Danger, if he was left without the Help of Physicians. This prevailed so much, that the Czar permitted him to be carried to *Petersbourg* for some Weeks, and to be provided with necessary Attendance.

A Prince born to the Czarewitz.
On the 22^d the News was brought from *Petersbourg* to the Czar, that the Day before the *Czarewitz*'s Consort was brought to Bed of a Prince.

The Czar's Pretensions on Sleutelbourg, and other Conquests.
The same Day we set out on our Return to *Petersbourg*, and on the Road the Czar took the Opportunity of discoursing about *Sleutelbourg*, and other Conquests, assuring us that they had been in the Possession of his Predecessors, which could be made out from the original Records kept in the Archives of *Moskow*. On occasion of which Discourse, a certain foreign Minister, talking with me afterwards on the same Subject, communicated to me a State of the Case drawn up some Months before in Latin, by a learned Swedish Officer in *Siberia*, relating to the Causes of the

The Present State of Russia.

War depending between *Sweden* and *Russia*, which I shall insert hereafter, with the Russian Answer to it.

I am now come to speak of the Decease of the *Czarewitz's* Consort, and to relate some Particulars of her Life, as far as they make part of the Russian History. It is known, that the said worthy Princess was of the Family of *Brunswick-Wolfembuttel*, and Sister to the present Empress. The occasion of her Marriage with the *Czarewitz* was as follows: The Czar had already long ago taken the Resolution of allying himself with some powerful Family of *Germany* by the Marriage of his Son, with a View at the same time of reclaiming the latter from his Indolence by the Conversation of a Princess of noble Education, for the said Prince had by continually frequenting vicious Company contracted such corrupt Habits, as could not fail producing an Aversion to him in all honest Minds; and notwithstanding all Representations, he was so far sunk in Sensuality that he went on in his former Courses, not considering that by doing so he indangered his Succession to the Crown. For the Czar being at length by his Son's perverse Conduct wrought into an Abhorrence of his Person, began to drop broad Intimations, that, unless he gave timely Hopes of Amendment, he might be sure of having his Crown shaved and being thrust into a Convent, it being better to sever an useless Member from the Body, than to suffer the Corruption to spread through the whole. The *Czarewitz's* own Favourites grew sensible of the Danger, and did not fail to acquaint him with it, zealously and earnestly intreating

Of the Czarewitz's Consort, with several Particulars concerning her Life and Death.

intreating him to have his own Welfare at Heart, to conceal that Hatred he shewed against Foreigners, and to look out for a Consort in some potent Family of *Germany*, in order to secure to himself the Succession to the Throne by the Interest of her Relations, and in the mean to induce the Czar, his Father, to use him with more Kindness, at least in Consideration of his Consort: This Representation made so much Impression on his Mind, that he followed their Advice and went to throw himself at his Father's Feet, declaring his firm Resolution of entering into a regular Course of Life, to which nothing being more conducive than the Conversation of a virtuous Lady, he instantly desired his Majesty to give him Leave to make a Tour to *Germany* in order to chuse himself a Wife. Accordingly he repaired to the Court of *Saxony*, where the Princess at that time lived with the Queen of *Poland*, and their Marriage was solemnized at *Torgau* in the Year 1711. But after he had brought her to *Russia*, he shewed not the least Complaisance in endeavouring to divert her, on the contrary I observed that on all publick Occasions he never exchanged a Word with her, but carefully avoided her Company. The *Czarewitz* had the Apartments of the right Wing of their House, and the Princess those of the left; but they saw each other scarcely once a Week, so that had the *Czarewitz* not looked upon the begetting of an Heir, as the support of his own Safety, that Couple would have been entirely invisible to each other. He even neglected the Repair of the House to that degree, that the Princess was exposed to the Injuries of the Air and
Weather

Weather in her own Bedchamber, and if the Czar happened to expostulate with him for it, he loaded her with Reproaches as if it was she who accused him to the Czar, whereas that wife Princess bore her unhappy Fate with an uncommon Resignation and Constancy, and had no other Witnesses of her Complaints and Tears, besides the Princess of *East-Frizeland* her Companion, and the Walls of her own Apartments. To enter into Particulars of her Sufferings would require a Volume; I shall content my self with making mention of a Finlandish Woman a Captive, whom the *Czarewitz* took openly into his House for a Mistress, and was never out of her Company Night or Day. This State of their Domestick Affairs lasted till the Princess's Death, which was occasioned partly by her continual Grief and Affliction, partly by the Neglect of the Midwives at her Lying-in. The Princess having been delivered of Prince *Peter Alexiewitz* on the 21st of *October*, was six Days after seized with so dangerous an Indisposition, that her Recovery was immediately despaired of. When she observed that her End was approaching, she desired to see the *Czar*, for the *Czarina* was so near her Time that she could not go abroad. The Czar being indisposed at the same Time, was carried thither on a Machine rowling upon Wheels. Being arrived, the Princess took her Leave of him in the most moving Expressions, and recommended her two Children and Servants to his Care and Protection; whereupon she embraced her two Children in the most tender manner imaginable, almost melting away in Tears, and delivered them to the *Czarewitz*

witz, who took them in his Arms, and carried them to his Apartments, but never returned afterwards. Then she sent for her Servants, who, to the number of two hundred Persons and upwards, lay prostrate on the Ground in the Antichamber, praying and calling to Heaven to assist their dying Mistress in her last Moments. She comforted them, gave them several Admonitions and at last her Blessing, and then desired to be left alone with the Minister. The Physicians were endeavouring to persuade her to take some Medicines, but she flung the Phials behind the Bed, saying with some Emotion, *Do not torment me any more but let me die in quiet, for I will live no longer.* At length on the 1st of *November*, having continued all that Day in fervent Devotion till eleven at Night, she departed an unfortunate Life, after having endured for the last five Days the most acute Pains, in the twenty first Year of her Age, having been married four Years and six Days. Her Corpse was according to her Desire interred without being embalmed in the great Church of the Fortress, whither it was carried on the 7th of *November* with a Funeral Pomp becoming her Birth. Her two Children are still alive, the one being a Princess, *Natalia*, and the other the Prince *Peter Alexiewitz*, who gives early Proofs of uncommon Endowments both of Body and Mind.

A Son born to the Czar, and named Peter Petrowitz. The next Day being the 8th of the said Month, the *Czarina* was brought to Bed of a Prince to the *Czar's* unspeakable Joy: The Rejoycings ordered to be made on that account lasted eight Days successively. On the 17th

17th the new-born Prince was baptized and named *Peter Petrowitz*. The Godfathers were the Kings of *Denmark* and *Pruſſia*. The Solemnities made on that Occaſion were attended with extraordinary Pomp. What was moſt curious was a Pye ſerved up on the Table of the Gentlemen, which being opened, a well-ſhaped Woman Dwarf ſtept out of it, being ſtark-naked, except her Head-dreſs and ſome Ornaments of red Ribbons; ſhe made a well-ſet Speech to the Company, filled ſome Glaſſes of Wine which ſhe had with her in the Pye, and drank ſeveral Healths; after which ſhe was carried off again. On the Ladies Table a Man Dwarf was ſerved up in the ſame manner. In the Duſk of the Evening the Company broke up and went to the Iſland *Jenneſſari*; where a noble Fire-work was plaid off in Honour to the young Prince. I was too far off to diſtinguiſh the Deviſe on the Theatre, but above it was a Motto in large Ruſſian Characters: *Hope with Patience.*

On the 4th of *December* the Czar received Advice of the taking of the Iſland of *Rugen*, which News arrived juſt at the time when I had the Honour to entertain his Majeſty with his Miniſters and Generals at Dinner at my Houſe. The Czar gave a ſplendid Entertainment upon that account on the 9th, where among other Curioſities were ſeen two hundred Melons, brought from *Aſtracan* by Water, which were diſtributed among the Company.

Decemb. 1715. Rejoycings on the taking of Ruſſian gen.

His Czariſh Majeſty was pleaſed to tell us, that *Aſtracan* is ſo fruitful a Country that it might be counted a Paradiſe, if it had a Communication by Water with *Indoſtan*, *Perſia*, and eſpecially with the *Black-Sea*, by which it

Of Aſtracan and its Trade.

it might impart its noble and cheap Produce to other Countries: That it was true, Commodities might be carried into *Perſia* by the *Caſpian-Sea*, but there was no Poſſibility of carrying them further up into that Kingdom by Water; and as to the intended Communication between *Aſtracan* and the *Black-Sea*, and ſo on to the *Mediterranean*, the ſame was not yet opened, becauſe of the Difficulties and Obſtructions attending the cutting of the Canal between the Rivers *Wolga* and *Don* which was attempted in the Year 1707.

January 1716. Precautions againſt the Tartars.

The Czar being apprehenſive that the *Tartars* at the Inſtigation of the Turks might intermeddle with the Affairs of *Poland*, and approach the Frontiers with their Swarms, ſent Orders to General *Weiſsbach*, who during the Summer had his Station near *Kioff* at *Baſtoff*, and in Autumn at *Starodub*, to march with ſix Regiments of Dragoons behind *Veronitz* on the *Don*, to keep a watchful Eye on the Motions of the *Tartars*. The *Zaporovian* and other *Coſacks* under the Ruſſian Dominion were likewiſe ordered to be in a readineſs to mount on the firſt Notice.

Death of the Czarina Dowager Marvea.

The Czarina Dowager *Marvea Matweofna*, Relict of the late Czar *Fedor Alexiewitz*, (who was the preſent Czar's half Brother) died on the 14th of January. She was Siſter to the preſent Grand Admiral *Apraxin*, and died 51 Years old. All Genealogiſts have long ago reckoned her among the Dead; it is probable the occaſion of their Miſtake was, becauſe ſhe lived but four Weeks in the State of Matrimony with her Conſort, and upon his premature Death in the Year 1682, ſhut herſelf up in her own Apartment out of immoderate

derate Grief, and was for seven Years together not to be seen by any body but her own Servants. Her Corpse was carried with great Pomp to be interred in the Evening at Twilight. The Procession went from the Mourning-House to the Church in the Fortress over the Ice, the length of an English Mile, through a double Row of Flambeaus. The Privy-Councellor *Tolstoy* carried the Crown which was richly set with precious Stones: The Coffin was carried on a Sled, as were likewise two hundred Mourners in long Cloaks, and three hundred Persons more who attended the Corpse. The funeral Ceremonies being performed, the Coffin was put into the new Vault of the Czarish Family, where now are lying one Prince and two Princesses of the Czar's Children besides the said Czarina Dowager. The whole Russian Clergy, the *Archireje*, (Archbishop) the Metropolitans, the *Archimandrites*, (Abbots,) *Popes* (Priests), Singers, and all other Churchmen, preceded the Corpse dressed in their several magnificent Habits after the Russian Custom, with innumerable Tapers and Censers, during continual singing, all which added very much to the decency of the Procession. As to the Custom which of old had obtained on the like Occasions of immoderate weeping, making Lamentations and loud Groans, and Cries, and of which I have seen many Instances sincere as well as affected, the Czar will have it entirely abolished, and Orders were given before this Funeral to abstain from any such Lamentations. The generality of the common People hold that superstitious Opinion, that the Soul of the deceased

still

still haunts the Place where it left the Body, for six Weeks after, during which time the neareſt Relations perfume the Bed, and have daily Maſs ſaid near it. There is ſtill a Czarina Dowager, the Relict of *Iwan Alexiewitz,* another Half-Brother of the preſent Czar; her Name is *Proſcovia,* and mention has been made above of her and her three Daughters.

Antiquities dug up near Samarcand. Prince *Gagarin,* Governor of *Siberia,* having received Advice that ſome Oar hadbeen diſcovered on the Eaſt-end of the *Caſpian-Sea* in the Neighbourhood of *Samarcand,* (the Town where it is reported the Great *Tamerlan* was born,) ſent People from *Siberia* to make a further Search, who after having dug up the Earth in ſeveral Places, found many ancient Braſs Figures, which they ſent to the Prince, who tranſmitted them as a great Curioſity to the Czar to *Petersbourg,* where I had an opportunity of ſeeing them. They were all of them Pagan Idols, in the form of Minotaurs, Oxen, Geeſe, old deformed Men, and ſome in that of young Women. All thoſe Images which had the true Signs of Antiquity, and had within a ſtrong ſmell of Musk, had every one in their Hands or Claws a ſort of Candleſticks, which in all probability ſerved for the Candles burning during the idolatrous Worſhip. Both the upper and lower part of the Bill of the Gooſe, and the Mouth of the Minotaur as alſo their Tongues were made like Lids with a ſort of a Hinge, on which they moved; within one might diſcern that there had been a Pipe going to the Mouth, which it is likely the Prieſts made uſe of to impoſe on the People by ſpeaking through it. The Inſcriptions which

The Present State of Russia.

which appear etched in on those Images, seem inexplicable, though the Characters are said to have a Relation to those of the *Persian* and *Mongalian* writing. The Czar gave Orders to go on with digging about *Samarcand*, in hopes to find either more of these Curiosities, or even rich Veins of Gold Oar.

On the sixth of *February* both their Czarish Majesties set out for *Germany*, and solemnized at *Dantzick* the Marriage of the eldest Princess Daughter to the Czarina Dowager *Proscovia*, with the Duke of *Mecklenbourg*.

February 1716. The Czar goes to Germany.

Advice came to *Petersbourg*, that the *Cuban Tartars*, according to their yearly Custom, had made an Inroad into the Kingdom of *Casan* and carried between six and seven thousand Souls into Slavery. Colonel Schwartz, a German, who has already served the Czar eighteen Years, went in pursuit of them with six hundred Dragoons, formerly Swedish Prisoners, but now in the Czar's Service, and overtook them forty German Miles behind *Casan*; the Canon being pointed to play among the Tartars, they put the Russian Prisoners in their Front, which obliged the Colonel to attack them Sword in hand; he put them to Flight, took many of them and among them the commanding *Can*'s Son, whom he forthwith caused to be hanged on a Tree, he rescued the Russian Prisoners, and got fifteen hundred of the Enemy's Horses, which with other Booty he distributed among his Men. The said *Schwartz* came to *Petersbourg*, to make Report to the Senate of this Expedition, and afterwards returned with new Instructions.

Hostilities of the Cuban Tartars restrained.

The

The Present State of Russia.

The Author's Journey to Moskow.

The Absence of the Court, and other Circumstances, gave me an Opportunity of executing my long intended Design to make a Tour to *Moskow*. Having made Acquaintance with the Archbishop of *Resan*, I obtained from him an Order in Writing to all Russian Convents and Churches, to shew me without any Difficulty all that is remarkable, notwithstanding my being a Stranger, and that it is contrary to the Custom of *Russia*: Besides, I was furnished with the Czar's Orders to the Regency at *Moskow*, to shew me all manner of Complaisance; so that I had the fairest Opportunity imaginable of making the most exact Observations on my Journey. I left *Petersbourg* on the 24th of *February* in the Evening, and arrived at *Novogrod* on the 25th, at *Tweer* on the 27th, and at *Moskow* on the 28th, at eight in the Evening. So that in less than four Days I travelled upwards of one hundred and twenty German Miles, which Expedition is owing to the Conveniency of Sleds in Winter-time; whereas the same Journey takes up two or three Weeks in Summer, when it is very uneasy and troublesome, the Roads being for the greater Part laid with Timber.

Description of a Sled.

It would be impossible for a Traveller to bear the intense Cold in *Russia*, was it not for the convenient Contrivance of their Sleds. The upper Part of the Sled is so closely shut up and covered, that not the least Air can enter; on both Sides are small Windows and two Shelves, to lay upon it Provisions, as also Books taken along for Pastime; over the Head hangs a Lanthorn with Wax-candles, to be lighted when Night comes on. In the lower

The Present State of Russia.

lower Part of the Sled lies the Bedding, with which the Traveller is covered Night and Day, having at his Feet warm Stones, or a Pewter-case filled with warm Water, to keep the Sled in a Temperature, and to preserve the adjoining Box, in which Wine and Brandy is kept, against the Frost, notwithstanding all which Precautions, the strongest Liquors very often freeze, and are spoiled. In this moveable Apartment a Man is carried along Night and Day without stepping out, except in Case of Necessity; for there are no Inns to be met with on the Road, nor other Provisions to be had, beside coarse Bread, and very indifferent Brandy, so that one must make one's Meal in the Sled.

There are twenty four *Gama (Jam)* or Post-stages, between *Petersbourg* and *Moskow*, one at every fourth or fifth German Mile, where twenty Horses and upwards are kept ready, and maintained by Peasants appointed on purpose, who must content themselves with a Fare very easy for the Passengers, for which they are exempt from all Imposts, so that they have nothing else to mind, but to see Travellers dispatched. This great Conveniency, added to the Cheapness of Carriage, renders the Communication between *Petersbourg*, *Moskow*, and *Archangel*, extreamly easy; whereas otherwise it could not be kept up without great Difficulty. The Post-boys wear their ordinary Clothes like other Peasants, they have no Post-Horns, but only the Mark of the Spread-Eagle, which they tie to their Breast when upon Duty. In the Year 1718, the riding Posts were regulated on the same Foot as in *Germany*, and the Post-Boys

Regulation of the Posts in Russia.

begin now to blow their Horns as well as they can; they wear grey Coats with the Figure of a Poſt-Horn cut out of red Cloth, and ſewed on behind. When theſe Riding-Poſts firſt began, the Peaſants employed in them could not, without the utmoſt Difficulty, be brought to the blowing of the Horn, and to the exact Time fixed for their Courſe: I remember that once at *Petersbourg,* one of thoſe new Poſt-Boys out of Rage, gulped down ſuch a Quantity of ſtrong Brandy, that he was choaked on the Spot, thus reſolving rather to deſtroy himſelf than to blow the Horn, which is an Inſtance of the Stubbornneſs of that Nation. The other ſort of Poſtilions, of whom I ſpoke before, who drive Sleds and other Carriages, keep their own Country Habit, and uſe no Horns, inſtead of which they whiſtle with their Mouths, the ſhrill Sound of which makes their Horſes run, and gives Warning to thoſe they meet on the Road to get out of the Way: Upon their arriving at the next Stage they make a great Noiſe, calling out without Intermiſſion, *Davai,* that is to ſay, Horſes, Horſes, till they are put to, and ſo they let them run along in a continual Gallop, where there is the leaſt Poſſibility, though they are not bid by the Paſſengers ſo to do.

A new Road from Petersbourg to Moſkow. A certain Engliſh Mathematician at *Moſkow,* having propoſed to the Czar to cut out a Road from thence to *Petersbourg* in a ſtraight Line, and to make it paſſable, his Project met with ſuch Approbation and Encouragement, that this expenſive Work was brought to Perfection in the Year 1718, by which Travellers ſave upwards of thirty German Miles of their Way.

The

The Present State of Russia.

The principal Places on this Road are *No-* *Descripti-*
vogorod, *Tweer*, and *Waldei*. *Novogorod* is a *on of No-*
City of great Extent, fortified with old *vogorod.*
Walls and deep Ditches, almost all the Houses
are like wretched Peasants Cottages, built altogether of Wood. One and twenty Years
ago it was entirely burnt down, so that there
hardly appear at present any Remains of its
former Splendour, except that at a great Distance on both Sides of the Walls one may,
though not without some Difficulty, discern
how far that City extended in ancient Times.
Many Monasteries built of Stone have been
preserved from the Flames, which, together
with others built since, amount to the Number of about one hundred and eighty, reckoning those in the City and the adjacent Parts
together. *Novogorod* in former Times was
in the most flourishing Condition, on account
of its Commerce. It was comprehended in
the League of the *Hans-Towns*, and was the
Staple of the inferior Towns, so that its Power and Riches gave Birth to the famous Russian Saying: *Who can prevail against God and
Great Novogorod?* The Inhabitants make it
still their Boast, and the City is to this Day
in great Veneration among the Russians, on
account of St. *Anthony*'s Corpse kept there
uncorrupted, and of the Miracles by him performed: They shew there a Mill-stone, on
which they pretend he swam from *Rome* to
Novogorod, over the Ocean.

Tweer is a Town consisting of about two *OfTweer.*
thousand Houses, seventy Churches and Convents, and a fortified Castle on a Hill, in
which the Governor resides. The *Wolga* runs
by it, by the means of which River many
thou-

thousand Weight of Corn are yearly sent up thither from the Kingdom of *Casan*, so that *Tweer* is the true Staple of that Commodity, which is carried from thence on Sleds to *Petersbourg* and the Army.

Of Waldei.
Waldei is a Borough of small Importance. The Houses there, like others in middling Places, are all built of Wood, one Beam laid on the other, and without Chimneys, which makes them liable to frequent Fires.

The Nature of the Country, and the Inhabitants.
The Country as far almost as *Moskow*, is sandy, and not very fruitful, and there is nothing to be seen along the Road but Fir-trees; however, the Tract from *Petersbourg* to *Tweer* is somewhat better than that from *Tweer* to *Moskow*.

Their Houses.
I did not find the Villages to be very frequent; they never lie in Woods or Bushes, but in the flat Country. The Peasants Houses are wholly built of Wood, without Stonework, Iron, or Glass-Windows: They have extraordinary large Stoves, which take up one fourth Part of the Room. Such a Stove being well heated, and then shut up towards Evening, the whole Family go to lie promiscuously on the Top of it, and bake themselves thoroughly. If the Stove cannot hold them all, there are Shelves made under the Cieling, on which the rest stow themselves, for no body lies on the Ground. At *Tweer* I met a whole Family of twenty Persons, Master and Mistress, Children married and unmarried, with the Servants, lying thus together on Heaps on the Stove, and the Shelves above; and upon my asking them, whether they lay easy, and had Room enough to sleep; they answered

answered me, they rested perfectly well in such a warm Place, and wanted no Beds.

The greater Part therefore of the Country along the said Road yielding but little, so that in some Places the Harvest would not pay for the Pains of tilling the Land, the Peasants do not concern themselves much with Agriculture, but gather and make the best of what kind Nature produces of her self: Hay they have in abundance, and what they cannot consume themselves, they carry to Market, and exchange it for Corn to make Bread. Hops grow plentifully in the Woods without the least Care, which is another Article of their Subsistence; for they lead a poor Life, seeing they are but Slaves, who work for their Landlords; however, they bear their hard Fate with great Patience, forasmuch as they have no Notion of another way of living, and that their Ancestors fared no better. Among those Peasants all along the said Road, there are no Inns, nor any Victuals to be had for Money, so that Travellers are obliged to carry their own Provisions with them. They use no Candles, but long Shivers of Wood, which every one of the Family carries in his Hand, or a-cross his Mouth, and so they run about the House, and do their Work. *The Produce of the Soil.*

Some Time ago they wore long Clothes hanging down to the Ground, to which sort of Dress they stuck very obstinately; but the Czar, by a most expeditious Method, found means to make them quit it. Soldiers were appointed at the Gates of the Towns, who seized every Boor that came with a long Coat, made him sit down on his Knees, and with a Pair of Scissars cut it off by the Ground, and *The Peoples Dress.*

made

made him pay a Fine into the Bargain. Since this the Peasants wear a coarse Coat reaching to the Knee, and in the Summer-time they let the Shirt, which is but short, hang out over the Breeches, and gird it with a Girdle, into which they put a great Knife with a Sheath before, a Whip on one Side, and their Fur-Gloves and Hatchet behind. Their Hair is cropt to their Ears, and their Heads covered Winter and Summer with a Fur-Cap. Their Beards remain yet untouched, their Hands being too clumsy to handle a Razor. Their Shoes are tied together with Bast, for they know no better. About their Neck they wear from the Time of their Baptism a Cross, and next to it their Purse, though they commonly keep the small Money, if it be not too much, a good while in their Mouth; for as soon as they receive any, either as a Present, or as their Due, they put it into their Mouths, and keep it under their Tongue.

The Government of the Village. There is a Head-borough in each Village, whom they call the *Starosta,* who has but little Authority; the Differences which he cannot decide, are laid before the *Pricasse,* or Court of the Town to which it belongs.

Their Marriage. The Russians in the Towns, as well as the Country, marry very young, and their Houses are stocked with Children. A Peasant who marries into another Village, pays four or five Rubels for a Licence; but if he takes a Wife among his Neighbours, he pays but as many Farthings.

Their Religion. There are Churches in all Places; but as there is no Preaching, nor any Schools in the Country,

The Present State of Russia.

Country, the common People are very ignorant in point of Religion, and still more so as to Reading and Writing. But the present Czar, who has already established School-and Writing-Masters, for the Instruction of the Youth, in the Towns, is resolved to do the like in the Villages, and to banish the former Ignorance from among his Subjects. The People in general pay a blind Obedience to the Laws of their Religion, and observe them with the greatest Strictness imaginable. I have seen with Astonishment how zealous they are in observing their Fasts, and some of the Peasants are even so superstitious, that in those Times they refuse to sell Milk or Eggs to Travellers. They are of Opinion, that if they keep those Fasts holy, they may live afterwards as they please, which occasions great Disorders and Licentiousness, particularly during the *Maslanitza* or Butter-Week, which precedes the Easter Holydays, and is the Carnival of the Russians.

At the Buryings of their Relations they make great Lamentations. At *Petersbourg* indeed they begin to leave it off, since it has been expresly prohibited, as I mentioned above; but in remote Places the old Custom still prevails. In a certain Village I heard the most lamentable Cries on a Burying, which not only the Relations of the Deceased, but also old Women hired of purpose for it, made out of the Windows of the House whence the Corpse was carried, that the whole Village resounded with it. At *Petersbourg*, if any of the common sort die, their Friends expose the Corpse to publick View, and place a lighted Wax-candle near it, begging of all who

Their Buryings.

who pafs by, a Charity towards enterring it. Thofe who are compaffionate, fix the Money in the Candle; and the others who undertake the good Office for the Deceafed, having thus got a Sum which they judge fufficient for their Trouble, few the Corpfe up in a Matt, and tie it round with Ropes, then hang it like a Sack on a Pole, which two of them take upon their Shoulders, and befpeak fome more Friends to attend it to the Grave. Once I happened to fee two Ruffians, who had carried a dead Body after that manner already good part of the Way; but probably thinking they were not paid enough, laid it down again, fet up a Wax-candle, and fell a croffing themfelves after the Ruffian Way, and repeating their ufual Ejaculation, *Gofpodin pomilui*, (Lord, have Mercy upon us) in order to collect a larger Charity; but Night coming on before they got any thing, they were unwilling to carry it further that Night, in Hopes to compleat the Sum next Morning, and fo they pitched upon a narrow Corner under a Bridge, to depofite the Corpfe there in the mean time, which they did accordingly, after having turned it twenty different Ways before they could get the Head under, which done, they made a Crofs over it, and went away: The next Day they found Means to carry it to the Church-Yard. A little before *Chriftmas* the Ruffians have a Holyday, which they call *Raditeli Sabot*, the Relations Sabbath-Day; becaufe on that Day the Burying-places of the Deceafed are vifited by their neareft Relations, who carry thither Provifions and divers Prefents, and, with the moft lamentable Cries and Howlings, ask the Dead, how they
do;

do; why they died; what ailed them; and the like: after which they return home, and the *Popes* or Priests take care of the Presents left there, which they employ for the Benefit of the Church. This Custom of bemoaning the Dead is also observed on other Occasions, during some time after the Burial; and at *Moskow* I saw every Day People in the Church-Yards, weeping and making melancholy Gestures.

On my passing by a Village not far from *Tweer*, I was surprized to hear two Peasants talking together in a strange Language, which I found to be that of *Finland*; upon my asking them, whether they were Russians born, and had perhaps lived for some Time in *Finland*; they at first appeared not much inclined to answer my Question; however, they told me at last, that they were Russians, and had never been far from their Village, that they learned both Languages from their Parents; and as for the rest, they directed me to an old Man, who would satisfy my Curiosity. From him I learned, that his Father, together with several thousand Natives of *Finland*, had left their own Country in the Revolutions occasioned by the Wars between *Russia* and *Sweden*, and submitted to the Czar's Protection; which Colonies had settled as far as *Tweer*, and preserved their native Tongue, though at present corrupted. By the old Man's Computation, I found that the said Transmigration happened in the Time of *Gustavus Adolphus*, whose General *Jacob de la Gardie*, very much annoyed the Russians, and forced the Czar *Michael Fedrowitz*, to yield over to *Sweden*, *Kexholm* and *Ingria*; on which Occasion

A Finlandish Colony in Russia.

Occasion the Inhabitants of those Provinces removed thence, and settled in *Russia,* either of their own Accord, by reason of the Government's being changed, or forced to it by the Czar. All along the rest of the Road I met with no more of those People, but was informed, upon further Enquiry, that in a Slip of Land extending from both Sides of the High Road, (just as it is with the *Wenden* or *Vandals* in *Germany)* the Villages are full of the Posterity of those *Finlanders,* who indeed call themselves Russians, and outwardly profess their Religion; but in their Hearts are of another Faith, and keep up their own Customs, which they transmit from Generation to Generation, with so much Circumspection, that the Russians, in spite of all the Care with which they watch them, cannot lay hold of any of their Actions. There was a Time when they suffered much Persecution; but under the present Government they are connived at, because they live peaceably, and are regular in paying their Taxes. They have Russian Churches; but it is said, that, in remote Places, they do not care to frequent them, though they ring the Bells, as it were, for Divine Service; so that if by chance a Stranger comes there to be present at it, he may often find the Doors shut, and see neither Priest nor Congregation.

A Description of Moskow. The City of *Moskow* is situate in a large and pleasant Plain, and makes a fine Show at a Distance, by reason of its great Extent, and so many hundreds of Steeples gilt all over, which, when the Sun shines upon, cast a Brightness that pleases the Eye. But the Inside falls very short of its outward Appearance.

ance. It is one German Mile and half in Length, and one in Breadth, though in former Times it was nine in Circumference, according to Tradition. It is divided in four Diſtricts, each of which is ſurrounded with a Wall and a deep Ditch, which, however, would prove but a poor Defence againſt a regular Attack. Within the firſt Wall, through which the River *Moskow* runs, are the *Slabodas* or Suburbs, the greater Part of which are vaniſhed away, by the Incurſions of the Tartars in former Times, and frequent Fires. In the Compaſs of the ſecond Wall lies *Czar-Gorod* or the Czar's City. The third is called *Kitai-Gorod (Kitai* with the Ruſſians ſignifies *China)* or the Chineze Town, becauſe Chineze Goods are ſold there. The fourth Wall makes up *Kremelin*, which is the Czar's Reſidence, large enough to make a Town by it ſelf. Near and about the Czar's Palace ſtand the ſeveral Offices, the Patriarch's Houſe, and about forty Churches and Chapels. Before the Caſtle is a large Market Place, which is the fineſt in the whole Town. All the Buildings in *Kremelin*, are of Stone, and very durable. *Kitai-Gorod* is the proper Place for Trade, the Booths are ranged into ſeparate Quarters and Streets, according to the Goods ſold in them, which is a great Conveniency for the Buyers, in ſo large a City. A peculiar Spot is aſſigned for the Images of their Gods and Saints, where they are exchanged for Money; for it would be a Crime among the Ruſſians to ſay, they were bought or ſold, and for this Reaſon there is no bargaining about the Sum demanded, for one muſt either take them at that Rate, or leave them. This

Part of the Town defigned for a Market, how large foever, yet is fo crowded with People, that it is hard to get through; and I found by Experience, that in any of the moft noted Fairs in *Germany*, the People are not fo thick as they are there every Day. In *Czar-Gorod* are large Markets, where nothing but Wooden Wares are fold: Their Houfes are Part of that Commodity, for they ftand there by Hundreds ready made, and put up for Sale. If a Buyer is found for one, it is taken to Pieces, and carried to the Place where he wants to have it fet up, which is done in a few Minutes. This fort of Buildings, of which the greateft Part of *Moskow* is made up, confifts of Timber joined together in a fquare Figure, after which the Chinks are ftopt with Mofs, and a Roof made over it of thin Planks. There are alfo thoufands of Coffins of different Sizes to be fold there: They are nothing elfe but Stocks of Trees made hollow in the Form of Troughs, and covered with a Lid. When any of the common Sort dies, his Relations go and buy fuch a Coffin, and fo bury him without any further Ceremony. Moft of the Houfes in *Mofkow* are built as abovefaid, and differ little or nothing from thofe in the Villages. The frequent Fires that have happened there, have left, in many Parts of that City, wafte and empty Places; for the rebuilding of which there is the lefs Hope, becaufe of a late Order, forbidding not only to build any again, but alfo to repair any of the Stone-Houfes, which occafions a ftill greater Decay of that City. It feems the Czar's Defign in iffuing fuch an Order, was to divert his Subjects from laying

The Present State of Russia.

laying out Expences in repairing their Houses at *Moskow*, and to bring them to employ that Money in building new ones at *Petersbourg*; which End being in some Measure obtained, it is probable the Czar will not suffer the City of *Moskow* entirely to go to Ruin, but maintain it in the Condition it is in at present. It is reckoned that there are near three thousand Stone-Buildings in *Moskow*, very durable, and for the greater Part sumptuous, which would make a fine City, if they stood regularly together. But they lie dispersed up and down between Thousands of Wooden Houses, besides that they do not face the Streets, but are hid in Yards, and surrounded with Walls, to secure them against Fire and Thieves. The Streets are not regular, and paved but in few Places, the rest are laid or lined with Timber, which renders the Passage exceeding troublesome in Summer time. I was told for certain, that there are fifteen hundred Churches and Convents in and about *Moskow*, every one of which being provided with many Bells, there is no End of ringing: their Bells are not raised with the Feet or Hands, as in *Germany*, but tolled by a Rope tied to the Clapper. On *Prasnicks* or Holydays, the common People croud to the Belfries to pull the Ropes, being of Opinion, that the Sound of the Bells is a Preservative of hearing during the whole Year, besides other wholesome Effects which they attribute to it. There are some Clocks in the City, and the beautiful Church built by Prince *Menzicoff* has a Chime. In every Boyar's House stands a Watch-man, who marks the Hours by striking with a Wooden Hammer against a large Plank.

Plank. The common People count the Hours of the Day from Sun-Rise to Sun-Set.

The Streets unsafe at Night. Idleness produces such Numbers of Beggars and Rogues, and occasions so many Excesses and Disorders, that after Sun-set no body ventures abroad without sufficient Company. Those Villains place themselves at the Corners of the Streets, and throw swinging Cudgels, which they call *Dubines*, at the Heads of those that pass by, in which Practice they are so expert, that these mortal Blows seldom miss. The most dangerous Time is the Butter-Week, when all the Rabble are drunk and mad. During the last that was over before my Arrival at *Moskow*, above sixty Persons thus murdered were taken up in the Streets, and I my self found two lying on the Road in my Journey thither. This Danger on the Highways increases, and consequently obliges Travellers to be the more upon their Guard, when the Czar happens to be in remote Parts; for then it is a common Saying with those Villains: *Bog wissoko, Ossodar dalioko*; God dwells high, and the Lord (the Czar) is far off. It is the Custom at *Moskow* to carry those that are found murdered in the Streets out of Town, and to throw them into a deep Hole, and on a certain Day about *Whitsuntide*, Priests are sent thither to say Mass for the Repose of their Souls, whereupon they order Earth to be thrown upon them.

Three Colleges founded by the Czar. It is many Years ago since the Czar founded three Colleges at *Moskow*, and provided them with several learned Russian Monks, who studied in *Poland, Ukraina*, and *Prussia*. In the first are between two and three hundred

dred Scholars, *Polanders, Ukrainians,* and *Ruſsians,* divided in different Forms, where they are taught the Principles of Literature by Monks, who are able Men, and of good Senſe. They ſhewed me their Buildings and Churches, and gave me an Account of their Method of Teaching; and afterwards a Student of the firſt Form, who was a young *Knees,* made a handſome Speech in Latin, for which he had prepared himſelf, and which conſiſted of Compliments. The ſecond College is for all the Mathematical Sciences, in which are near ſeven hundred Scholars, who, according to their Capacity, are ranged in three Forms, and are kept under a ſtrict Diſcipline. The Maſters are *Ruſſians,* and their Head an *Engliſhman,* thoroughly verſed in the Ruſſian Tongue, who has already ſent many Youths well inſtructed both to the Sea and Land Service. At my being there he ſent, purſuant to the Czar's Orders, one hundred more to the new erected Academy of the Marine at *Petersbourg,* after having given them the firſt Tincture by his Inſtructions, and he himſelf has ſince been ſent for thither to be Profeſſor in the ſaid Academy. The Boys in the third College are only taught Navigation, and what belongs to it.

On the fourth of *March* I went to ſee the Cathedral in *Kremelin,* which is a large, ancient, and ſtrong-built Structure of Stone. On the right Side of the Altar was the Czar's Seat, and at the Left that of the Patriarch. A Silver Sconce of uncommon Size hung in the midſt of the Church. The Picture of the Virgin *Mary,* and other Ornaments of the Altar, were ſet with ſuch a Quantity of Pearls

March 1716. *The Cathedral in* Kremelin.

and

and precious Stones, that the whole Value was reckoned to amount to fifty thousand Crowns and upwards. The Priests shewed me another Picture of the Virgin *Mary*, pretended to be drawn by St. *Luke*. Three Saints of great Repute among the Russians, *Aeolus*, *Anthony*, and *Philip*, are buried in this Cathedral in Stone Coffins, guarded with iron Rails. They opened the Coffin of the first, in which his Corpse lay uncorrupted, but covered all over with divers Silks; the Priests only shewed one of his Hands, which the Russians, who had watched the Opportunity of getting in with me, kissed with a great deal of Devotion and Veneration. There was also kept in this Church the Image which a certain Russian Priest had cut and slashed with a Knife, for which he was, in the Year 1715, burnt alive as an Heretick, and Defiler of I-

Pag. 82. mages, as I related above. In a separate Room there was a vast Treasure of golden Chalices, Plates, and other Church Ornaments, as also a New Testament fairly written and bound in Silver, richly set with precious Stones. Moreover, I was shewn a Chalice of Jasper, of ancient Grecian Workmanship, which, as they pretend, St. *Anthony* threw into the Water at *Rome*, and, upon his miraculous Arrival at *Novogorod*, found it again in the River there. That Saint and his Miracles are mightily cried up among the Russians. In the Steeple of this Cathedral lies the famous great Bell, which has not its Fellow as to Bigness. It is all scrawled over with the Names of those that saw it, and the Descriptions which Travellers have given us of this Piece of Curiosity, are pretty exact. It was

The Present State of Russia.

was cracked in a great Fire, and fell down. Next to the Church is to be seen a Hole in the Ground, where it was cast, and which, for Remembrance sake, was never filled up. None of the Russians could give me an Account how that unwieldy Mass had been raised up. Some Germans born at *Moskow*, whom I took with me up to the Steeple, told me, by way of Tradition, that, for Want of proper Machines and Ingineers, they made use of Wedges, which they drove in one upon the other, and fastened them, till, after unspeakable Pains, they got the Load up to the desired Height, and let it slopingly into the opening of the Steeple.

Next to the Cathedral is the House in which the Patriarchs lived formerly. In a great Hall built after the manner of a Refectory, was a Chair raised on four Steps, on which the Patriarch used to sit when he dined, the rest of the Clergy being served on lower Tables. Above it was the Library consisting of old Books in the *Russian, Slavonian, Polish,* and *Oriental* Languages. I found there no other German Book but the Bible of Dr. *Luther*'s Translation printed at *Lunebourg* 1650. In their Churches and Convents I could never meet with the Old Testament, for they have only the New, in the binding and adorning of which they spare no Expence. But the Old Testament, the first Book of *Moses* excepted, they judge to be of no Edification to the common People. In the same Room were six wooden Chests, in which were very carefully kept seventy seven Patriarchal Habits, but as there is no Patriarch at present, they are of no use at divine Service.

The Patriarch's House.

Service. Some English who were with me and understood Jewels well, assured me that the Value of those Habits was inestimable. Those which were wore by the late Patriarchs, *Adrian*, who was the last and died in the Year 1702, and *Nicon* the Saint, one of his Predecessors, were laid up in two several Chests; one of them was of a Workmanship extraordinary precious, and was sent by a Grecian Patriarch for a Present about one hundred Years ago. The Miters and Crosiers, that were used to be carried before them, were tipped with Gold, and richly set with precious Stones; one of those Crosiers was a Present from the now reigning King of *Persia*'s Father to a Russian Patriarch. All the *Pontificalia* together belonging to the Habit of a Patriarch, consisted of so many Parcels and were so heavy that I was hardly able to lift them up with one Hand.

The Tombs of the Czars. On the 5th I viewed the Church of the *Archangel*, in which are the Tombs of all the Czars of *Russia*. The Priest, my Conductor, led me to a Chamber separated from the Body of the Church sideways behind the Altar, in which stood three Stone Coffins. In the first lay the Corpse of the famous Czar *Ivan Basilowitz*, and in the other two those of his two Sons. In a separate Place of the Church lies the true *Demetrius*, who was in the Year 1591. murdered by *Boris Gudenow*, then Great Steward to the Czar *Fedor* or *Theodor*, and after the latter's Death Usurper of the Crown. The said *Demetrius*'s Coffin stands near to a Pillar over against the great Altar, and is placed under a little Altar built in Honour to him, his Memory being almost in no less veneration among the Russians than that of a Saint, and the greater part of them do firmly believe that the said young Prince was actually killed by *Boris*'s Assassins at *Uglitz*, 180 Werfts from *Moskow*, where he lived with his Mother, and that this is truly his Corpse; for, according to what they say, the first counterfeited *Demetrius*, who by personating him got upon the Throne, was soon after miserably murdered and his Body burnt to Ashes, consequently could not be that which lies in the said Coffin. The present Czar's Father *Alexius Michaelowitz* with his two Sons *Fedor Alexiewitz* and *Ivan Alexiewitz*, who both wore the Crown, lie near each other almost in the middle of the Church in three Brass Coffins covered with most precious Palls; the Turcois in particular, which the Czar *Ivan* in his Life-time wore on his Body, and is now fixed on his Pall, is highly valued on account of its extraordinary Bigness. The other Czars lie in a row along one Side of the Wall, their Coffins being covered with the like Palls. The Princes of the Blood who never came to the Crown, have their separate Places: I counted about thirty odd of their Coffins in this Church which are of no great value. All the Palls belonging to the Coffins of the Czars, are put over them only on great Festivals, or when Strangers come to see the Tombs, as was done on our coming thither; they are of an admirable Workmanship after the Russian manner, the Bottoms are of Silk or Velvet, on the Tops of most of the Coffins lie Crosses of massy Gold, and about the Borders of each Pall are the respective Lives and Characters

racters of the deceased in some thousands of Russian Letters, expressed by Pearls joined together and set with precious Stones of divers sorts. Moreover they shewed me in this Church the Sepulchre of St. *Alexius,* as also a Piece of Wood of our Saviour's Cross. On a Desk before the Altar I saw a Shrine divided in upwards of thirty Cases, in each of which lay a small piece of Bone, with an Inscription denoting what Saint's Relict it is; Devotees use to pitch upon one according to their several Cases and Concerns, to kiss it and put up their Prayers before it.

A Nunnery called Tchude Monaster. Next I went to a Nunnery called *Tchude Monaster*, and sent to acquaint the Abbess with my desire of seeing her Convent. At first she seemed startled at my Servant's Proposition and made some difficulty to comply with my Request; but upon my sending the Diak, or Clerk of the Office of State, who accompanied me everywhere, and his shewing her the Archbishop of *Resan*'s Order in Writing, she forthwith caused the Churchdoor to be opened and me to be conducted into it by two old Matrons. But one of them held me continually by the Sleeve, and as my Curiosity to view a very ancient and noble piece of Painting on the Altar, made me break loose, I was civilly reprimanded, and immediately Frankincense brought to purify all the Places where I had walked. This done, they shewed me the Burying-places of all the *Czaritzas* (or Czarinas) and *Czarennas* (or Czarish Princesses) which are adorned after the same manner as those of the Czars, and make a fine Appearance; the Corpses lie in Stone Coffins ranged in the same Order as they

they died. They further shewed me the Sepulchre of St. *Ailtulus*, who lived three hundred Years ago, and of whom they related abundance of Miracles. The Abbess or *Igumene*, (as the Russians call her) of this notable Nunnery, had the Curiosity to invite me into her Apartment, though she was indisposed, and is otherwise but seldom to be seen. She was attended by many Nuns who shewed a great deal of respect to her: After having complained to me of the ill State of her Health, she cut several Slices of Rye-bread, which she dipped into a sweet, and to me unknown, Liquor, and offered them to me eat. Then a Nun brought some Silk-work made in their Monastery, which the Abbess presented to me to keep in Remembrance of her, after which she asked me many Questions about the Manners of *Germany* and the Nunneries there, and was very attentive to the Account I gave her in answer to what she asked. Last of all to give me a Mark of her Friendship, she ordered some of the principal Nuns to entertain me in their common Cell, which they did accordingly with much Civility and no less Affability, and after having made me drink five Cups of Brandy almost against my Will, they desired me to come soon again to see them. I was but just returned to my Lodging when one of their Servants came with a Letter and divers small Presents of their Nun-work; as I was told by a Friend that this was as much as civilly asking a Return of a handsome Present for having been shewn the Convent, I made my Acknowledgment by sending them some

religious

Of the Russian Nuns.

religious Pictures for the Ornaments of their Cells.

In this Nunnery are also married Women, who either chuse that Life of their own accord on some Discontent in Marriage, and for other weighty Reasons, or are thrust into it by their Husbands, which in this Country is very easily done. The Women in *Russia* are kept very close and live in perfect Slavery; their Husbands use them so ill that many a Woman conceives an Aversion to Matrimony and prefers a Convent to it. On the other hand, if married Men turn Monks, the Marriage is thereby also dissolved. Many of the Maiden-Nuns are forced to monastical Life either by their Parents for Disobedience, or by their Brothers and Relations out of Interest to keep the Estate to themselves; hence it is that there are many young and handsome Nuns, and of good Families in the abovesaid *Tchude Monaster* as well as in other Convents. They wear long black Gowns with wide Sleeves, a Girdle about their Waste, and on their Heads wide black Hoods hanging down on the Shoulders, and when they are at Divine Service they cover the upper part of the Face with a Crape. They perform their Canonical Prayers Night and Day, and sing in two Choruses after Russian Notes, but there is no great Variation or Art in the Musick.

Of the Russian Church-Service.

The Russians suffer no Instrumental Musick in their Churches, for they say that God can only be praised by human Voice; neither have they any Seats, but either they stand or kneel before the Images, crossing themselves without Intermission and repeating their *Gospodin Pomilui*, Lord have Mercy upon us, all the

the time the Priest says Mass. They have a high Notion of the Sign of the Cross, which they make with two Fingers first from the Head to the Breast, and then from one Shoulders to the other, a Ceremony which a Russian never fails to perform even in the Streets, at the sight of a Church or a Cross.

About an English Mile from the City stands another Convent called *Dewitz Monaster*, or Maiden-Nunnery, which is a very magnificent Structure, in which the Princess *Sophia* the present Czar's Sister of the half Blood, was kept Prisoner during Life for being concerned in the great Rebellion, and now lies buried there. No body was admitted into it without the express Leave of the Knees *Fedor Jurgowitz Romadonofsky*, then Vice-Czar of *Moskow*. He was a Man of strict Justice, but withal of a strange Humour, for it was his Custom to force his Guests to drink a Cup full of strong Brandy mixed with Pepper, which a huge Bear was artfully taught to present to them with one of his Paws, and even for Diversion sake to pull off their Hats and Wigs, and to lay hold of their Clothes if they scrupled to pledge. I had known, the said Knees at *Petersbourg*, and was treated by him with great Civility according to his own way, but at *Moskow* I would not venture upon paying him a Visit for fear of being made welcome like others, so that I missed the opportunity of seeing the said famous Nunnery within. It is situate in a pleasant Plain; and has a Prospect all over the adjacent Country. It contains three hundred Nuns, who lead a strict Life and never come abroad; the only Diversion they have

Another Nunnery called Dewitz Monaster, the Prison of two half Sisters of the Czar, Sophia and Catharine.

is on Festivals when they are allowed to walk upon the great Wall. The Princess *Catharine* another half Sister to the Czar, was also shut up for some Years in this Nunnery on well-grounded Suspicion, but was set at Liberty again seven Years ago upon the Intercession of the Princess *Mary* also a half Sister to the Czar, (who lately fell her self under her Brother's Displeasure on occasion of the Inquisition against the Czarewitz) and of the Princess *Natalia*. The said Princess *Catharine* lived at that time in *Moskow*, in her own Palace quite at the End of the Suburbs, and was maintained suitably to her Quality; a Lady of excellent Sense of and an heroick Spirit. The Czar had ordered her to come and live at *Petersbourg*, but at her instant Request she was excused. They shewed me the Apartment on the Wall next to the Convent, in which the Princess *Sophia* was kept in the beginning of her Imprisonment, and from the Windows of which she was obliged to see those Rebels executed who had sided with her. She died fifteen Years after in this Monastery, and I remember that upon a certain occasion when mention was made of her, the Czar himself gave her this Character, that she was a Princess endowed with all the Accomplishments of Body and Mind to Perfection, had it not been for her boundless Ambition and insatiable desire of governing.

The Convent Simonov-Donskoy Monaster. Within two English Miles of the City are several other Convents, which are noble and strong built Edifices, surrounded with large Walls. Among them there is the *Simonov-Donskoy Monaster*, which is inhabited by Monks who are Natives of *Ukraina* and the

The Present State of Russia.

the Country along the *Don:* The Prior of it told me, that the finding of an Image of the Virgin *Mary* near that River one hundred Years ago, had been the occasion of the Foundation of that Convent.

On the 10th of March I made a Journey to the *Woskresenskoy Monaster*, attended by a Guard of eight Dragoons and a Corporal, which was given me for my Security. That Monastery lies eight German Miles from *Moskow*, and is surrounded with a wide and high Wall, and a River full of Fish. Within all along the Wall are the Cells of the eighty Monks maintained there, and the Rooms in which four Swedish Prisoners are kept, *viz.* two Lieutenant-Colonels, an Adjutant-General, and the Privy-Secretary or Clerk of the Privy-Council *Cederhielm:* They have Permission to go a hunting with their Guards, but during my being there they were not allowed to come abroad. This Monastery is in great Veneration and much frequented by reason of its being built within in imitation of the holy Sepulchre, by the Patriarch *Nikon*, who with great Expence sent several able Architects to *Jerusalem* to take the exact Dimensions of the Original. The Structure of the said Holy Sepulchre and of the rest of the Church is of Free-Stone, as are almost all other Monasteries, and is divided into many By-places, Recesses, little Chapels and Galleries above and under the Ground, each of which has its own Altar, so that I counted above seventy Altars in that Church. Before the Entry of the Sepulchre where the Stone-cover is rolled off, and the Guards painted on, hangs a Light which burns very dim,

The Convent Woskresenskoy-Monaster.

near

near which sate an old Monk asking Alms. After I had seen all that is remarkable, as for instance the Coffin of the Patriarch *Nikon* who is buried there, the Church-Plate and other precious Ornaments, I went to see the *Archimandrita* or Abbot, and after some Discourse turning upon religious Affairs, he told me that the Patriarch *Nikon* had lived twenty Years in a desart Place an English Mile from the Convent, almost inaccessible at that time by reason of the deep Snow. However as I had heard so much of that Man who is extremely cried up by the Russians, I resolved to go and see the Place. I was two Hours on the Way and had a very troublesome Journey, the Snow lying to the height of a Man.

The Hermitage of the Patriarch Nikon.

I found a very small Chapel, incompassed with a few Trees and railed in. Two old decrepit Monks, hearing the Noise of our coming, came out of the Chapel and appeared surprized at so unexpected a Visit of Soldiers, but upon the Diak's approaching and acquainting them with our intent, they recovered from their Fright and bid us come into the Yard. I crept through a winding Stair-case which was so narrow that one Man could hardly pass, first to the little Chapel of about a Fathom in the Square, in which the Patriarch had used to perform his solitary Worship. Then I went into the Room where he had lived, which was not much larger; in it hung a broad Iron-plate with a Cross of Brass fixed to a heavy Chain weighing twenty odd Pound, all which the said Patriarch wore about his Neck Night and Day for twenty Years together. His Bed was

The Present State of Russia.

was a square Stone two Ells in length, and scarcely one in breadth, over which had been spread nothing else but a Cover made of Rushes, which is now preserved and shewn in the Monastery, the Pilgrims having begun to handle it as a Relick, and to tear it to Pieces. Below in the House was a small Chimney in which the Patriarch used to dress his own Provisions. The foresaid two old Men live in this Hermitage Winter and Summer, and subsist by the Alms arising from the Pilgrimages that are made thither.

It may be said in general that there is a tolerable good Order kept in the Russian Monasteries; each is governed by a Prior or *Archimandrita*, to whom the Monks pay all imaginable Obedience and Respect. Their Revenues were very great in former Times, at present they are stript of what is superfluous, yet they have still their Competency. It is astonishing to see the immense Treasure kept in the Monasteries and Churches of *Russia*, consisting of Jewels, Pearls and Gold, which is in some Measure lost to the Publick, but since the Battle of *Narva* when the Affairs of *Russia* had but an indifferent Aspect, the Clergy were forced largely to contribute towards publick Charges, and a good many of their Bells were transformed into Guns. The Czar not judging proper as yet to nominate a Patriarch, the Church is governed with a Dependance upon his Majesty's Supremacy, by Metropolitans and *Archi-Rejés* or Archbishops, and the Convents of Monks by *Archimandrites*, and those of Nuns by *Igumenes*. Only *Popes* or secular Priests are allowed or rather obliged to marry, though but once, pursuant

The State of the Monasteries and of the Clergy in general.

pursuant to the Interpretation which the Ruffian Church puts upon that Sentence of the Scriptures: *A Bishop must the Husband of one Wife.* The Clergy let their Hair grow as long as they please, contrary to the general Custom of the Country. They have hitherto preserved the Liberty of wearing Beards, which they tender almost as their Lives, and have a high Veneration for them, in as much as they think they make them resemble God Almighty, whom their Painters represent with a Beard.

Other Curiosities in and about Moskow. The publick *Dispensary* in the City of *Moskow*, is, if not to be preferred to any in *Europe*, at least to be counted one of the chief. It furnishes the Armies and all the great Towns of *Russia* with Medicines, and is recruited every Year with Drugs to the value of twenty thousand Rubels and upwards. The Building is one of the most splendid in the City, and all those belonging to it, are *Germans*. There is also a little House built of purpose for a terrestrial *Globe* nicely contrived, made many Years ago in *Holland* by a masterly Hand: Next to it lies a Sloop with four Oars which the Czar *Michael Fedrowitz* wrought with his own Hands, as is kept as a Rarity. At the End of the City is the *Park*, in which are kept live Lions, Tigers, Panthers, white Bears, black Foxes, Lynxes, Sables, and a great number of valuable Birds of different sorts. The *Woods* about *Moskow* are very pleasant and stored with singing Birds, of which there are but few in the barren Neighbourhood of *Petersbourg*; to supply this Defect several thousands of Birds to the value of 1500 Rubels were bought up some Years

The Present State of Russia.

Years ago at *Moskow* and in the neighbouring Villages, and carried to *Petersbourg*, where they let them fly into the Woods, in which they have confiderably multiplied fince.

The live *Sables* in the faid Park look almoft like Cats: They are killed with Bows and wooden Crofs-bows. The Value of their Skins is known, and I have feen a Gown made of Sables of the deepeft black, which the Czar fent to the *Grand Signior* valued upwards of 4000 Crowns. The ancient Hiftorians relate many Fables and different Opinions about the *Golden Fleece:* But if one reflects on the Trade which its probable the *Scythians* of old carried on with the Inhabitants of the Country which is now called *Siberia*, whence they had among other Commodities thofe Sable-skins, which they carried to *Colchis*, and the People of *Colchis* further to *Greece*; there is large room for Conjecture, that the *Grecians* receiving thofe precious Furs at the fecond or rather third Hand, paid a good deal of Gold for them, and for this Reafon gave them the Name of *Aureum Vellus* or the *Golden Fleece*. The Kingdom of *Siberia* pays its yearly Taxes chiefly in this Commodity; all the Furrs are firft delivered to the Governor of *Siberia*, and after being prepared, are marked with a Seal and fent to the Ruffian Senate.

Of the Sables of Siberia, and the Golden Fleece of the Ancients.

Seventeen Years ago an *Arfenal* of extraordinary Bignefs and Strength was begun to be built by the Czar's Orders, of which now appear only the Foundations and the Outwalls, the reft remaining unfinifhed, fince the Czar fet his Mind upon the building of *Petersbourg*.

An Arfenal unfinifhed.

The Caftle of Kremelin. As to *Kremelin*, or the Caftle it felf, and the Czar's *Throne* in it, I could not fee them till a little before my Departure, the *Knees Proforowsky* High Treafurer (Father to the Princefs *Gallizin)* being always indifpofed, and yet unwilling to truft any body with the Key to the Room in which the Throne ftands. The faid Caftle is fituate clofe upon the River *Moskow*; the whole Structure is of Free-ftone and very durable, but without any Regularity or Symmetry by reafon of the Alterations and Additions that have been made from time to time. In the inmoft Court ftands a little old Church, which has been hitherto preferved on account of its Antiquity, it having been built before the Foundation of the City. The Czar's Apartments are empty at prefent and for the moft part unfurnifhed; a broad Stair-cafe leads up to them, before which is fhown the Place, where the *Strelitzes* ftood in the Rebellion of 1682, and received at the Points of their Pikes all thofe Ruffian Lords who were thrown out of the Windows and from the top of the Stairs. There is as a Gallery leading from the Apartments of the Czarifh Family to the Czar's Chapel, where they continue to perform divine Service. The Czar's Seat is over-againft the Altar, all open before, but that of the Czarina and the Princeffes is clofe fhut up, and only an opening left of the breadth of an Inch, through which they could look into the Church: Even the feparate Gallery through which they ufed to go thither from their Apartments, is covered on all Sides, fo that they could not be feen neither at Church nor any where elfe, conformably

ably to the old Russian Custom. The Crown and Scepter are lockt and sealed up in a Room, of which the Great-Chancellor Count *Golofkin* having the Keys and Seals, and being then absent, I could not see them. The Chair on which the Czar sate when he gave Audience, has been removed out of the Audience-Chamber into another Room, the Czar but seldom observing those Solemnities any more. There is another such Chair besides; both of them were above sixty Years ago sent for a Present to the Czar *Alexius Michaelowitz* by the King of *Persia*. They are like common easy Chairs, except that a Foot-stool is fixed to each of them, and that the Seats are somewhat higher from the Ground than ordinary. The Sumptuousness of them consists in the quantity of divers precious Stones with which they are richly set: The first exceeds the other as to the Value, and on the Back of it is written with golden Letters a Latin Dedication to the Czar, in which the *Persian* styles him *Potentissimus & felicissimus Ruthenorum Imperator*, the most potent and most fortunate Emperor of the Russians. There is also a third Chair of half the size and not near so sumptuous as the other two, which was a Present from the King of *Persia* for the *Czarewitz* at that time, who used to sit in it at publick Audiences. I found nothing very remarkable in the Castle besides what I have already observed.

The Day before my Departure, the Abbess of *Tchude-Monaster* sent Word to me, that if I was willing to see a Nun take the Habit, I should have the Liberty of seeing the Ceremony of her Consecration in her Monastery. Upon my entering the Church, I found all the

A young Nun takes the Habit in Tchude Monaster.

the Nuns singing, and a great Congregation of Women, among whom were the principal Ladies of the whole City, who are otherwise but seldom seen. No other Men were admitted besides me and my Servants, and two old Women placed me, notwithstanding my declining it, upon the Altar, in order to see the better, and to be the better seen. The singing of the two Choruses of the Nuns having lasted for some Time, they went out of the Church through two Rooms into a third to fetch the Candidate of their Order. She wore a black Gown, and her fair and long Hair was combed quite over her Face. She walked on stooping, and being arrived in the middle of the Church where a Priest stood before a Desk, threw her self upon the Ground thrice, and continued afterwards in that Posture. The Priest, after having said a Prayer, asked her divers Questions, *viz.* Whether she entered into Monastical Life out of Constraint? Whether she entirely renounced the World? Whether she would obey the Laws prescribed? &c. to which she returned proper Answers with a loud Voice, always adding the Asseveration of *Je Je Bog*, By God. Then the Priest began another Prayer, after which he bid her rise, and shew her Face. Upon which some old Nuns parted her Hair, and she appeared a young, well-favoured Person of about twenty Years of Age. She stept up to the Desk, took a Pair of Scissars that lay upon it, presented it to the Priest, kissed his Hand, and desired him to cut off her Hair; but he declined it, and laid the Scissars aside. This Ceremony being repeated a second and third time, the Priest at last took the Scissars, and having parted her Hair into four Tresses,

cut

The Present State of Russia.

cut them cross-ways over the Crown of her Head, the Choruses singing certain Hymns in the mean time. This done, two old Nuns put the Girdle about her Waste, and dressed her in the Habit, during which her Relations, who stood by, were bathed in Tears, and bewailed the young Woman, as now dead and lost to the World. Last of all the Priest read to her the Statutes of the Convent; after which she was led out of the Church with the same Ceremonies as in the Beginning, and carried before the Abbess, whom I went also to see upon her Invitation. I found her still indisposed; she asked me how I liked the Ceremony, and so on; and as for the rest, entertained me as she did on my first Visit.

My coming into the Church occasioned no small Surprize among the female Congregation there, who knew nothing of my having Leave for it from the Abbess and the Archbishop; the Curiosity of some of the Ladies was such, that they began to pull me by the Sleeve, and to enter into Conversation with me. They not only asked me, what Country I was of, what Business I had at *Moskow*, and the like, they even enquired whether I was baptized, and a *Christian*, because I did not bow, and fall to the Ground as they did; which I excused, by saying, that this was an outward Ceremony, which was not customary with us. However, this Conversation made Room for another after the Solemnity was over, when they detained me with great Civility near an Hour, asking many Questions relating to *Germany*; particularly about the Ladies there, and whether they were kept so close and low as they are in *Russia*. They seemed

Of the Women in Russia.

seemed greatly pleased with the Account I gave them, and on our parting gave me to understand, that they should be glad to be married in that Country. I have observed above, that the Russian Wives and Daughters are kept extremely retired, and never go abroad, unless it be to Church, or to see their nearest Relations. I have seen many a beautiful Face among them, but they are disgraced by their old Customs, which they cannot yet leave off, the Court being too far off to break them of them. Ladies of Quality are dressed after the *German* Fashion, which indeed they prefer to their old antick Dress; but as to their Courtesies, still the old Custom prevails of bowing with the Head to the Ground. There are those Ladies, who have made some Stay with their Husbands in foreign Countries, but, upon their Return to *Moskow*, are obliged to throw off foreign Manners, and conform with the old Way, for fear of being laughed out of Countenance by their former Acquaintance; but at *Petersbourg* they have the Czar's rigorous Orders on their Side. All the Comfort the old-fashioned Ladies have in this spreading Reformation of Manners, is now and then to remember with Pleasure, the good old Time, when the Court Ladies attended a Czarina's Coach on Horse-back in *Amazons* Dress. If a Russian gives an Entertainment to Persons not related to him, the Mistress of the House does either not appear at all, or only just before Dinner, to make the Guests welcome with a Kiss and a Cup of Brandy, after which she makes her *Poclan* or Courtesy, and gets out of the Way again. Five Years ago there was a Project on foot, for sending the youngest and handsomest Russian Ladies to travel abroad, as well as their

their Brothers, at the Expence of their Parents, to *Koningsberg, Berlin, Drefden,* and other Places, to board in Families, in order to learn foreign Cuſtoms and Languages, and all ſort of Female Work. But upon the Remonſtrances of the Parents, that the Freedom of foreign Converſation would expoſe their Children to great Temptations, and endanger their Virtue and Reputation, this Deſign was dropt. He that endeavours to oblige a fine Woman by a Compliment, calls her *Crafna Dewitza,* or *red Maid*; for they think, the more red, the greater Beauty; hence it is, that the Sex paint to Exceſs in this Country, and thoſe of a middling Rank put abundance of Patches on their dawbed Faces, which Extravagance was carried ſo far not long ago, that they wore Patches of Variety of Figures, even Trees, Coaches and Horſes, and the like. The Women in general, the Quality excepted, ſtill wear Furs under their Coats, even in Summer time; thoſe who frequent the Court, appear indeed perfectly well dreſſed after the foreign Faſhion; but in Converſation with Strangers, they cannot yet conquer their in-born Baſhfulneſs and Awkwardneſs. As for what concerns the common Tradition, that the Ruſſian Women judge of the Love of their Husbands by the Blows they receive from them, the ſame ought to be taken in a right Senſe. They are indeed very ill uſed, and kept under a ſevere Diſcipline; but who would imagine them to be fond of being beaten? The Truth is, they are ſo given to Drinking, and other ill Habits, (I ſpeak of the common Sort) that they neglect their Houſhold Affairs, whence it

happens

happens, that the Man, if he has the Education of his Children and other domestick Concerns at Heart, either provoked by the Carelesness of his Wife, or even sometimes prompted by his own ill Humour, lashes her as long as he thinks that rude Way of Correction may reclaim her, or at least till his mad Fits are over. But if he finds her past Hopes, or falls into ill Courses himself, he begins to leave his Wife and Children to themselves, and to follow other Women. In this Case it is natural for a Woman to infer from her Husband's beating her no more, that he has withdrawn his Affection, and abandoned himself to forbidden Pleasures.

Of the Nobility at Moskow. The principal Families are already removed from *Moskow* to *Petersbourg*; however, many *Boyars* are yet remaining there, who keep up a great Figure in Town, by the Number of their Servants, Horses and Sleds. Those of the old Stamp wear, for the greater Part, their own Hair still, though they have parted with their Beards, which some of them cut off themselves with Scissars. They wear the German Dress; but it is easy to observe on many, that they have not been long used to it.

The present State of the City of Moskow. *Moskow* is a City of vast Extent, the Streets are crouded with People, among whom are so many Vagrants and idle young Fellows, as would make a tolerable Army. Its Situation is one of the most pleasant that is to be seen any where; and the Foreigners who live there, very much extol the Variety of Diversions, which the many Walks cut in the Woods, the Gardens, Country-Houses, Manors, and Farms of the neighbouring Country afford

afford in Summer time. Some *English* Merchants (who keep very good Houses) had already in *February*, and even sooner, Roses, Gilliflowers, and well-tasted Sparagrass, in their Gardens on forced Ground. The Country thereabouts produces all the Necessaries of Life, which, as well as the Houses in the City, are very cheap, so that a Man may live at *Moskow* for one third of what it will cost him at *Petersbourg*, where every thing is excessive dear. This Time of Plenty has augmented still more, since the Court's removing to *Petersbourg*: But, on the other Hand, the Price of Land has abated in proportion, so that an Estate which before was valued at ten thousand Rubels, is now sold for four thousand, which is a great Loss to the Nobility; but Strangers and others, who have no Land, fare the better by it. There is Plenty of Cattle, Venison, Corn, and Garden-fruits. From Time to Time Rain-deer are brought killed from *Samoiedia* on Sleds by the Way of *Archangel*; their Flesh eats almost like that of red Deer, and is looked upon as a great Dainty. But Fish bear a high Price, by reason of the frequent Fasts, and the great Number of Inhabitants; particularly Sterlets, Belugas, and other nice Fishes out of the *Wolga*, in the Dearness of which the Russians place the Sumptuousness of their Feasts; they dress them with Wall-nut Oil during their Fasts. At the Time of my being at *Moskow*, the Prince *Gagarin* gave but an ordinary Entertainment, at which fifty odd Dishes of Fish were served up of all Sorts, and dressed as they use in Fast-time. He was served in Plate, and lived splendidly; his House and Train

Train were Princely, especially when he was in his Government of *Siberia*. He carried me to his Closet, and shewed me his *Bog* or God, which was covered almost quite over with Diamonds of great Value; and the Jewellers there assured me, that this Image stood him in one hundred thirty thousand Rubels.

The Administration of Justice in Russia.

The Russians have their own Laws, and a most summary Way of proceeding. Their Law-Suits do not require much Writing, but chiefly depend on the Penetration and Justice of the Judge, who hears the Parties himself, and pronounces Sentence. The Chancery at *Moskow* decides in Country Affairs, and collects the Taxes. I was present at one of their Sessions, where above two hundred Suitors and Petitioners appeared, being *Russians*, *Siberians*, *Astracanians*, *Cosacks*, *Calmucks*, and *Tartars*, some of whom came with Complaints, and others to give in their Accompts; thirty of them were dispatched that Morning. The Vice-Czar, *Knees Fedor Jurgewitz Romadonofsky*, whom I mentioned above, was then Lord Chief-Justice at *Moskow*. He punished the Criminals without Controul, and there was no appealing from his Sentences. His severe and rigorous Executions had rendered him the Terrour of the Country; he knew nothing of Mercy, his Speech and Looks were enough to make People tremble. He was in great Favour with the Czar, notwithstanding his strange Humour; for no Respect of Persons, nor Bribes were able to bias him in the Administration of Justice. Numbers of Robbers and Murderers, which some Persons assured me, amounted to six thousand and upwards, have been executed

The Present State of Russia.

cuted by his Orders, yet this proved no sufficient Remedy against those Crimes, forasmuch as a Russian values neither Life nor Death, and undergoes capital Punishment with an unparalleled Indolence. But towards the latter End of his Administration he caused two hundred such Offenders at one time to be hanged up on iron Hooks by the Ribs; the Horror of which Death struck such Terror among the rest, that their Number soon diminished. The Prisons in *Moskow* are crouded with such Criminals, they subsist by begging, and many of them continue there all their Life-time without working. When the Country begins to be pestered again with that Vermine, the said *Knees* uses to cause a Parcel of the convicted Prisoners to be executed, to serve for a publick Example. It is absolutely necessary in this Country, that Justice be executed in the severest manner, for otherwise no Person of what Rank and Degree soever, would be safe. Some Years ago Prince *Menzicoff*, passing through a certain Borough, was attacked by all the Inhabitants, who knew him well enough; several Persons of his Retinue were killed, and he himself would not have escaped the Hands of the furious Multitude, had it not been for the Swiftness of his Horse. He soon after caused all the Inhabitants promiscuously to be hanged to one Man, without even sparing the Curate. To return to the Vice-Czar *Romadonofsky*: I shall take notice, that when he was at *Petersbourg*, the Czar, as *Vice-Admiral*, paid to him, as *Vice-Czar*, all the Honours that are due to a crowned Head: His Son, who has succeeded him in that Dignity, is now treated upon the same Foot.

Of the Caspian Sea. Of the River Daria, which carries Gold Dust, and of the Calmucks

I have made mention above of *Alexander Bekewitz*, a *Circassian* Prince, and his being sent to the *Caspian* Sea. When I was at *Moskow* he returned from thence, and proceeded to *Riga*, to make Report of his Commission to the Czar, who sent him a second time, furnished with new Instructions. M. *Blüher*, a Gentleman versed in mineral Affairs, who had been sent to accompany him as far as *Astracan*, was also returned to *Moskow*, where he tarried, and gave me the following Account of both their Commissions. A certain River, called *Daria*, runs out of the Country of the *Calmucks* into the North side of the *Caspian* Sea, carrying along with it a great deal of Gold Sand: This Discovery had been made a good while before; but because some Difference had arisen with the *Calmucks* about Trade, those People had not only turned the Channel of the said River another Way into the Sea, but also, by choaking up the Mouth of it, rendered it so shallow, that the Russians could not enter it with their Ships. But as the said River might have proved very beneficial, not only on account of the Gold Sand, but also for settling a Communication of Trade with the *Usbeck Tartars* and the *Indians*, it had been for some Time under Deliberation, how to maintain the Possession and Navigation of it. With this View the Czar sent the Prince *Bekewitz* thither to make an exact Draught of that Side of the *Caspian* Sea, which accordingly he had done, and was then carrying the said Draught to the Czar, to whom he was to propose the raising of a small Fort for a Garrison of two or three hundred Men, to command the said River. As
to

The Present State of Russia.

to the Occasion of the Discontent the *Calmucks* had conceived against the *Russians*, he told me the following Particulars. The *Calmucks* use to carry on a Trade, some to *Astracan*, others to *Tobolsky*, the Metropolis of *Siberia*, by the River *Irtis*, with Tea, divers *Chineze* Stuffs, and especially great Quantities of Salt, which, in some Rivers of their Country, shoots out above the Water, in the Shape of Sugar-Loafs, and is said to be extraordinary good, for which they take from the *Siberians* Money, Russia-Leather, Iron, and Furs. But as this Nation is very unruly, the Czar would rather have his own Subjects to gather the Salt; and as the *Chineze* Goods may be had by another Way, his Czarish Majesty a Year ago, and better, commanded Major-General *Bucholtz*, a *German*, to march with three Regiments of Dragoons above a thousand *Wersts* beyond *Tobolsky*, into the Heart of the *Calmucks* Country, to take Possession of those Places where the Salt grows, and to raise a Fort, to keep those People in Awe. But they would not be dealt with after such a Rate, and not only from that Time left off frequenting the Fair at *Tobolsky*, but also, in Resentment of the Russian Proceeding, choaked up the River, as abovesaid.

As to the Commission with which M. *Blü-* of Circassia. *ber* was charged in particular, he related to me, that, pursuant to his Orders, he parted with the Prince *Bekewitz* at *Astracan*, and turned to the Right into the Country of the *Circassians*, to take a View of the Mines there, which, according to the repeated Informations given to the Czar, were stored with rich Silver-Oar. When he arrived at those

those Places the Country People confirmed, that there was such Oar, but laughed at his coming to search for it in the Winter-time, when all the Earth was covered with Snow and Ice; upon which he applied to their Princes or *Kneeses*, who gave him Pieces of Oar, which, upon Essay, he found to contain a great deal of Silver. With these Informations he returned to *Moskow*, expecting, as well as Prince *Bekewitz*, the Czar's further Orders. To this Relation he added, that the *Kneeses* of *Circassia*, upon his producing the Czar's Order, received him very civilly; but that they had a Mind for every thing he had about him, which they exchanged for Horses: The Chief of the Country wear Coats of Mail, with Silk Gowns over them, their Arms are Bows and Arrows; they are generally well mounted; in Summer they live in the Woods under small Tents, during which their Families dwell in ordinary wooden Houses, and take care of their Husbandry. M. *Blüher* assured me, that though he had been a great Traveller, yet he never met any where with such a Variety of beautiful and ugly Women as in *Circassia*: The Land having been visited the Year before with a great Dearth, he could not get a Morsel of Bread all over the Country; yet they have Plenty of Cattle; the Peasants lead a poor and uncomfortable Life. In some Places he found ancient Tombs with Latin Inscriptions, most defaced; the *Circassians* told him, they were the Burying-Places of some Christians, who, in former Times, inhabited their Country, which M. *Blüher* refers to that Time, when

the

The Present State of Russia.

the Christian Emperors had their Residence in the East.

At the same Time arrived at *Moskow* M. Pouſſet, a French Refugee, a Gentleman of fine Parts and good Senſe, coming from *Aſtracan*; of which Kingdom, and the Buſineſs in which he had been employed there, he gave me the following Account. *An Account of the Kingdom of Aſtracan.* The Czar ſent for him five Years ago from *Berlin*, and ordered him to go to *Azoff*, to try the Soil of the Neighbourhood of that Place, whether it it was fit for planting Vines. But he was hardly arrived there, when the Town fell again under the Dominion of the *Turks*; whereupon the Czar ordered him for *Aſtracan* for the ſame purpoſe; accordingly he planted French Vines there with great Care, which produced divers Sorts of Wine, which indeed had the ſame Colour, and ſomething of the Flavour, though not the ſame Spirit as thoſe in *France*. He brought with him ſeven different Sorts for the Czar to taſte, in order to know whether he ſhould go on with planting, or leave off. At the ſame Time he was to communicate to his Majeſty a Project, by which he engaged to produce in a few Years ſo many Silk-worms, and ſuch a Quantity of Silk, in the Country about *Aſtracan*, as would enable *Ruſſia* not only to do without Perſian Silk, but even to export that of their own Produce to other Countries, provided he had ſixteen or twenty thouſand young Mulberry Trees. The Kingdom of *Aſtracan*, ſaid he, yields to the Czar by its Trade upwards of two hundred thouſand Rubels a Year. It is ſituate in an excellent Climate, and would be one of the moſt fruitful

Countries

Countries in the World, if it had Rain from time to time: But, except some little Sprinklings which fall in the Spring, it is entirely deprived of all Moisture from the Air all the Summer long, which is so dry and scorching, that the Earth, in most parts of that Kingdom, is not able to produce a Handful of Corn, Garden Fruits, or any of those Things which are necessary for the Support of human Life, consequently the Inhabitans cannot subsist without the Trade they have with their Neighbours. The many sorts of delicious Melons which grow there, are planted on the Banks of the Rivers, out of which the Water is raised by Mills, and conveyed among the Melon Beds; which Method M. *Pousset* applied to his Vineyards, and designs also to make use of it to water the Mulberry Trees, if his Project takes with the Czar. However, kind Nature supplies this Defect of Rain in another manner: The *Wolga*, like the *Nile* in *Egypt*, swells in the Spring, and overflows the adjacent Country for ten, twelve, and more German Miles on each Side, which inriches the Ground to that Degree, that, after the falling of the Water in some Parts, and the melting of the Snow in others, the Grass shoots up in a Month's time two Ells high, which furnishes the Country with some Pasture. Corn and Garden-fruits they fetch from the Kingdom of *Casan* on the *Wolga*, and the many *Caravans* of the *Calmucks* supply them every Year with Cattle to kill, with Leather, and other Commodities, for which they take in return Money, Melons, Rice, Stuffs, and all sorts of Goods, which those of *Astracan* get by the Trade
with

with *Perſia*. This Intercourſe therefore with the *Calmucks* being ſo beneficial to *Aſtracan*, they are uſed civilly by the Inhabitants, and gently by the Czar, whoſe Vaſſals they are.

The Nature of the *Caravans* of thoſe roving *Calmucks*, is as follows: Thoſe People live in no fixed Habitations, they come from the Frontiers of *Great Tartary*; after having joined, for their mutual Security, in a great Swarm, to the Number of ſix, and even twelve thouſand Souls, they break up, driving and carrying along with them near as many Camels, Horſes, Oxen, Cows, Sheep, all ſorts of Poultry, &c. they begin their March in Spring, after the Inundation of the *Wolga* has made the Graſs come up, as above mentioned, on which they let their Cattle feed, as they come along in eaſy Journeys, and leave every thing bare behind them. They have a ſort of Huts of Leather, called by them *Kubits*, which M. *Pouſſet* compared to our Ladies Hoop-Petticoats; they put them up with Poles, make Fire in them to dreſs their Victuals, and when the Fire is gone out, they ſtop the opening above to keep themſelves warm at Night. In the Morning they take their Huts down again, load them on their Beaſts of Burthen, and ſo jog on. When they have diſpoſed of their Merchandize at *Aſtracan*, they return home in the ſame manner, by the Help of a ſecond Crop of Graſs that is ſprung up in the mean Time. Theſe Journies they make from Year to Year. They are Idolaters, and carry their Idols, of different Shapes, every where with them; their Worſhip conſiſts in very ridiculous Ceremonies

Of the Caravans of the Calmucks.

monies; and as for the reft, they live in the grofleft Ignorance.

The Calmucks defeated by the Cuban-Tartars.

I informed my felf of the faid M. *Pouffet,* and fome other Perfons, concerning a remarkable Incident, of which I had heard fomething before at *Petersbourg,* but could never learn any Certainty as to the Particulars. About Chriftmas 1715, the *Cuban-Tartars* (of which Nation I fpoke above) affembled to the number of thirty thoufand Men, and upwards, to furprize the Caravan of *Calmucks,* of which they had Information, that they incamped within fome German Miles of *Aftracan*; being three times their Number they defeated them, and cut off above three thoufand *Calmucks,* after which they retreated without doing any Harm to the Ruffian Inhabitants. But the Governor of *Aftracan* and Prince *Bekewitz,* at the Head of three thoufand Men, coming to the Affiftance of the *Calmucks,* overtook them, and were going to renew the Fight, when, to their great Surprize, the *Cubanian* Leader produced the Czar's Orders in Writing, giving them Leave to annoy the *Calmucks,* wherever they could meet them. The Governor refpected the Orders, and returned to *Aftracan*; upon which the *Cuban-Tartars* fell on a fecond time, and killed a great Number of *Calmucks.* No body could ever penetrate into the Truth of this Affair, whether the faid Orders were counterfeited, or whether the Czar had in Reality given them to the *Cuban-Tartars,* in order to humble and punifh the *Calmucks* for choaking up the River *Daria,* and abandoning the Fair at *Tobolsky,* as has been mentioned above, or whether it was done with a

View

The Present State of Ruſſia.

View to ſecure the *Cuban-Tartars* to the Ruſſian Intereſt, in caſe of any Difference that might ariſe with the *Turks*.

I learned on the ſame Occaſion, that the ſaid *Alexander Bekewitz* is a *Circaſſian* Prince, whoſe Father, ſome Years ago, ſhook off his Obedience to the King of *Perſia*, and ſought the Czar's Protection. There are alſo two Princes in *Georgia*, who are weary of the *Turkiſh* Yoke, and deſign to follow his Example, to which End they have charged Prince *Bekewitz*, to deſire two or three thouſand Men of the Czar for their Protection. *[marginal: Of the Prince Bekewitz.]*

The greater Part of *Tartars* inhabiting the Provinces about *Aſtracan*, are *Mahometans*, though ſubject to the Czar. For it would be difficult to endeavour at a Change of their Religion, ſeeing they are a vagrant People, who, upon the leaſt Oppreſſion, would throw off their Obedience, and ſubmit to ſome other Power. M. *Pouſſet* related, that as he had frequent Dealings with them, he found many ſenſible Perſons among them, and met with the moſt grateful Acknowledgments at the Hands of ſome of their principal Men, whom he inſtructed in ſeveral profitable Methods of improving their Husbandry. To give me an Idea of their way of living, he told me the following Story: In the Year 1715, a *Tartar*, in Token of his Gratitude, invited him and his Wife, who was a French-woman, to his Habitation, ſixteen German Miles from *Aſtracan*. He had ſome Suſpicion, and declined the Viſit, but was at laſt perſwaded. Their Guide brought them to a pleaſant Grove, where they found the *Tartar* in his Summer Habitation, ſitting under *[marginal: An Account of the Tartars inhabiting the Kingdom of Aſtracan.]*

under a handsome Tent in a fine Dress, smoaking his Pipe: He received them with great Friendship, and entertained them with Coffee and Sweet-meats. M. *Poußet* having lived very familiarly with the Tartar at *Aßracan*, took the Liberty to enquire after his Wives, and whether he might see them. The Tartar having let him know first, that this was not usually allowed among them; yet in regard of his being a Stranger, and his particular Friend, he sent for them. About half an Hour after appeared seven Women nobly dressed, whom any Man might have ventured to call so many Beauties, coming out of an Arbour of Rose-trees, at the Distance of a Stone-throw from the Tent, which they entered, and, by the Man's Order, saluted and kissed the Strangers, after which he made them forthwith return, for fear of being observed by his Neighbours. The Women, being curious of viewing a Stranger of their own Sex, the like of whom they never had seen before, took M. *Poußet*'s Wife, though much against her Inclinations, along with them to the Arbour. Just when the Men were at Dinner, they heard the French Gentlewoman crying for Help in a most lamentable manner. The Men in great Haste running thither, found those seven Women, full of Mirth, pulling and haling about their new Acquaintance, whom they had almost unrigged, withal telling the Men, that they had stript first, and that the French Woman had been greatly delighted with it, so that now it was her Turn to do the same; with which Words they all fell on again, fully resolved to have their Will. The Tartar, upon M. *Poußet*'s

pressing

The Present State of Russia.

pressing Instances, interposed his Authority, and parted them; but at the same Time gave his Guest to understand, that in their Country it was the greatest Piece of Civility among Women thus to undress on their first Visit. However, our Strangers, apprehensive of being exposed to more of such coarse Compliments, hastened away to *Astracan*, whither the Tartar sent the next Day divers Presents to appease them. M. *Pouffet* further told me, that the Lewdness of those People is beyond what can be imagined; but at the same time he extolled their orderly Life, in other Respects, and that they place their Point of Honour in being extremely officious and hospitable.

Before I end my Account of what I observed at *Moskow*, I shall relate some Particulars touching the State of the *Swedish* Prisoners in *Russia*, great numbers of whom are dispersed at *Moskow* and over all the Russian Empire. Ever since the Battel of *Pultava*, (upon the Name of which Place, so fatal to the victorious Arms of the late King of *Sweden*, one of his own Subjects plaid by transposing the Letters into *Vapulat*, He is beaten,) the Prisoners who were common Soldiers received but twice Remittances from *Sweden* for their Subsistance amounting to three Crowns a Head, but nothing was sent to the Officers. The latter were at first more gently used than the common Soldiers; but when many of them, who upon their Parole had Leave to go, did not return, and others who had entered themselves into the Russian Service, under this Cloak made their Escape; they began in general to be more closely watched,

The State of the Swedish Prisoners in the Russian Dominions.

watched, they were separated, and many of them dispersed into remote Parts, where they now are under strict Inspection; those who were become Securities for their Companions who kept away, were even put under close Confinement, so that there are now some of those Prisoners in all Provinces and Towns of the Russian Dominion. It is reckoned that there are at present above two thousand superior Officers remaining, and as not one tenth part of that Number can subsist by their own Means, the rest have been obliged to learn all sorts of Arts, Handicrafts and Trades to get their Bread. It is astonishing to hear by how many different Methods those unfortunate Gentlemen make shift to get a Livelihood, and to what degree of Perfection they have attained in those Works of their own Hands, which are carried about for Sale all over *Russia*. *Siberia* is the Prison of near a thousand superior Officers, who set up all sorts of Manufactures: There are among them Painters, Gold and Silver-smiths, Cardmakers, Turners, Joyners, Shoemakers, and Taylors, of all which respective Work I have seen Samples at *Moskow*, with which the best Masters can find no Fault: It is said, that only Periwig makers and Hatters are not among them: Some make the best of Gold and Silver Tissue and Brocade, others are turned Musicians, others again are Inn-keepers; those who have fallen into a Trade and Traffick as Merchants, have liberty of travelling up and down the Country, the Passes being so well guarded that there is no Possibility of escaping; there are even some who are reduced to do Chair-work for the Russians,

ans, others whose Misfortune it is, not to have been brought up to any other Business, if they have but found Limbs and sufficient Strength, go into the Forests and cut down a Load of Wood in a Day, for which they receive an *Altin* in the Evening. Others still who have some Tincture of Learning, have set up publick Schools, and have divided them into Forms, into which they receive not only the Children of their Fellow-Prisoners, many of whom either had their Wives with them, or married Russian Women, but also the Children of Russians committed to their Care. They teach them Latin, High-dutch, French, and other Languages, Morality, the Mathematicks, and divers bodily Excercises. One of those Schools is grown into such Repute among the Russians, that they send their Sons thither from *Moskow*, *Wologda* and other Places. The Masters who have been Officers of Distinction, are said to lead a holy Life, and to have entirely devoted themselves to spiritual Exercises, being maintained by their Disciples and the charitable Contributions raised by the celebrated Mr. *Francke* at *Hall* in *Saxony*. At *Moskow* there are others who subsist by teaching Youth, and whose Conduct is irreproachable. Some have embraced the Russian Religion, engaged into their Service and married Russian Women, and so found means to live. A certain Lieutenant, a Native of the Dutchy of *Bremen*, having lost his Health in the cold Winter near *Pultava*, and being brought up to no Trade, set up a Puppet-shew at *Tobolsky*, to which there is a great Resort of the Inhabitants who never saw the like before. It is very lucky for all

those

those Prisoners that they live in so cheap a Country, where they may have their Provisions all the Year round for twelve to twenty Rubels; besides, Prince *Gagarin*, who was at that time still Governor of *Siberia*, never let any Prisoner, who applied to him, return without Relief. The Swedish Officers could not enough praise his Generosity and Compassion, and would often say that their only Misfortune was to be confined to a Country so remote from their own. They have all free Habitation, and are not kept to hunting of Sables or any other Labour; their own Industry is enough to supply them with Necessaries. A Swedish Colonel, whose Name is *Schönstrom*, has employed the time of his Captivity in *Siberia* in making curious Observations and Remarks on the Country and its Inhabitants. He wrote to his Friend at *Moskow*, that on the Frontiers of *Siberia* he met with a Heathen Nation, and upon a narrow Enquiry into their Religion and Customs found many things which bear a great Resemblance to ancient Heathenism; and seeing that in their Worship they make use of the Names of *Thor*, *Fregga* and *Odde*, which were the ancient Heathen-Gods of the *Swedes* at *Upsal*, he conjectured, that the said Heathen Nation who have their own Language, are descended from those *Goths* who in ancient Times left *Sweden* and landed on the other side of the *Baltick*, from whence part of them proceeded towards the *Black-Sea*, and part of them went to settle in the Russian Provinces, and that probably some of them were forced by the growing Power and Oppression of their Enemies to abandon those

those Settlements again, and to retire to the hindmost Recesses of *Siberia* where they would be secure against the Pursuit of their Adversaries. It is reported that the said Colonel has gathered very curious Arguments and Observations which he intends to publish on a proper Occasion to support his Assertion. As to the common Swedish Prisoners they are kept to Labour, and are at present reduced to above one half of their former Number. The Names and Places of Abode of the Officers are all regularly set down in writing, so that upon an ensuing Peace they will be easily found out. But this will be more difficult with regard to the common Soldiers, who are not marked down by their several Names, besides that they are dispersed far and wide in the Towns and on the Estates of the Boyars, where many of them by marrying among the Natives and embracing their Religion, are so fixed that they are not like to return home again. Above one thousand of them are employed on the Works at *Petersbourg*, where they have a daily Allowance of Meal, Salt, &c. and as for the rest have liberty to beg. In the beginning of the present Northern War, when the Russians made use of the *Calmucks* and *Tartars* to ravage *Esthonia*, *Ingria*, and *Finland*, many thousands of the Inhabitants of those Countries were carried into Captivity into the Country of the *Calmucks*, who sold them to the *Siberians*, *Tartars*, *Cosacks*, and even to the *Turks* and *Persians*; I spoke with divers Persons who had seen some of those Exiles among the said several Nations in a tolerable Condition, but some of them had renounced the Christian

Christian Faith, which makes the Russians reflect upon this Captivity and Dispersion of the *Swedes* all over the World as a particular Punishment inflicted by Providence on that Nation.

An Account of a Journey to China, with the Observations made in it.

The *Caravan* which had been of late in *China,* and arrived at *Moskow* four Months ago, brought much Riches with them. When I was at Prince *Gagarin*'s at *Moskow*, the Commissary and *Fiscal*, or Sollicitor of the Caravan happened also to be there. The Prince at the Request of his Guests ordering them to give an account of the most remarkable Things they had observed on their Journey, they related the following Particulars. They set out from *Moskow* three Years ago. The first strange People they met with were the *Ostiacks*, inhabiting a Country beyond *Siberia*, blind Heathens worshipping their Idols. Their whole Dress is made of the Skin of Sturgeon, and they live on the Flesh of that and other Fishes, which they shoot with their Arrows in the Water. Of Bread they know nothing, and if any is given them, they spit it out again; a little Brandy will overcome them; they take no Money, of the Use of which they know nothing, but prefer to it Tobacco, Wooll, and other Trifles. The said Caravan navigated on the River *Oby* almost as far as *Jeniseskoy*, a Town on the River *Jenisea* tolerably fortified, where the Land already begins to be better and bears Corn. They arrived next at the Town of *Ilenskoy*, in the Neighbourhood of which lived another strange People called the *Tonguses*, who know nothing of God or Providence; in Summer they go naked; leading

withal

The Present State of Russia. 169

withal a miserable Life; they run as swift as Stags, four Days together without eating any thing Their Dead they do not bury, but lay them on high Trees; they have no fixed Habitations but remove from Place to Place; they have a strange way of beautifying their Faces, as they reckon it; in their younger Years they sow their Cheeks with black Thread in the Forms of different Figures, which they leave for some Days in the Skin, after which they draw out the Thread which leave black Points and the Marks of the intended Figure; the more a Man has disfigured his Face by this painful stitching, the more beautiful and the greater he is counted among his own Nation. The Caravan went further to the Town of *Burat*, and from thence to *Jekutskoy*, meeting thenceforward almost nothing but Heathens. Then they proceeded into *Dauria*, where they met the *Konni-Tongufes*; the Prince who reigns over them is called *Larimuh* of about thirty Years of Age; his Father being persecuted by the *Chineze* threw off their Obedience, and put himself under the Czar's Protection, embracing the Grecian Faith with all his Family, and above three thousand of his Subjects; the rest remain Idolaters. After the Caravan had past the last Frontier Town of the vast Russian Empire, they had fifteen Weeks still to travel; upon entering the *Chineze* Dominions, their Expences were defrayed by the Governors of the Places; they were conducted by two hundred Soldiers through the Chineze Wall, which wonderful Structure they could not enough admire; at *Peking* their Quarters were assigned them in the

Suburbs

Suburbs in a great Inn built of purpose for the Russian Caravans, where they were obliged to deposite their Merchandize and stay for their Buyers, because they are not permitted to go into the City with their Goods to expose them to Sale. They dispose first of the Czar's Merchandize, and then of that of the Merchants, by exchanging them for Gold and Silver Bullion, and all sorts of Chineze Commodities. The *Chineze* are very impudent in asking their Price, but often they come down to the tenth part of their first Demand: They value very much precious Stones, Watches and the like Curiosities, and pay more than triple the Price for them. As for the rest they are a discreet People who are easily to be dealt with. The City of *Peking* lies within three Walls. In the inmost which is called the red Wall, is the Emperor's Residence. That Prince is never to be seen in publick: During the Caravan's being there, he once set out on Horseback to go a hunting, of which publick Notice was given by two Trumpeters in the Streets where he was to pass, whereupon the People either retired, or lay down with their Faces to the Ground, till the Emperor was gone by. He is at present sixty odd Years of Age, and highly commended for his good Government: He has nineteen Sons, who all appear in publick; he whom the Father chuses from among them, succeeds to the Empire after his Death. The eldest desired the Commissary to come to him with some Russians, he being curious to see some of that Nation; accordingly he went with thirty of the most personable well dressed and provided by him

with

with good Wigs: The Prince received them kindly, asked them many Queſtions, treated them with Tea, and made them ſmall Preſents after the Chineze way. Among the *Jeſuits* who are at *Peking*, is one Father *Kilian Stumpf* *, who is in great Favour and Eſteem with the Emperor, and obliged to be continually near his Perſon, for which Cauſe he has a Bed at Court: He tranſlates many Books into the Chineze Tongue; he has made great Progreſs in propagating the Chriſtian Religion and is building many Churches, towards which Expence the Emperor lately gave a large Bounty. His leaving an entire Liberty and Power to the Jeſuits, makes it believed, that he is inwardly perſuaded of the Truth of the Chriſtian Religon. The famous Diſpute between the *Jeſuits* there and the *Dominicans* ſtill continues. The unconverted Chineze generally ſpeaking, ſome Idolaters among them excepted, have little or no Religion at all, but place their greateſt Happineſs in worldy Pleaſures. By the Treaty for ſettling the Limits between the Chineze and Ruſſian Empires, for twenty three Years, ſome Chineze Subjects fell under the Ruſſian Dominion, as on the other hand ninety Ruſſian Families were made over to the Scepter of *China*. The Emperor out of particular regard has taken all the latter to *Peking*, and formed himſelf out of the young

---

* [*It is ſince adviſed from* Peking *by Letters dated* January 12. 1721. N. S. *that the ſaid Father* Kilian Stumpf, *who was Preſident of the Academy, erected there for teaching the Mathematicks, died on the* 24th *of* July 1720. *after a languiſhing Illneſs of three Years, and was ſucceeded in his Preſidency by Father* Ignatius Kellern.]

Russians a Life-guard who have the Rank above all others of his Guards, and are looked upon as the most faithful of any of them: They are inviolably maintained in the Exercise of their Religion, and as the Russian Priests whom they took with them to *China* died one after another, they petitioned the Emperor for Leave to send for others from *Russia*, which he readily granted, and even dispatched Letters to Prince *Gagarin* (who confirmed it to me to be true) to desire some Russian *Popes*, or Priests. The Prince upon the Czar's Orders accordingly sent two *Archimandritas*, with some *Popes* and *Protopopes*, (Priests and Arch-priests) whom the Caravan met near the Wall of *China*. After a stay of sixteen Weeks at *Peking*, the Caravan was reconducted to the Frontiers in the same manner as above, and the Expences of their Journey thither defrayed. But at *Peking* their free Entertainment lasted only one hundred Days, as being the Time agreed on between the two Courts. As for the rest they said, that this Journey is one of the most fatiguing that can be undertaken, and however successfully it is made, yet it takes up at least sixteen Months in going thither, and as many in coming back, so that it would be difficult to find Persons to undertake it, was not the Trouble so amply recompensed by the great Gains. To this Relation the Prince *Gagarin* added, That the *Can* or Emperor of *China* negotiated all his Affairs with *Russia*, not directly with the Court it self, but with him the said Prince, nor did he send any Embassy to the Czar, who avoided that Ceremony, but to him the Prince

The Present State of Russia.

Prince to *Tobolsky*, with Credential Letters written in the *Chineze*, *Mongalian* and *Latin* Tongues.

The Prince took notice on this Occasion, that, considering the vast Extent of the Russian Empire and that many parts of it are almost inaccessible, it was no wonder that so many of those Heathen Nations remain unconverted: However that his Czarish Majesty had made already a Beginning of their Conversion, and was resolved to continue in his Zeal for propagating the Christian Religion all over his Dominions. The same was confirmed to me by some of the Clergy at *Moskow*, who told me that two Years ago by the *Czar's* Orders several Persons were singled out from among them, and sent in the Capacity of Priests and Schoolmasters to divers Pagan Nations, especially the *Ostiacks*, which laudable Undertaking had in several Parts already met with the intended Success: A more particular Account of the said *Ostiacks*, not only with respect to their Conversion, but also in general to their way of Life, is contained in the curious Description of that Nation, composed by *John Bernard Müller*, a Swedish Captain of Dragoons during his Captivity in *Siberia*. It is among other Pieces annexed to these Memoirs, according to a Manuscript of it which was communicated to me at *Petersbourg*.

The Conversion of several Heathen Nations under the Czar's Dominion.

On the 26th of March I arrived at *Petersbourg* on my Return from *Moskow*. The following Injunction of the Czar to the Clergy, had been published in my Absence, of which I will give a literal Translation:

The Czar's Order or Charge to the Clergy.

His

" *His Great Czarish Majesty's Order to the
" High Illuminated* Job *Metropolitan of
" Novogorod and Weliki Luki.*

" HIS Great Czarish Majesty has issued
" a special Order, to send to you,
" the *Archirejés,* (Archbishops) the Copy of
" the Promise made by the *Archirejés* of *A-*
" *strakan* and *Wologda* on their Presentation
" at *Petersbourg,* to the End you, the other
" *Archirejés* do inviolably conform thereto in
" every Particular; and the High illumina-
" ted *Job* Metropolitan of *Novogorod* and
" *Weliki Luki* is hereby injoyned to observe
" the said high Order as a general Rule in all
" Cases, in pursuance whereof we *Archirejés*
" have promised the same, according to the
" Sense of the Holy Scriptures, and the Ca-
" nons of Councils, for the better ruling of
" the Flock and the benefit of Souls, *viz.*

" I. I promise that I will not excommu-
" nicate nor exclude from the Sacraments of
" the Church, any Person either for himself
" or with his whole Family out of private
" Passion, or on account of any Differences
" whatsoever, that he may happen to have
" with me or any who are subordinate to
" me; pursuant to the 4th Canon of the se-
" venth General Council, and the 134th Ca-
" non of the Council of *Carthage, item,* pur-
" suant to the 39th Law of the † Emperor
" *Justinian:* Unless such Person appears to
" be a notorious Offender and Transgressor
" of God's Commandments, or an Heretick
" against the Church, and has first been

[† L. 39. Codice, de Episcopis & Clericis.]

" thrice

"thrice admonished without humbling or a-
"mending; however I will excommunicate
"and sever him from the Church only for
"his own Person, and not with his whole
"Family.

"II. That I will deal with those who op-
"pose the Holy Church, with Judgment, in
"a regular Way, and with Meekness, pur-
"suant to the Doctrine of *Paul* the Apostle,
"that a Servant of the Lord must not strive
"but be gentle unto all Men, apt to teach,
"not angry; that I will reprove all Oppo-
"sers with Meekness, that God in time may
"bring them to Repentance and Acknow-
"ledgment of the Truth; according to the
"66th Canon of the Synod of *Carthage*.

"III. That I will keep the Monks toge-
"ther according to the Canons and Rules
"prescribed to them, and will not permit
"them to run out of their own into other
"Monasteries, nor to enter into secular
"Houses, unless upon pressing Occasions and
"for the Good of their Friends, with my
"special Knowledge and Consent in writing,
"if they shall desire it; pursuant to the 4th
"and 11th Canons of the fourth General
"Council.

"IV. That I will not build any new
"Church my self without Necessity, nor al-
"low others to do it, that the same may not
"happen afterwards to be left unfinished;
"pursuant to the 84th Canon of the particu-
"lar Synod of *Carthage* and the 27th Law of
"*Justinian.*

"V. *Item*, I will not make many Priests,
"Deacons and other Church-Officers, with-
"out due Necessity, or for filthy Lucre
"sake,

"sake, but for the sake of the feeding of the Flock, and for the Advantage of the holy Church. Pursuant to the 6th Canon of the fourth General Council.

"VI. Moreover I promise, that I will visit the Diocese committed to my Charge, every Year if possible, or at least every third or fourth Year, my self and in Person so as the Apostles did, and have Inspection thereof, not for Lucre, Fame or Honour sake, but after an Apostolick manner and in the Lord, to the End the Faithful may remain in Faith and in the Practice of good Works; particularly I will be careful in observing, instructing and correcting the Priests, that they do prevent Schism, Superstition and Worship contrary to God's Command, and that no Shrines which are unknown and have not the Testimony of the Church, be honoured as sacred Relicks, and that they cause those Sorcerers who feign themselves to be possessed, and go about naked, or only in their Shirts, to be carried before the Judge of the Place and punished; that they do not countenance any fictitious and deceitful Works carrying an outside of Godliness, be they performed by Ecclesiastical or Secular Persons; that they do not set up the holy Images for Deities, nor ascribe to them lying Miracles, which give a Handle to the Adversaries of calumniating the Orthodox, but that they may honour them according to the Sense of the holy Orthodox Catholick Church.

"VII. That I will not intermeddle with any worldy Affairs and Strife except when
there

" there appears open Injuftice, in which Cafe
" I will firft admonifh, and afterwards even
" make Report to his Czarifh Majefty, pur-
" fuant to the Doctrine of the Apoftle: *Sup-*
" *port the Weak.*

During the Czar's Abfence abroad, nothing or little remarkable happened in his Dominions, except that there came Advice to *Petersbourg*, that the Harbour of *Revel*, the building of which had coft immenfe Sums, was near half deftroyed by a Tempeft. The Repair of it was finifhed two Years ago, and the Works put in their former Condition.

The Harbour of Revel damaged by a Storm.

On the 30th of *June* died at *Petersbourg* the Princefs *Natalia Alexevna*, the Czar's only Sifter by the whole Blood: Her Corpfe was embalmed and depofited in her Palace till the Czar's Return.

June 1716. Princefs Natalia, the Czar's Sifter dies.

The choice *Library* of the late Duke of *Courland* confifting of four thoufand Books, was carried to *Petersbourg* and lodged in the Fortrefs.

The Duke of Courland's Library carried to Petersbourg.

The *Houfes* at *Petersbourg* were again counted and found to be above fifty thoufand in number.

The Houfes at Petersbourg numbered.

Two Merchants propofed to the Senate to make a *Communication* between feveral navigable Rivers and Lakes, by the means of which the Ruffian Merchants might carry their Goods from *Archangel* to the *Eaftern Ocean*, and fo by an eafy and fhort way trade to *Japan* and the *Eaft-Indies*, to the incredible Advantage of the Ruffian Dominions. The Connexion was to be by the Rivers *Dwina, Tafta, Irtis, Oby, Keta, Jenifea, Angur,* the Lake *Baikal,* the Rivers *Schulka* and *Amur,* the

A Communication between Archangel and the Eaftern Ocean projected.

the latter of which runs through *Dauria* into the *Eastern Ocean*. So that there would be no occasion of finding out the North East Passage by *Nova Zemla*, the Discovery of which has been hitherto found impracticable.

An Attempt of a Discovery on the Eastern Ocean.

The Master of the Ordnance, M. *Bruce*, of Scottish Descent, but born in *Russia*, is a great Mathematician, and for that Reason frequently consulted and employed by the Czar in the like Affairs relating to the Russian Dominions and the Provinces of *Asia*. He assured me that the Kingdom of *Japan*, of whose true Situation and Extent nothing certain is known as yet, must needs joyn with *Great Tartary*. He told me that two Years ago he procured from the Czar an Order to the Governor of *Nertzinskoy* in *Dauria*, where the Prince *Gagarin* formerly commanded, to send two Men along the Boundaries of the Russian Dominion to the Coast of the *Eastern Ocean*, who were to embark there on board a Vessel and sail in quest of some unknown Country that may lie in that Ocean. Those Men who had not the least Knowledge of Navigation, having travelled for some Weeks along the Coasts, spied a Continent about four great Leagues off; they built a Boat and went over; two Days after they returned, but when they were already near the Shore, they were cast away in a Hurricane, in the sight of the People who waited for them on the Coast but were not able to save them, so that it could not be known what Discoveries they had made. General *Bruce* added that he would advise the Czar to send a second time able Men skilled

The Present State of Russia.

in Astronomy and Navigation, well accompanied, on the same Design, who he did not doubt if they did build there a strong Vessel, would make some extraordinary Discovery which might open a most beneficial Trade to *Japan*. The said General has collected a fine Cabinet of *Chineze Curiosities*; he told me it was pity, that the Nature and Situation of *China* was not better known, the Reason of which was that the Russian Ambassadors and Merchants are not allowed to stay there above three or at furthest four Months, unless they resolve to continue there all their Life-time.

During the Height of the Summer, *viz.* in *July* and half of *August*, the Heats at *Petersbourg* were almost intolerable, by which the Corn, and other Fruits of the Earth, were so suddenly ripened, that from sowing to reaping there was but an Interval of six Weeks, when the Air was so hot, that even the Nights were not cool, the Sun disappearing but a few Hours from the Horizon. However, frequent Rains falling immediately after, the Corn was gathered in wet, and dried in the Stoves. During the great Heats one is hard put to it for Drink, considering the Beer which is brewed for publick Sale in the Czar's Brew-Houses, is so strong, that it does not quench one's Thirst, besides that no outlandish Person can resolve to send for it to the Publick Tap-houses, where it is enough to see but once their manner of selling it, to be put out of Conceit for ever with all Russian Beer. The Liquor stands there in an open Tub or Cooler, to which the common People croud, taking it out with a wooden Vessel,

July, 1716. Hot Summers at Petersbourg.

Veffel, and drinking it, holding their Mouths over the Tub, that nothing may be fpilled, fo that if by chance any of it miffes their Mouths, it runs down their Beards (which the Day-Labourers, and other common People, are connived at ftill to wear for want of Barbers) and falls again into the Tub. If fuch a Cuftomer happens to have no Money, he leaves his old Fur Coat, a Shirt, a Pair of Stockings, or fome other Part of his wearing Apparel, to pawn, till the Evening, when he receives his Hire; mean time thofe filthy Pledges hang on the Brim, round the Tub, nor is a great Matter whether they are puſhed in by the Throng of the People, and fwim there for fome time. The Czar has Englifh and Dutch Brewers for his Houfhold, who make good Beer of divers Sorts after the way of their Countries, and not with red-hot Stones or iron Bullets, as all the reft is made at *Petersbourg*.

The new Academy of the Marine. This Summer the *Academy of the Marine* was opened: I dare aver, that there was not one noble Family within the Boundaries of the vaſt Ruſſian Empire, but was obliged to fend thither one or more Sons or Relations above ten, and under eighteen, Years of Age; and we faw Swarms of thofe young Plants arriving from all Parts of *Ruſſia* at *Peterſ-bourg*; fo that this Academy at prefent contains the Flower of the Ruffian Nobility, who, for thofe four Years paſt, have been inſtructed in all the Sciences belonging to Navigation; befides which, they are taught Languages, Fencing, and other bodily Exercifes, by the ableſt Profeffors and Maſters, and are kept under ſtrict Difcipline.

There

The Present State of Russia.

There arrived twenty Shepherds from Silesia, who were afterwards sent to *Cafan*, to shear the Sheep there, and to teach the Ruffians how to prepare the Wooll, which was to be employed in the *Manufactures* designed to be set up, that there might be no longer any Necessity of sending ready Money to *England* for Cloth to cloath the Armies. But this Project has not yet met with the intended Success; the chief Cause of which is said to be, that the Wooll is too coarse, the Flocks of Sheep and Goats having, Time out of Mind, mixed and engendred together. *(Woollen Manufactures to be set up.)*

But it is otherwise with respect to the *Linnen Manufacture*, which has been established a League from *Petersbourg*; for they make Linnen there of Russian Flax, which, for Fineness, does not yield to the best *Holland*. The Master is a Dutchman, and has under him twenty odd Journeymen, who are Germans. The Flax is spun in a Work-house newly established, where an old Dutch-woman is set over eighty odd loose Women, to teach them with the Whip how to handle the Spinning-wheel, the Use of which was unknown in *Russia* before; several other good Regulations have been made, to improve the Growth of Flax in *Russia*. *(A Linnen Manufacture established.)*

Four Leagues from that Work-house, beyond *Duderhoff*, the Czar has caused a *Paper-Mill* to be erected, and a little further a Mill for making *Cut-straw*; the Masters, who are Germans, and receive each eighteen Crowns Bank-Money a Month, have already put those Works in such a Condition, that nothing can be added to them, so that they perfectly answer the Ends proposed. Hitherto the *(Paper- and Powder-Mills, Rope-Yards, Founderies, a Printing-House, &c.)*

the Ruffians were Strangers to the Use of Cut-ftraw. They knew as little of making good Butter; their Way was to take the Cream, and melt it in a Pan for prefent Use. Towards *Sleutelbourg*, along the River *Neva*, are divers *Corn*-and *Saw-Mills*; and near *Petersbourg*, as alfo at *Moskow*, are fet up *Powder-Mills*, *Laboratories* for Gunnery and Fireworks, and Houfes for preparing Salt-peter and Brimftone, for which Ufe *Ruffia* produces all the neceffary Materials; as alfo all the Hemp for Cables, for the making of which a large *Rope-Yard* is fitted up at *Petersbourg*, where fome hundreds of *Ruffians* are daily at Work, and furnifh the Fleet with all the neceffary Ropes in abundance. There is alfo a *Foundery*, in which they are cafting new Guns without Intermiffion. Vaft Quantities of Iron-Oar are found at *Alonitz*, and Major-General *Hennings*, who is Governor of that Place, caufes not only Guns, Mortars, and fmall Fire-arms, to be caft there, but alfo all other fort of Arms are made there by outlandifh Mafters and Ruffian Journeymen, to fuch Perfection, that in Time the Ruffians will be able to furnifh foreign Countries with their own Work. The great *Forge* that is eftablifhed at *Petersbourg*, furnifhes Anchors, and all other Iron Work for Ships and Houfes. The many *Brick-kilns* provide *Petersbourg* with a fufficient Number of Bricks and Tiles for the building of new Houfes; however, they prove not very durable, and as their Mortar is likewife none of the beft, or at leaft is moftly prepared and ufed in Winter, (building going on all the Year round) it is no Wonder, that the new Houfes and Palaces

laces want to be repaired every second or third Year. The Streets of that vast Place are at present all paved, which indeed causes a great Expence to the Inhabitants, because there are but few Stones found in the marshy Ground of that Neighbourhood; however, it has added very much to the embellishing of that City, where besides every Housekeeper is obliged to plant Lime-trees before his House. The *Printing-House* is beyond Exception, and they have begun to print in it Weekly News-Papers in the Russian Language by the Czar's Orders, who will have his Subjects get an Insight into the Affairs of the World, and it is with this View that four Monks at *Prague*, who are well versed in the *Slavonian* Tongue, are now actually translating from the *High-Dutch* the great *Historical Dictionary* of M. *Budæus*. The Translations of *Pufendorf*'s *Introduction to History*, the *Colloquia*, or familiar Dialogues of *Erasmus* of *Roterdam*, *Arnd*'s *True Christianity*, *Commenius*'s *Orbis Pictus*, and other useful Books, were printed three Years ago.

Being fallen upon the Subject of the Introduction of so many Sciences in *Russia*, it is proper to speak here of the Improvements and Amendments the Czar has since made, down to the Year 1710. Besides Ship-building, his Thoughts chiefly turn upon opening *Mines* in *Russia*, and bringing to Light those Treasures which have hitherto lain buried for want of searching. In the Year 1718, a Board (or *College*, as they style it) for Mines was established, who have begun with making proper Regulations for the Improvement of Minery. Besides their Iron Works, which are

Mines.

are already upon a good Foot, they have discovered Gold Sand in some Rivers, and have learned how to refine and separate it from the Dross, which gives them Hopes of discovering great Store of Gold, Silver, and other less precious Metals, by digging into the Entrails of their Mountains, after the Method of other Countries. If they meet with Success in this Point also, it is easy to conclude, that all those new Regulations together, will at last enable the Czar, to provide and maintain his Armies out of his own Stock, without any Aid or Supplies from foreign Countries.

Silk-Manufactures.

And as he is very sensible what immense Sums his Country is drained of by the Importation of Silks, Woollen Stuffs, and Linnen, which it cannot do without, he has been endeavouring, ever since the Year 1718, at establishing also a *Silk Manufacture* in his Dominions, to which End he has sent for great Numbers of Manufacturers from *France*, and many of the Russian chief Nobility did, of their own Accord, advance Sums of Money to raise a Stock for an Undertaking, in which they hoped to find their own Account. But as those Manufacturers were vexed and oppressed by the rest of the Russians, who put them to endless Difficulties, chiefly as to the Provisions they were to furnish them with, the greater Part of them left the Country, nor can I tell how it stands with those Manufactures at present.

The Gardens, the Library, Antiquities, and other Curiosities at Petersbourg.

I should tire my Reader, should I expatiate on this Subject, by relating the several Regulations made by the Czar; as for Instance, the Introduction of an Ordinance of Police or Polity, for keeping his new City in

good

The Present State of Russia.

good Order, the great Encouragements given to Architects, Mechanicks, and all other imaginable Sorts of Artificers, and the like: I shall content my self with shewing, that the Improvements which the Czar has made in his Dominions, were not merely calculated for Profit, but for Delight also. He has built splendid Pleasure-Houses, raised noble Gardens, and adorned them with Greenhouses, Aviaries and *Menageries*, Grottos, Cascades, and all other sorts of Water-works. He has placed on the Steeple of the great Church a Chime made in *Holland*. He has ordered Assemblies to be kept in the Winter; Operas, Plays, and Concerts of Musick, are to be set up for the Diversion of his Court, and, in order to engage Foreigners to frequent it, Draughts have been already made, and proper Places marked out to build Houses for those Purposes. Nor has the Czar neglected any thing that might render his Residence celebrated among the learned World. If they continue to augment the pretious Library at *Petersbourg*, it may in a few Years be reckoned one of the best in *Europe*, if not for the Number of Books, yet at least on account of their Value. The Czar has a Collection of Pictures that is inestimable. Only the Presents which he and his Predecessors received from all Parts of *Asia*, and which are now at *Petersbourg*, would make a complete Cabinet of Curiosities. The Antiquities that were found in the Years 1716 and 1718, among the Ruins of Pagan Temples near the *Caspian* Sea, are enough to furnish a separate Cabinet of Idols; and if a Man versed in the Oriental Languages, their Antiquities, Mythology,

thology, and Hieroglyphicks, ſhould undertake to examine thoſe Images, Veſſels and Inſtruments for Sacrifices, and the ſeveral Parchments, on which I obſerved a Writing tolerably legible, he would give great Light to the Learned in thoſe Branches of Science, and open a Way for the Diſcuſſion of things hitherto unknown. There are likewiſe at *Petersbourg* ſo many Chymical and other Natural Curioſities, monſtrous Productions, Mathematical Inſtruments, the famous Globe of *Gottorp* repreſenting the Copernican Syſtem, and abundance of other Rarities; (the Care of all which was committed to M. *Areskin*, the Czar's firſt Phyſician) that it is to be wondered, how ſuch a Collection could be made in ſo few Years. Another thing ſtill deſerving the Attention of the Curious, is the Houſe in which ſtrange Beaſts are kept; among which are the fine Lion and his Lioneſs, which were brought from *Perſia* two Years ago by M. *Wolinsky*, whom the Czar had ſent Ambaſſador thither.

Aſſemblies ſet up at Peterſbourg.

As to the Aſſemblies in *Petersbourg*, I ſhall mention a few Particulars. They were begun in the Year 1719, and are kept thrice a Week during the Winter. The Czar cauſed a Regulation to be printed on that Occaſion in the Ruſſian Tongue, which I thought worth tranſlating and inſerting here:

Regulation for keeping Aſſemblies at Petersbourg.

" ASSEMBLY is a French Term,
" which cannot be rendered in Ruſſian
" in one Word: It ſignifies a Number of
" Perſons meeting together, either for Diver-
" ſion or to talk about their own Affairs.
" Friends

"Friends may see each other on that Occa-
"sion, to confer together on Business or o-
"ther Subjects, to enquire after domestick
"and foreign News, and so to pass their
"Time. After what manner We will have
"those Assemblies kept, may be learned from
"what follows:

"I. The Person at whose House the As-
"sembly is to be in the Evening, is to hang
"out a Bill or other Sign, to give Notice
"to all Persons of either Sex.

"II. The Assembly shall not begin sooner
"than four or five in the Afternoon, nor con-
"tinue later than ten at Night.

"III. The Master of the House is not ob-
"liged to go and meet his Guests, to con-
"duct them out, or to entertain them; but
"though himself is exempt from waiting on
"them, he ought to find Chairs, Candles,
"Drink, and all the Necessaries asked for, as
"also to provide for all sorts of Gaming, and
"what belongs thereto.

"IV. No certain Hour is fixed for any
"body's coming or going, it is sufficient if
"one make his Appearance in the Assem-
"bly.

"V. It is left to every one's Liberty to sit,
"walk, or play, just as he likes, nor shall a-
"ny body hinder him, or take Exception at
"what he does, on pain of emptying the
"*Great Eagle*, (a Bowl filled with Wine or
"Brandy.) As for the rest, it is enough to
"salute at coming and going.

"VI. Persons of Rank, as for Instance,
"Noblemen, and superior Officers, likewise
"Merchants of Note, and Head-Masters,
"(by which are chiefly understood, Ship-
"builders,)

"builders,) Perſons employed in the Chan-
"cery, and their Wives and Children, ſhall
"have Liberty of frequenting the Aſſem-
"blies.

"VII. A particular Place ſhall be aſſigned
"to the Footmen, (thoſe of the Houſe ex-
"cepted) that there may be ſufficient Room
"in the Apartments deſigned for the Aſſem-
"bly.

At thoſe Aſſemblies there is dancing in one Room, in another People are playing at Cards, Draughts, but particularly at Cheſs, in which even the meaneſt Ruſſians excel; in a third Room there is a Company ſmoaking and diſcourſing together, and in the fourth are Ladies and Gentlemen diverting themſelves with Queſtions and Commands, Forfeits, Croſspurpoſes, and other ſuch little Plays, that create good Humour and Laughter. Though none of the Company are obliged to drink any more Wine or Brandy than what they ask for, except one tranſgreſſes the eſtabliſhed Rules or Laws of the Aſſembly, which happens very often, yet there are many good Ruſſians, who lay hold of that Opportunity, of making much of themſelves at other Mens Coſt, and look upon Aſſemblies as one of the moſt laudable Innovations that have been introduced in their native Country. It falls to the Turn of every great Man of the Court to keep an Aſſembly once in a Winter at leaſt; and if the Czar pitches upon a particular Perſon for it, Notice is given to him by the Maſter of the *Police.*

Operas, Plays and Muſick. Operas and Plays will alſo be in Faſhion in Proceſs of Time, and they are now looking
out

out for a Fund for thofe Diverfions, though the Czar himfelf has as little Inclinations that Way as he has for Hunting, or the like. His Subjects indeed have made fome Attempts for acting on the Stage, but with very indifferent Succefs, for want of proper Rules. The Princefs *Natalia* once had the Direction of a Tragedy, which was reprefented before the Czar's laft Travels, and at which every body was admitted. She had caufed a large empty Houfe to be fitted up, and to be divided into Pit and Boxes. The Actors and Actreffes were ten in Number, all native Ruffians, who had never been abroad, fo that it is eafy to judge of their Ability. The Tragedy it felf, as well as the Farce, were in Ruffian, and of the Princefs's own Compofition, being a Compound of facred and profane Hiftory. I was told, that the Subject related to one of the late Rebellions in *Ruffia*, reprefented under difguifed Names. The Piece was interfperfed with the Drolleries of a *Harlequin*, who was an Officer of the Army, and ended with an Epilogue, fetting forth the Contents of the Tragedy, and concluding with a Moral reflecting on the Horrors of Rebellion, and the unhappy Events it commonly iffues in. The Orcheftre was compofed of fixteen Muficians, all Ruffians, whofe Performance was fuitable to that of the reft. They are taught Mufick, as well as other Sciences, by the Help of the *Batogs*, without which Difcipline nothing goes down with them, as I have been told by divers Officers, and is confirmed by daily Experience. If a General pitches upon fome fpare Fellow in a Regiment, whom he will have to learn Mufick, notwithftanding he
has

has not the least Notion of it, nor any Talent that Way, he is put out to a Master, who gives him a certain Time for learning his Task; as, first, the handling of the Instrument, then to play some Lutheran Hymn, which are their Airs, or some Menuet, and so on; if the Scholar has not learnt his Lesson during the Term prefixed, the *Batogs* are applied, and repeated till such Time as he is Master of the Tune. The same Method is made use of in all other Things, particularly in military Exercises. This severe Discipline produces such a blind Obedience among these People towards their Superiors, as appears particularly among the Soldiers, who shew themselves faithful and indefatigable in the Service, and, notwithstanding their gross Ignorance, learn to practise what is required of a good Soldier.

Whether Petersbourg is likely to be resorted to in time by Foreigners. I will conclude this Discourse concerning the intended embellishing of *Petersbourg*, with what I once heard the Prince *Menzicoff* say, viz. that *Petersbourg* should become another *Venice*, to see which Foreigners would travel thither purely out of Curiosity. Setting aside the perpetual Objection of the raw Climate of the Place, it is possible his Saying might prove true in time, if the Russians would be less refractory to the Czar's Intentions, and use Strangers better than they do at present, as likewise if Passengers were allowed more Liberty than hitherto, in going thither, and returning from thence, and if Care was taken to provide against the excessive Dearness of all Necessaries of Life at *Petersbourg*.

On the 31ft of *August* the Duchefs-Dowager of *Courland*, attended by her firft Lady or Groom of the Stole, the Countefs *Matweoff*, (who had been formerly in *England* and *Holland* with her Husband, then Ambaffador) fet out from *Petersbourg* for *Mitau*, to take Poffeffion of her Dowry. The Countefs *Matweoff* died in the Year 1720 at *Petersbourg*, and was fucceeded in her Employment by General *Ronne*'s Widow.

Auguft, 1716. The Duchefs-Dowager of Courland goes to take Poffeffion of her Dowry.

During the Winter fome Hundreds of noble Families arrived at *Petersbourg*, purfuant to the Czar's Orders. They complained, that, by this Change, they loft about two thirds of their Eftates, confidering they were obliged to build Houfes at *Petersbourg*, and pay ready Money for what they wanted; whereas in *Ruffia* they could live cheaper, and fubfift on the Produce of their Land. The Country People, who are in the fame Manner hurried away from their own Habitations, and forced to fettle at *Petersbourg*, fuffer ftill worfe by that Change. However it is furprifing to fee with what Refignation and Patience thofe People, both high and low, fubmit to fuch Hardfhips. The common Sort ufe to fay, that Life is but a Burthen to them: If they fall fick, they lie down on the Floor without the leaft Concern, whether they fhall recover or die, and for this Reafon they will not take any Medicines. A certain Lutheran Minifter in *Ruffia* related to me, that upon an Occafion when he examined fome fimple Ruffian Peafants about their Belief, and asked whether they knew what they ought to do, in order to obtain eternal Salvation? they anfwered, that it was very uncertain,

The planting of Peterfbourg a national Grievance, to which they patiently fubmit.

even

even whether they should go to Heaven at all, for they believed everlasting Happiness was reserved only for the Czar and his great Boyars.

January 1717. An Interval of some Months during the Czar's Absence.
In *January* 1717, I set out from *Petersbourg* to meet the Czar in *Germany*, and, upon his Return to *Petersbourg* in *October* next, I followed him thither. His Czarish Majesty had been near two Years abroad at *Dantzick*, in *Denmark*, *Holland* and *France*. The Transactions of that Time are foreign to my Design, and therefore I shall resume my Account of the domestick Affairs of *Russia*. The most remarkable, and almost only Occurrence, which had happened during my Absence, was the Czarewitz's Flight, of which I shall speak more at large hereafter.

October 1717. An extraordinary Court of Justice established.
The Czar after his Return, which, as I have mentioned, happened in *October*, employed the remaining Part of the Year to redress, with an indefatigable Application, the great Disorders that had crept into the Administration during his Absence, and to bring the Authors of it to condign Punishment. He assisted in the Senate every Morning at four a Clock, and was at the Pains himself of hearing and examining the Accusations and Defence of the Parties concerned. But as the Affairs of this Inquisition appeared to be of a deeper Die than was at first expected, and that a great deal of Time was required for convicting some of those who stood accused of Breach of Trust; an extraordinary Court of Justice was established, and in the mean Time the Prince *Wolchinsky*, Governor of *Archangel*, who had been fully convicted of his Crimes, was shot to Death. The said Court of

The Present State of Russia.

of Justice was divided into several Committees, each of which consisted of a Major, a Captain, and a Lieutenant of the Guards, who were to examine into the respective Causes laid before them, and to give Sentence according to common Sense and Equity. And so Things were come to that pass in *Russia*, that the Members of a venerable Senate, composed of the Heads of the greatest Families in the Czar's Dominions, were obliged to appear before a Lieutenant as their Judge, and be called to an Account of their Conduct.

In order to remedy the great Want of Money which appeared then, the Czar issued an Order prohibiting the Use of Gold and Silver on wearing Apparel; several useless Mechanicks, who had been brought into the Country, were discharged, others were reduced to Half-pay, and divers other Methods were tried, that were thought conducive to that End. It was on this Occasion that several Russians of Distinction entered into a Society for the manufacturing of Silk-Stuffs, of which I made mention above; to encourage which Undertaking, the Czar granted them a Privilege for many Years, and raised the Duties on the Importation of foreign Stuffs to double the Price for the middling sort, and treble for the best, which Impost was to commence with the 1719, and was judged to be a proper Method for obliging foreign Merchants to trade to *Russia* with ready Money instead of Stuffs.

Novemb. 1717. Provision against Scarcity of Money.

The young *Great-Prince* (so the *Czarewitz*'s Son was styled) was presented by the Czar with his Picture set with Diamonds, and

Of the young Great-Prince, the Czar's Grandson.

as he gave early Proofs of a martial and lively Genius, he was not only declared Serjeant in the Guards, and cloathed accordingly, but also taught the military Exercise, which he very readily learned to that Degree, that a Year ago he was able to perform the principal Part of his Function himself.

Decemb. 1717. A new Ambassador from Bucharia. In the Beginning of my Account I related some Particulars of *Atscherbi*, a *Bucharian* Ambassador, who had been at *Petersbourg* in the Year 1714. On his Return home, he was informed at *Astracan*, that, during his Absence, the Affairs of his native Country had put on quite a different Face by a general Revolt. This made him tarry at first for some Time at *Astracan*, but at length he resolved to proceed. He was hardly arrived in his own Country when he was put to Death, with a great Number of other Persons, by the Orders of *Gamalie*, the new Can, who sent one *Batucha* his Ambassador to the Czar, to make his Submission to him, and to renew the ancient Alliances, as also to implore the Czar's Assistance against the Can of the *Karakalpakes*, and others of his Neighbours. The said *Batucha* had his first Audience of the Czar on the 20th of December, at the *Chancery* or Office of State, where there was a numerous Appearance of the Russian Nobility, and though they were all standing, yet the Ambassador asked for a Chair, on which he sate down with a particular Air of Gravity; but when the Great Chancellor came out, and made a Sign to him to go in to the Czar, he rose in great Haste, threw his Scimetar to his Servants, who were well dressed, and entered the Room with low Bows.

Bows. The Audience being over, the Czar came out with him; an old Tartar, *Batucha*'s firſt Officer, approached his Majeſty with a low Bow, and gave to underſtand, that he had ſomething to ſay; having obtained Leave, he began with a loud Voice, and abundance of Geſticulations, to make a Speech ſtuffed with high-ſtrained Flouriſhes and empty Compliments, concluding with this Wiſh, *That as there is but one Sun in Heaven, who illuminates the whole Earth, ſo the Czar might be the ſole Ruler over it.* The Ambaſſador, who talked Ruſſian, having interpreted it, the Czar laughed at the poor Orator, without returning an Anſwer.

On the 31ſt of December the Czar ſet out for *Moskow*, where he had not been for eight Years together. *The Czar goes to Moſkow.*

At the ſame Time a Jeſuit arrived at *Peterſbourg* from *Perſia* with Advice, that the Ruſſian Ambaſſador, *Artemi Wolinsky*, had made his Entry at *Iſpahan*, and that M. *Wenigerkind*, a German by Birth, and Secretary to the Embaſſy, as alſo thirty of the Servants, had died of Fevers on the other Side of the *Caſpian* Sea. The Secretary was a Man of Learning, well verſed in Philoſophy, whoſe Death was the more to be lamented, becauſe it was his Deſign, and he had Orders for it, to make particular Diſcoveries in *Perſia*, and in the reſt of his Travels. I had many curious Letters from him during his Journey, but by ſome Misfortune I once loſt them in my Travels. *Advice from the Ruſſian Embaſſy in Perſia.*

The Ruſſian *Caravan*, which was gone to *China*, had been detained many Months on this Side of the great Wall, the Mandarin com- *Of the Caravan for China.*

commanding on the Frontiers refusing them Admittance, on divers trifling Pretences; but a Courier having been dispatched to *Peking* with earnest Representations, they were at length admitted.

January 1718. Apprehensions of an Invasion from the Cuban Tartars. An Express from *Ukraina* arrived at *Petersbourg* in January 1718, with the unwelcome News, that the *Cuban-Tartars* were drawing together in great Numbers, and approaching the Frontiers of *Russia*; and this so far from being set on by the *Porte*, that the Turkish Governor of *Azoff* had sent Notice of their Design to the Russian Officers commanding on the Frontiers, and declared that it was out of his Power to check those Robbers, who, having found their Account by the Inroad which they made into *Russia* last Year, seemed resolved to try a second Visit. Upon this all necessary Orders were given at *Petersbourg* for opposing them, the *Cosacks* were ordered to mount, five thousand Dragoons, and the like Number of Infantry, were ordered to join them, and to guard the Lines on the River *Don*, which the Czar had caused to be cast up last Summer at a vast Expence, in order to cover his Frontiers against the like Insults. The Grand Seignior afterwards, in order to remove all Suspicion, sent a Letter under his own Hand to the Czar, promising that in Case those Plunderers, being defeated in their Design, should take their Refuge in his Dominions, he would cause them to be pursued with Fire and Sword, being willing to discharge, in every Respect, the Obligations of a faithful Neighbour and Confederate.

The Present State of Russia.

February 1718. The unfortunate Issue of an Expedition near the Caspian Sea.

On the 4th of February they received more disagreeable Advices at *Petersbourg*, relating to the Expedition near the *Caspian* Sea, of which the Prince *Alexander Bekewitz* had the Command. The Reader will recollect, that the said Prince was two Years ago sent a second time sent to take Possession of the River, in which the Gold Sand is found, and to discover Mines in the Mountains of *Great Tartary*, at the Head of three thousand Men, among whom were three hundred *Saxons*, who were taken Prisoners at *Pultava* in the Swedish Service. Their Design was to raise two Forts on the *Caspian* Sea, to facilitate the Commerce, and to cover the Gallies that were built for that End; accordingly they erected Forts with Shells, which lye in prodigious Quantities on the Shore, at first without the least Opposition from the *Tartars* and *Calmucks*. But when the Army penetrated further into the Country, through the great *Step* or Desart, extremely harassed in their March for want of Water, and arrived at the Place where the Gold Sand is found; the Subjects of the Can of *Schirvan* began to take Umbrage, gathered to the Number of fifty thousand, and refused to accept the Presents that were tendered to them on the Part of the Czar; however, they feigned Compassion to see so fine an Army in so great Distress, and offered to supply them with Water and Provisions, on Condition that they should separate, and return home in several Bodies. The General was drawn into the Snare, and, either pressed with great Misery or for want of Experience, consented to those Terms, dividing his Forces into several Detachments,

tachments, some of three, some of five hundred Men, in order to march off, and so they all fell a Sacrifice to the deceitful Enemy. The Prince himself was carried before the Can's Tent, where a Piece of red Cloth was spread on the Ground, the usual Sign of Blood among the Tartars, and upon his refusing to kneel down, and submit to his melancholy Fate, they first cut him with their Scimeters in the Calves of his Legs, and afterwards massacred him in a most miserable Manner. His divided Forces were likewise all cut to pieces, except those of the Artillery, who obtained Quarter, and were afterwards employed by the Enemy in the Siege of *Mezetz*, a Frontier Place of *Persia*, and, by the Help of those Gunners, and of the Cannon and Ammunition which they had taken from the Russians, they forced the Governor to surrender upon disadvantagious Terms, and got a rich Booty in the Place, where there was a Monastery, the Walls of which were lined all over with Gold Plates. The Musicians, as also several young Voluntiers, who were most all Sons of Boyars, had likewise their Lives spared, and were afterwards sold. One of them, after having passed through the Hands of divers Masters, at last had the good Fortune to meet with his Countrymen, and lives at present at *Petersbourg*.

Of the Circassian Prince Alexander Bekewitz. The said *Alexander Bekewitz* was a *Circassian* Prince, whose Father died some Years ago at *Moskow*, whither he was fled from his own Country and put himself under the Czar's Protection. He was a Vassal of the King of *Persia*, whose Disgrace he drew upon himself by refusing to resign to him his Wife,
who

who was a very beautiful Woman. The Czar had received him with great Civility and extraordinary Honour, and promifed to reftore him to his Territories. Prince *Alexander Bekewitz* was his only Son, who inherited from his Father the great Treafure he had faved when he fled, and had married a Princefs *Galitzin* who was reckoned the greateft Beauty of *Ruffia*. She was unfortunately drowned in the *Wolga*, fometime before the unhappy Fate of her Husband.

The great *Step* or Wildernefs mentioned a little before, is a champian Tract of Land extending many hundred Werfts in length, in which there is indeed plenty of all forts of Fruits, dwarf Fruit Trees, Flowers, Rice, and Shrubs of an aromatick Smell, yet there are few or no Springs at all, and but little Grafs, inftead of which there grows a fort of Reed or Sedge, fo tall that it hides a Man on Horfeback, which the Soldiers are obliged to burn down for many Werfts to get fome Grafs for their Horfes and to provide for their own Security. *Defcription of the great Step or Wildernefs.*

It is firmly believed the Czar will take the firft opportunity of revenging himfelf on thofe Tartars, (in their own Language called *Kibicks* from their Tents) who have nothing to defend themfelves but their Scimiters, Bows and Arrows, and very fwift Horfes; and that for this Reafon he will fend a lefs numerous Army againft them, which may more eafily be furnifhed with Water and Provifions, and caufe new Forts to be raifed in their Country for covering thofe Mines which he intends to open there. The *Perfians* have already long ago had an Eye upon the *The State and Importance of the Gold Mines near the Cafpian-Sea.*

the Gold Sand there, but the Inhabitants have choaked up the Mouth of the River *Daria* on the *Caspian Sea*, which gave Passage up to the Mountains from which the Gold Sand is washed down, and diverted its Course into the flat Country. Part of the Prince *Bekewitz*'s Commission was to restore things to their former Condition with respect to the said River, in order to keep open that Communication with the Mountains, and to avoid the troublesome and dangerous Passage thither by Land through the *Step*. M. *Blüher*, who had been formerly a Refiner in the Mines of *Saxony*, from whence he was sent for to *Russia* and made a Commissioner of the Mine-works, returned a second time from that Country to *Petersbourg* with Essays of the Gold Sand and Oar found there, three Ducats weight of which appeared to contain two and one quarter of pure Gold.

The Czarewitz brought back from Naples. Advice came to *Petersbourg* from *Novogorod* that the Privy-Councellor M. *Tolstoy* had passed there with the *Czarewitz* coming from *Naples*, on their way to *Moskow*.

The Vice-Czar Romadonofsky dies at Moskow. We were informed from *Moskow* of the death of *Knees Romadonofsky* Vice-Czar of that Metropolis, and that his Czarish Majesty had conferred that high Dignity upon his only Son, who being the last of the Male Line of that noble and ancient Family and having no Issue, the Czar, to prevent that Name's becoming extinct, designed to give the new Vice-Czar's two Sisters in Marriage to two of the chief Nobility of the Country on condition of exchanging their Family Names for that of *Romadonofsky*.

About

The Present State of Russia.

About that time the Affair relating to the Czarewitz began to be unravelled. On the 18th of February at Midnight the House of M. Kikin Commissioner of the Admiralty and formerly the Czar's great Favourite, was surrounded by fifty Grenadiers; the Czar's Displeasure being signified to him in his Bed, he was forthwith put in Irons, and carried away in such haste that he hardly had time to take Leave in a few Words of his Lady, who, and the Princess *Cyrkasky*, were reckoned the two greatest Beauties in *Russia*. The *Siberian Czarewitz* and all the Servants of the Russian Czarewitz had the same Fate, and were most of them carried away fettered on the 22d of February for *Moskow*, from whence a Friend sent me the following Advices:

The beginning of the Grand Inquisition against the Czarewitz.

"The Privy-Councellor M. *Tolstoy* being arrived with the *Czarewitz* at *Tweer*, the former proceeded hither and having received new Orders, returned to *Tweer*, from whence he arrived some Days ago with the *Czarewitz*, who having thrown himself at his Father's Feet, was by him received with very pathetick Expressions. It is impossible to express the Consternation which has seized the Russians of the old Stamp, who look with Abhorrence on *Petersbourg*, Shipping and Sea Affairs, foreign Customs and Languages; and as great part of the present Events are charged on the Russian Clergy, it is easy to judge of the Reason why the Czar has so much clipped their Wings by reducing them to a moderate Maintenance, and enjoined them to mind solely the Duty of their Office and the Service of the Altar. The whole Proceed-
" ings

"ings of the present Inquisition will be print-
"ed and published, I shall therefore content
"my self for the present with telling you,
"that the *Czarewitz* has made publick Re-
"nunciation of the Succession, and has been
"pardoned on condition of making a full
"Discovery of his Advisers. *Kikin* has had
"Spies in the Czar's very Closet, and has
"engaged the Page of the Bedchamber *Bak-*
"*lanofsky* by an Assignation of twenty thou-
"sand Rubels, that in case of approaching
"Danger he should give him timely warn-
"ing in order to make his Escape. Accord-
"ingly when the Czar was writing with his
"own Hand an Order to the Prince *Menzi-*
"*coff* to send *Kikin* Prisoner hither, *Bakla-*
"*nofsky* who had stood behind the Czar all
"that time, went directly to the Post-house,
"and dispatch'd an Express to *Kikin* for *Pe-*
"*tersbourg*, who arrived there almost at the
"same time with the Courier of the Czar,
"but yet too late. The Czar suspecting the
"sudden disappearing of the Page, sent into
"the City to enquire what he had been do-
"ing, and so his Practices were discovered,
"and he was confined with the rest of the
"Prisoners. Something very diverting has
"lately happened here, with an Account of
"which I shall conclude my Letter. You
"know, that ever since the great Rebellion
"of the *Strelitzes* the Heads of those who
"were concerned in it, have stood on the
"Tops of high Poles before the Palace and in
"other Places of this City. Those Rebels were
"Men of Quality, and have left Descen-
"dants and near Relations, who make a
"good Figure both in Town and Country,
"and

"and have resolved in the present Juncture
"to deliver a *Tchelobit* or Petition to the
"Court, representing, that the Heads of
"their Friends have long enough stood Sen-
"try in the Air, and therefore desiring they
"might be relieved, to which End they of-
"fered to discover to the Czar tenfold the
"number of Villains, Thieves and Traitors,
"whose Heads might supply the vacant
"Places, &c. *Moskow* $\frac{6}{17}$ *February*, 1718.

Mention being made among the said Prisoners of the *Czarewitz of Siberia*, it is proper to take notice that in *Russia* the Title of
Czarewitz is only given to the Czar's Sons
and to the Descendants of the ancient *Czars
of Siberia*, other Russian Princes being only
styled *Kneeses*. A Czarina is called by them
Czaritza, and a Princess of the Blood *Czarewna*.

The Signification of the Appellations of Czarewitz, Czaritza and Czarewna.

The *Siberian Czarewitz* is a Grandson of
the *Czar of Siberia*, who was subdued by the
Russian Czar *Fedor Ivanowitz* in the Year
1587, since which time *Siberia* has been annexed to *Russia*. This great Work being
brought about by the powerful Assistance of
a wealthy Russian Farmer *Stroganoff*, he and
his Posterity were rewarded with great Privileges and Grants, and are generally known
in *Russia* by the Name of the *rich Peasants*.
There is now at *Petersbourg* the eldest Son of
the said *Stroganoff*, who died three Years ago.
The foresaid *Siberian Czarewitz* is the last of
his Family and has no Issue. There lived
formerly another such *Czar* in *Russia*, *Simeon*
the King of *Casan*, whose Kingdom was conquered by the Russians the middle of the sixteenth Century, and himself with his Wife

Of the Czars of Siberia and Ca-san, and of the Fa-mily of Stroga-noff.

carried

carried to *Moskow*, whose Family is quite extinct.

State Prisoners in the Affair of the Czarewitz.

The Prince *Menzikoff* received Orders at *Petersbourg* to seize the Knees *Waſſili Wolodimirowitz Dolgoruki*, and to send him with a strong Guard to *Moskow*. He was Lieutenant-General, Colonel of the Guards of *Preobrazinsky*, Knight of the Danish Order of the Elephant, and till that time General-Inquisitor or Director of the Commission established for enquiring into the Mismanagement of the Czar's Revenue. Accordingly the Prince *Menzicoff* went to his House with a good number of Soldiers, and notified to him his Disgrace, upon which the Prince *Dolgoruki* delivered his Sword to him with these few Words: *I have a good Conscience, and but one Head to lose.* He was carried to the Fortress the same Evening, and in the mean time the Prince *Menzicoff* went with the like Commission to the Senator *Peter Matuewitz Apraxin*, the Great Admiral's Brother, who was afterwards cleared, to *Abraham Fedrowitz Lopuchin*, who till then was only confined in his House, to the Senator *Samarin*, to *Woinoff*, to *Woroff*, to *Ivan Waſſilewitz Kikin, Alexander Kikin*'s Brother, and to nine Persons more.

Mineral Waters discovered at Alonitz.

A Spring of Mineral Waters being lately discovered near *Alonitz*, a Physician was sent thither to inquire into the Nature of the Water, and to give it to some sick Persons to drink. The Waters proving beneficial to those People, others made use of them to good Effect, and even the Czar himself which in time made the Wells of *Alonitz* so famous that they were frequented by People from all Parts,

Parts, and the Waters are at present looked upon in *Russia* as an universal Medicine. They are of a chalybeate Quality and their Virtue consists in purging and creating an Appetite; they leave a reddish Sediment, and from an Experiment which I saw made, it is judged that the chalybeate Particles of Steel make up one third Part of the Substance of this mineral Water. The Spring lies sixteen Leagues further North than the Iron-works; and as a great deal of Exercise is required with the drinking of it, which the deep Snow and other Inconveniences of the cold Climate will hardly admit, the Czar has caused a Billiard-Table to be set up there, with which Exercise and the making of Turners-work his Czarish Majesty diverts himself when he is there. Some People are of Opinion that the Czar has a particular View in frequenting that Place: He has observed at *Pyrmont*, *Carlsbad* and *Spaw*, that many Persons of Distinction use to go to those Places rather for Diversion than with a design of drinking the Waters, which brings Trade to those Places and makes them flourish; therefore considering that the Handicraftsmen who live in the small Town of *Alonitz*, have scarcely any other Profit besides the Wages the Czar pays them, and that every Year abundance of fine Fire-Arms, Swords, and the like of their Manufacture are left upon their Hands; the Czar's Intention is, by his Example, to draw his People thither to use the Waters, (the Russians in general preferring natural Remedies to those out of the Apothecaries Shops, for which they even shew an innate Aversion,) and by this

Means

Means to encourage the Trade of Fire-Arms, which are made there under the Direction of M. *Hennings* Major-General of the Artillery, and to render the Town of *Alonitz* more flourishing.

March. 1718. Prince Peter Petrowitz declared next Heir to the Crown.

The *Czarewitz* having made a publick Renunciation of the Succeſſion at *Moskow*, an Order was ſent from the Czar to the Prince *Menzicoff* and the whole Senate at *Petersbourg*, to convene the Army, and the States of the Nobility, of the Burghers, and of the Peaſants, to take the Oath of Fidelity to Prince *Peter Petrowitz* the Czar's Son as next Heir to the Crown, which Ceremony was accordingly performed with great Pomp on the 9th of *March* in the Church of the Holy Trinity.

The Author's ſecond Journey to Moſkow.

The ſame Day I ſet out for *Moskow*, but I could not make that Journey in three Days as I had done the firſt time, by reaſon of the deep Snow and the exceſſive Cold. On the Occaſion of this my ſecond Journey into *Ruſſia* I made a Computation, that the diſtance between *Hambourg* and *Moskow* is exactly four hundred German Miles.

The Jeſuits in China in Diſtreſs.

At *Moskow* I met M. *Laurence Lange* lately returned from *China*, the Journal of whoſe Travels I have annexed to this Work. The Czar was well pleaſed with his Negotiation, and had ſince his return received freſher Advices from *China* in the Month of *March* by another Opportunity, giving an Account that the Emperor of that Country at the Inſtigation of the *Mandarins* had reſolved to extirpate the Chriſtian Religion in his Dominions, and that the Perſecution had actually begun. The Jeſuits in their Diſtreſs had written

ten a very moving Letter to the *Emperor* of *Germany*, which they sent by the Way of *Russia*, accompanied with another to the *Czar* in Latin to this Effect.

Most Great and Mighty Czar,

"A Prohibition issued last Month of this "present Year 1717, by the nine Su-
"preme National Tribunals, has put the
"Christian Religion in this great Empire of
"*China* in the most eminent Danger of utter
"Ruin, which only *Rome* could prevent, if
"the true State of Affairs was known there.
"But at this time there being no Ships sail-
"ing from hence, and considering the Re-
"moteness of the respective Countries, I am
"at a Loss where to apply unless to your
"Czarish Majesty, at whose Feet I throw
"my self, most humbly beseeching your Ma-
"jesty to be graciously pleased to give Or-
"ders that the Report of this whole Event,
"which I have drawn up and furnished with
"all the necessary Evidences, be sent through
"your Majesty's Dominions with safety and
"speed to *Vienna* in *Austria* to his Imperial
"Majesty *Charles* VI. your Czarish Majesty's
"near Relation. I hope your Czarish Ma-
"jesty will vouchsafe me this Request for the
"Love of God and the Faith of the Lord,
"as your Majesty, actuated by a religious
"Zeal, have often ventured your own high-
"est Person, Blood and Life against Turks,
"Tartars and other Infidels, not without
"the most glorious Victories, which by the
"Blessing of Almighty God, your Majesty
"has obtained over your Enemies, and
"thereby extended your Dominions. I will
"always

" always with profound Gratitude acknow-
" ledge the granting of such a Favour, and
" together with about eighty Preachers of
" the Faith and two hundred thousand Chri-
" stians, never cease instantly to pray to God
" that he may further bless your Czarish Ma-
" jesty, and your whole most great and migh-
" ty Royal House and Government, pro-
" sper them and heap on them all terrestrial
" and eternal Blessings. *Peking* the 25th of
June, 1717.

Your Great Czarish Majesty's

Most humble Servant, though unknown

Kilianus Stumpf, of the Society
of *Jesus*, Visitor in *China* and *Japan*.

The said Missionaries had already for two Years been in great Danger, because the Deputies whom they had sent from among their Brethren at the Desire of the new Converts to obtain a Dispensation from the Pope for worshipping *Confucius* and keeping up certain Pagan Ceremonies, were never heard of after; for which Reason with the Concurrence of the Council of the *Mandarins* they caused Revocatory Letters to be printed in the *Latin*, *Chineze* and *Tartarian* Languages, and to be sent to all parts of the World.

Proceedings of the Grand Inquisition, with relation to the Clergymen concerned. In the mean time the Grand Court of Inquisition at *Moskow* went on with their Proceedings against the Prisoners carried thither from *Petersbourg*, and against Major-General *Glebof*. There were two different Processes, one of which related to the *Czarewitz*, and the other to the late *Czarina*, (who had been carred carried from the Monastery of *Sufdal* to *Mofkow*) and Major-General *Gleboff*; the former of which two several Processes was finished at *Petersbourg*, and the latter at *Moskow*. The frequency of People at *Moskow* was extraordinary on this Occasion: The whole Court was there with the greater part of the Generals and other superior Officers, the Chiefs of the Clergy and Nobility of all *Ruffia* had also been summoned thither. The Processions of the Clergy, who at different times went in their Coaches and with their whole Train to the Czar's Palace, to the Trial of their Brother the Bishop of *Roftoff* made a noble Appearance: But what most deserved every one's Attention was to hear the *Czar* himself, contrary to the Custom of his Predecessors make Speeches to the Clergy and the great Men of his Dominions in the great Hall, representing to them and the People with his natural Eloquence, (in which Accomplishment as well as that of expressing himself in writing he has no Equal among his Subjects) the Danger to which his Government had been exposed, and the Horror of the Crime of High Treason. Upon which *Doffifei* the Bishop of *Roftoff*, and *Puftinoi* the Confessor of the late *Czarina* were divested of their Ecclesiastical Habit, and delivered up to the secular Arm.

On these Solemnities the *Czar* appeared in his usual Dress, nor can any body remember ever to have seen him in that extraordinary Pomp in which his Predecessors used to appear, he being naturally an Enemy to all Pageantry, notwithstanding he has inherited precious Jewels and pompous Attire enough of his Ancestors, of which Baron *Herberftein*, Ambassador *The Czar himself appears without any Pomp on that publick Occasion.*

Ambassador of the Emperor *Ferdinand* I. says, "That on his Audience the *Great Prince* had upon his Head a Crown adorned with precious Stones, which as to its Value did not yield to that of the Pope or any other Prince: His Robes were set with Rubies, Diamonds and Emeralds, some as big as small Nuts: The *Czarewitz*, says he, was also magnificently dressed. The Audience being over the Czar went to Dinner, which was served up by one hundred Noblemen in so many golden and silver Dishes, and in such Plenty that twenty Waggons might have been loaded with it." Those who have seen the Solemnity of the present *Czar*'s Marriage with the *Czarina* his present Consort, report that they were astonished at the quantity and great Value of the precious Stones with which her Crown was adorned, and that the value of her Jewels was beyond what can be imagined. But the *Czar* himself loves a plain Dress and a small Retinue, and even at the time we are speaking of, in the midst of the Disturbances in his own Family, he had never above two or three Servants attending his Sled, in which he was carried up and down the City both Night and Day, he being the most active Person in the Affair of the Inquisition, though the Direction of it was committed to the Privy-Councellor M. *Tolstoy*, and the Senator *Mussin Puschkin*.

Proceedings against some of the Nobility.

The Senator *Samarin* was acquitted; as was also Count *Peter Matuewitz Apraxin*, Senator and formerly Governor of *Astracan*, because nothing could be made out against the latter except his advancing three thousand Rubels

Rubels to the *Czarewitz* upon his Departure from *Petersbourg* for *Germany*, without knowing what were his Designs. But the Prince *Waffili Wolodimirowitz Dolgoruki*, Lieutenant-General was ordered to be continued under close Confinement.

The principal Persons who were involved in this Grand Inquisition, were (besides the *Czarewitz* and *Kikin*, of whom frequent mention has already been made) the former *Czarina Eudochia* or *Afdokia* of the Family of *Lopuchin*; her Father Confessor; *Maria Alexevna*, the Czar's Sister by the half Blood; the *Czarewitz* of *Siberia*; the Boyar *Stepan Gleboff*; *Doffifei* Bishop of *Roftoff*; and the Treasurer of the Monastery of *Sufdal*. *The principal Persons under Inquisition.*

On that Occasion a Paper was published setting forth the Crimes of the Prisoners of *Sufdal* as they were proved by intercepted Letters and their own Confessions; but as I lost it by some Accident, I can only give here the Copy of a Letter of *Doffifei* the Bishop (who by his pretended Visions was the chief Cause of the unhappy Fate of most of the Prisoners) to the Princess *Maria Alexevna* the Czar's Sister of the half Blood, which Letter relating to his pretended Revelations was of his own Hand writing, and found in the Princess's Apartment, to this Effect. *Fragments of Evidences of one of the Processes.*

" God bless Thee, my most gracious Prin-
" cess, and preserve Thee, my Light *, in
" Health. I have offended God and Thee,
" my gracious Princess, and brought Thee
" under great Affliction, and even heaped up-

---

* *This Expression*, my Light, *in the Russian Language denotes a particular Respect.*

" on

"on my self a great deal of Grief, that I do
"not care to live any longer upon Earth;
"because I did not take a Journey to Thee;
"had the Danger on the Road been never so
"great, yet it would have been better than
"now; but I will not let Thee be ignorant,
"why I am not come to Thee at present, my
"Light; a good while before *Christmass* and
"for above a Month I have been sick to
"Death, so that I was not able to stir out
"of my Cell, much less to go any where
"else, and for this Sin I have been forced to
"stay. I would willingly not live, had not
"the Time then passed away thus to no pur-
"pose, and there are no proper Days now
"for setting out, but to stay till next Week
"would make me think one Day longer than
"a whole Week, and after all I do not
"know how to contrive it as not to deprive
"my People of their Diversion. I am se-
"parated from Thee, my Light, and I have
"not seen Thee a long time. I hear already
"what a cursed Man and unfaithful Servant
"I am, because I have offended my Pro-
"tectors, and this Sickness has seized me,
"which though not over-violent, yet has
"been prejudicial. God's Will be done, I
"give it over to Him and the Saints. I beg,
"my most gracious Princess, not to take it
"ill, that I have been so backward in wri-
"ting. On the fourth instant I was in the
"*Tolstian* Monastery at *Jareslow*, where our
"Master of the Horse delivered to me thy
"Highness's Letter. On the fifth being re-
"turned home I wrote about every thing,
"but why the Letters did not come to
"Hand, God knows. I sent them with a
"safe

The Present State of Ruſſia.

" ſafe Meſſenger, who travelled with his Ma-
" jeſty's Caſh, and was aſſured by him, that
" he would deliver them without delay. I
" therein wrote at large, particularly that *Fe-*
" *dor Stephanowitz* might ſpeak with me if
" poſſible. (A) (X) Concerning the *Hermits*
" I tell you that they know nothing of this
" Affair. They think, that he is with the
" Father, but how I ſhall go to them, ve-
" rily I do not know. This Winter I was
" once already on the Road, and went as
" far as the Village *Ankowa*, where I baited
" and met *Dimitri* and returned back with
" him, whereupon the Robbers on the High-
" way attacked others inſtead of us, robbed
" and murthered them. But He, our Light,
" preſerved us. However I wiſhed as much
" to concert Meaſures with them, as I wiſh
" to come to God; laſt Summer I was with
" them, as Thou well knoweſt, *N. B.* I told
" them that I had taken a Journey thither, but
" I had been with the *Hermits*, with whom I
" concerted many things, *&c.* and as ſoon
" as I had left them I forgot all: Alas! Poor
" Man, I almoſt loſe my Memory; was it
" not for the Friendſhip of our Acquain-
" tance there, I ſhould not be able to pre-
" ſerve my right Senſes. I have ſufficiently
" experienced their Friendſhip there; if Thou
" hadſt alſo been there, Thou wouldſt like-
" wiſe have been ſenſible of it, and not ſo
" much as think of thy Acquaintance here.
" Upon this Letter *Dimitri* was quite ſtruck
" dumb, and things draw towards an End
" with him: As for what relates to *Paul*, I
" knew already long ago, that he was, but
" is no more, and his Father will fare no
" better,

"better, who knows when it will be their
"Turn? There are many who fervently
"pray to God for it; God grant a speedy
"Issue to the Affair, which the *Hermits* very
"much wish, for his sake, and that God may
"bring him to right. *Dimitri* will stay away
"a long time, he is in another's Custody, and
"is very sick on account of the finishing of
"the Structure, because it lasts so long.
"*Wissarion* and all the others exalt their Voice
"to Thee, and desire thy Assistance, where-
"in verily I do not lie; I hear by them
"that thy prevailing Prayers and good Re-
"gulations can afford a great deal of Ease;
"do not leave them helpless; for they value
"thy Comfort higher than any other, which
"I truly swear to as an upright Christian,
"so as I heard it from them; they desire
"Thee, to lend them all possible Help; I
"can prescribe no certain Rule, how it may
"be best contrived according to the utmost
"of our Power. Concerning the *Hermits* I
"expect thy Czarish Highness's Advice, how
"things ought to be contrived with them,
"that they may not look upon me with
"Suspicion, seeing it cannot be concealed
"from them. I see no way how to go to
"*Wlodomir*, because I have communicated
"my Project to every one; however I will
"not recede from thy Commands. I fret
"and grieve for not having been able at first
"to go. Had I been with Thee, Things
"would be in another Situation at present.
"I believe the Adversary hindered me, and
"threw me into great Affliction against
"which there was no Help. A great
"deal of Grief surrounds me, and despica-
ble

"ble Sickness besides; it had been better, I
"had gone then. It was not well done in-
"deed, yet God's Will and thy Destiny re-
"quired it thus, without whose Will no-
"thing happens; I am a sinful Man! thy
"Intercessor with God falls with Tears to
"thy high and holy Feet and embraces them,
"instantly begging thy Forgiveness, as I
"likewise humble my self and bow to the
"Earth towards all the others, &c.

"Concerning this Letter *Rostriga Dimit.*
"† owned publickly that it was his own
"Handwriting, and that he had written it
"to the Princess *Maria Alexevna*, and the
"obscure Passages in it he explained as fol-
"lows:

The Words of the Letter.

Because I did not take a Journey to Thee.

The Explication.

Upon the Princess *Alexevna*'s return from *Carlsbad.*

L. *The Master of the Horse came from the Princess, and gave me the Letter in the* Tolstian *Monastery on the fourth Instant.*

E. I have forgotten what were the Contents of that Letter.

L. *On the fifth I returned home, and the next Morning wrote about every thing at large, why it did not come sooner to Hand, God knows. For I sent it with a safe Messenger, who travelled with the Cash, who promised to deliver it without delay, this happened on the sixth, and I wrote at large.*

---

† By this Name the *Bishop* was designed in the *Russian* Original, which was written in a Style so harsh and obscure that in some Passages one could hardly guess the Sense of it.

E. I have forgotten the Contents of the Letter, by whom I sent it, or who he was.

L. Particularly that Fedor Stepanowitz *might come, if possible.*

E. That I might speak with him concerning his Indisposition.

L. The Letters (A) and (X) or Sch in Parenthesis.

E. They signify: AFDOKIA SCHIWOFLI; is *Afdokia* alive?

L. Advice will come in concerning the Hermits.

E. Concerning the late *Czarina,* whom they called an *Hermit.*

L. I acquaint you that they know nothing of it, thinking he is with the Father.

E. Of the *Czarewitz Alexei,* as if he was with the *Czar,* but that the Princess wrote to him the Bishop, that he was already in the Emperor's Dominions, and that he would take a Journey to the late *Czarina* to acquaint her with it.

L. As for what relates to Paul, *I knew already long ago, that he was, but is no more, and that his Father will fare no better, who knows when it will be their Turn.*

E. That he had indeed written this of the *Czarewitz,* and that he had learned from the Saints, that the *Czar* should soon die, and that the *Czarewitz Paul* was already dead, but that in all this he lied in order to make the Princess rejoyce; that indeed he knew of the Death of the *Czarewitz Paul,* but only by Information from the Princess.

L. There are many who fervently pray to God for it, God grant a speedy Issue to the Affair.

E. That he wrote this, because he wished that the *Czar* and all those who were in his Favour,

vour, might soon die, of which he had also talked to the Princess.

L. Which the Hermits earnestly wish, and that God may bring him to right.

E. This the late *Czarina* desired, viz. that his Czarish Majesty might take her again.

L. Dimitri stays away a long time, and is in another's Custody.

E. That he lied, as if the *Czarewitz* was sent by God to protect his People.

L. How I shall go thither I do not know.

E. That the Princess wrote Word to him to go to the late *Czarina*.

L. This Winter I was already once on the Road, and went as far as the Village Ankowa, *where I baited and met* Dimitrio, *and returned back with him, whereupon the Robbers on the Highway attacked others instead of us, robbed and murthered them; but He, our Light, preserved us. However I wished as much to concert Measures with them, as I wish to come to God. Last Summer I was with them, as Thou well knowest,* N. B. *I told them that I had taken a Journey thither, but I had been with the Hermits, with whom I concerted many things,* &c. *and as soon as I had left them I forgot all. Alas! Poor Man, I almost lose my Memory; was it not for the Friendship of our Acquaintance there I should not be able to preserve my right Senses, which I sufficiently experienced there, hadst Thou been there, Thou wouldst likewise have been sensible of it, and not so much as think of thy Acquaintance here.*

E. That by *Dimitri* was meant the *Czarewitz*, who had not been with him, neither did he, *Rostriga*, go to *Susdal*, but stayed at *Rostoff;* all the rest were Lies.

Upon

L. Upon the Letter Dimitri *was quite ſtruck dumb, and things draw towards an End with him.*

E. That he told a Lie of the *Czarewitz,* when he told him what had happened, and alſo that the *Czar* would die.

L. He is very ſick on account of the finiſhing of the Structure, becauſe it laſts long.

E. That he wrote this of *Dimitri* the *Czarewitz,* as if he laid it to Heart for the People's ſake, and that what was aboveſaid was ſo long a coming, and the *Czar*'s Life was not abridged; which was telling a Lie of him.

E. Wiſſarion *and all the others exalt their Voice to Thee, and deſire thy Aſſiſtance, wherein verily I do not lie; I hear by them that thy prevailing Prayers and good Regulations can afford a great deal of Eaſe, do not leave them helpleſs, for they value thy Comfort higher than any other, which I truly ſwear to as an upright Chriſtian, ſo as I heard it from them; they deſire Thee, to lend them all poſſible Help. I can preſcribe no certain Rule, how it may be beſt contrived according to the utmoſt of our Power.*

E. That what he wrote was done merely out of Flattery to her, to value her higher than the Saints, likewiſe as if the Saints had told him, that her Prayers were of more weight with God than theirs.

L. Concerning the Hermits I expect thy Czariſh Highneſs's Advice how things ought to be contrived with them, that they may not look upon me with Suſpicion, ſeeing it cannot be concealed from them.

E. That he wrote to the Princefs, whether fhe permitted that he might fee the late *Czarina*, but that he had no Mind to it, becaufe he could not do it fecretly, and publickly to do it might have proved prejudicial to the *Czarina* as well as to himfelf.

L. I fee no way how to go to W lodomir, *becaufe I have communicated my Project to every one; however I will not recede from thy Commands.*

E. That he wrote he could not go to *Wlodomir*, left he might render himfelf fufpected in the Monaftery of *Sufdal*, and if he fhould go to *Wlodomir*, he could not pafs *Sufdal*, as for the reft he referred it to her Judgement, and that he would go if fhe commanded him.

L. I fret and grieve for not having been able at firft to go, had I been with Thee, Things would be in another Situation at prefent. I believe the Adverfary hindered me, and threw me into great Affliction, againft which there was no Help; a great deal of Grief furrounds me and defpicable Sicknefs befides, it had been better, I had gone then, it was not well done, yet God's Will and Fate required it thus, without whofe Will nothing happens.

E. That he wrote all this when he was with the Princefs at the time of her return from *Carlsbad*.

On the 26th of March Part of the Prifoners were executed in the publick Market Place of the City of *Moskow*. The Boyar *Stepan Glebof* was empaled alive, the Bifhop *Doffifei, Kikin*, one who was Treafurer of the Monaftery of *Sufdal*, and another Ruffian, were broken upon the Wheel; the Corpfe of the Bifhop was burnt, but his Head, with thofe of *Kikin*, and of the other two Ruffians, were

Executions at Mofkow.

put on high Poles, on the four Corners of a high square Wall erected to that End, and the empaled Corpse of *Gleboff* placed in the middle. The Page *Baklanofsky*, and some Nuns, had their Sentences mitigated, and suffered severe corporal Punishments, and the remaining Prisoners were carried to *Petersbourg*. This Execution gave me an Opportunity of judging of the great Number of the Inhabitants of *Moskow*, the Spectators who appeared then together, being reckoned between two and three hundred thousand Souls. A certain Person congratulating the *Czar* on this Occasion, for having restored his own Government to its former Tranquillity, by the indefatigable Care and Intrepidity he had shewn, in discovering and punishing a Conspiracy against his own Person; the *Czar* made this Answer: *If a Fire meets with Straw and other light Stuff, it soon spreads; but if it finds Iron and Stone in its Way, it extinguishes of it self.*

The State of the Russian Clergy and Nobility, and whether there is any Danger of an Insurrection? And here I cannot but take notice, how ill-grounded were the Reports, with which the World was filled at that Time, as if a Revolt was actually broken out in *Russia*, or at least apprehended: For even supposing that some of the Czar's Subjects had been big with rebellious Designs, out of Disaffection to the Administration, yet the blind Populace, who, without Leaders, seldom venture on the like Attempts, were so well awed, and the Safety of the Czar's Throne so firmly established, that they would have paid dear for the least itching Desire of revolting, the *Czar* being able to rely on his Forces, as entirely devoted to his Interest. Therefore they must have been

been ſtirred up or headed, either by the Clergy, or by the chief Nobility of the Country. But conſidering on one Side, that the greater Part of the Prieſts are of vulgar Extraction, without powerful Relations and Wealth; and that, on the other hand, the *Czar* has drawn all the topping Temporality to *Petersbourg*, where he keeps a watchful Eye over them, it is not probable this Monarch will ever have any thing to fear during his Life. It is notorious, how much the Power of the Clergy has been limited and clipped; nevertheleſs, the Czar does not pretend to turn out any Prelate of his own ſole Authority, but does it with the Concurrence of the Clergy; and for this Reaſon ſo many Difficulties aroſe about the Degradation of the Biſhop of *Roſtoff*, before he was executed at *Moskow*, his Brethren pretending, that, for want of a Patriarch, it was not in their Power to diveſt him of his Dignity; but the Czar propoſing this Queſtion to them, *Whether it was in their Power to create and inveſt a Biſhop?* And they anſwering in the Affirmative, he made this Inference: *And ſo you may as well diveſt him of that Dignity.* As to the Nobility, though their Subjection to the Czars has been very great at all Times, it is much greater at preſent beyond all Compariſon. *Theodor*, the Brother of the preſent Czar, made way to this Form of Government, by calling together the Nobility of all *Ruſſia*, with Orders to bring with them to Court their Family-Writings, Privileges, and other Originals, in order to have them confirmed. Accordingly they all appeared to one Man with their Papers before the Czar, who, without giving himſelf the Trouble of reading them, wrapt

wrapt them up together in a Bundle, and threw them into the Fire in the Chimney, declaring at the same Time, that for the future, Privileges and Pre-eminence should be grounded solely upon Merit, and not upon Birth; a Law which the present Czar has since fully enforced.

The Insufficiency of the History of Russia. Having made mention here of the Privileges and other Writings of the Russian Nobility, I shall take notice by the Way, that the History of *Russia* might be considerably improved, and several Points of it cleared up, if those Manuscripts and Memoirs, which lie concealed among divers Russian Families, were brought to Light, and communicated to the Publick: For there have always been some Persons among the great Families, who, for some Ages past, notwithstanding the Ignorance of those Times, have committed to Paper, and transmitted to their Posterity from Generation to Generation, the Transactions of their Czars, in which their Families and Relations were concerned. The Russian Counsellor of War, Baron *Huyssen*, finished three Years ago a great Historical Work, containing his present Czarish Majesty's glorious Atchievements, which ever since has lain ready for the Press; a good Performance in the main, and worth reading; but as the Author, though otherwise a Person of great Learning, had no Supplies for that Work, either out of the Russian Archives and publick Records, or any other Materials, but what a Collection of News-Papers, historical Mercuries, and the like ordinary Writings furnished him with; the said History falls short of what ought to be expected from it, and it is

The Present State of Russia.

to be wished, that, before its Publication, the Author may get better Light, to enable him to give the World a more substantial Account of the Czar's Actions.

Before the Czar's Departure for *Petersbourg*, several Conferences were held with the Ambassador of the *Bucharian Tartars*, as also with the General of the *Cosacks*. I had an Opportunity of getting acquainted with the former, and endeavoured to be informed by him of divers things relating to his Country, and its Neighbours; but I had such silly Answers from him, that some of his Retinue were obliged to help him out, and to satisfy my Curiosity. I learned afterwards, that he was a Merchant, who lived at *Astracan*, and was employed by the *Can* of those *Tartars* in this Embassy or Commission, merely because he understood the Languages, and had had Dealings long before with the Russians. This Ambassador begged of the *Czar* a Number of Swedish Girls to go along with him, or to give him Leave to buy some, his Master having heard, that the *Swedes* are a very warlike Nation, which had made him desirous to have some of their Race in his Dominions. This ridiculous Request met with a Repulse; however, he found Means to get two *Swedish* Girls, whom he carried along with him. Those *Bucharians* are not properly subject to the Czar; but as their Country is very much infested by their Neighbours, the *Calmucks* and *Mongalians*, who extend towards the River *Argun*, almost as far as the Wall of *China*, they commonly apply to the Czar for Aid; and, in Return, own themselves bound to be at his Service upon the first Warning.

Of the Bucharian Ambassador.

We

April 1718.
A dangerous Journey from Moskow to Petersbourg.

We left *Moskow* on the 1ſt of *April,* after having firſt had Intimation from Court, that ſeeing the Peaſants along the High Road had been extremely haraſſed for ſome Time paſt, another Rout ſhould be marked out for us further on the right Side, towards the Sea of *Ladoga :* This Way probably might have proved practicable in Winter; but as there happened a Thaw during our Journey, and that we had above twenty open Rivers to paſs, where there were neither Bridges nor Ferries, we were obliged to make Floats for our ſelves as well as we were able, the Country People, who were not accuſtomed to ſee Travellers that Way, being fled, upon our coming, with their Children and Horſes to the Woods. In all my Life-time I never had a more troubleſome Journey, and even ſome of our Company, who had travelled over great Part of the World, proteſted, that they never underwent the the like Fatigues before. After great Difficulties we at length arrived at *Kaſchna,* where the *Woywode Alzofioff* ſent us ſome Refreſhments of Beer, Mead, Brandy, and Bread, and afterwards came himſelf, and repreſented to us the Danger of purſuing that Courſe: Upon this we forthwith reſolved to turn to *Tweer,* where we came again into the uſual High Road, and at laſt, after three Weeks Time, arrived at *Petersbourg.*

Great Honours ſhewn to the Vice-Czar.

They were then making Preparations there for the Reception of the *Vice-Czar* of *Moskow, Romadonofsky,* who accordingly arrived before the Eaſter Holidays, being ſaluted with a triple Diſcharge of the Artillery. His Czariſh Majeſty himſelf, in the Quality of Vice-Admiral, went with a great Retinue to meet him, received him with profound Submission, and placed himself into the Vice-Czar's Coach, riding backwards with Lieutenant-General *Buturlin*, and so conducted him to Court, where he was welcomed with no less Respect by the *Czarina*, and all the Ladies; and after having been placed in an Elbow Chair, both their Majesties served him standing with Wine and Brandy. He is of about forty Years of Age, and is married to a Sister of the *Czarina* Dowager *Proskovia*.

The State-Prisoners arrived also at *Petersbourg* coming from *Moskow*, and the *Czarewitz*'s Mistress was brought Prisoner from *Leipzig*; but the Lord of the Bed-Chamber *Nariskin* a Relation of the *Czar* by the Mother's Side, was exiled to his own Estate, where he is since said to have run distracted. *The State-Prisoners removed to Petersbourg.*

A *Turkish Aga* arrived from the *Porte*, and delivered his credential Letters to the Great Chancellor and the Vice-Chancellor; but considering the ill Treatment the latter had met with at *Constantinople*, the *Aga* was used with a great deal of Coldness in his Audiences, which he was obliged to take standing. *A Turkish Aga at Petersbourg.*

The Czar made divers little Journies for Diversion sake; and his chief Attention was to see two and twenty Ships of the Line fitted out for putting to Sea. *New Ships on the Stocks.*

The *Czar's* Sister of the half Blood *Catharine Alexevna*, who had lived many Years at *Moskow*, without concerning her self with the late Troubles, died there on the 31ˢᵗ of May, and the Court went in Mourning on this Account. *The Czars Sister Catharine dies.*

Euphrosine (Afrosini) the Czarewitz's Mistress, was set at Liberty, not only in Consideration *Particulars concerning the Czarewitz' Mistress.*

deration of the open Confeſſions ſhe had made, but alſo becauſe ſhe had made it appear, that her Perſuaſions had much contributed to the *Czarewitz*'s Return. She is of very mean Extraction, being a Finlandiſh Captive; and ſhe pretended, that the *Czarewitz* forced her to comply with his Will with a Knife drawn, and threatning her with Death. It is maintained by ſeveral, that after her firſt Lying-in, and upon her conforming with the Ruſſian Faith, ſhe was actually married to the *Czarewitz*, when they were on their Journey, by a Grecian Prieſt, who was likewiſe ſeized at *Leipzig*, and carried Priſoner to *Ruſſia*. This Circumſtance appeared the more probable, becauſe the ſaid Miſtreſs having obtained his Czariſh Majeſty's full Pardon, and having had ſeveral Jewels reſtored to her, with this Declaration, that if ſhe had a mind to marry, ſhe ſhould receive a handſome Portion out of the Czar's Treaſury; ſhe made this Anſwer: *I firſt yielded to one Man's Will out of Force, henceforth no other ſhall come near my Side*; which Words gave then occaſion to divers Speculations.

June 1718. The Grand Inquiſition renewed. It was generally believed, that the bloody Execution at *Moskow* had put an End to the Grand Inquiſition, and that the Root of all further Troubles was thereby plucked up; the rather becauſe the great Secrecy which was uſed, ſince our Return to *Petersbourg*, in concealing any further Diſcoveries made by the Priſoners lately carried thither from *Moſkow*, made People at firſt believe, that the moſt material Points of the Conſpiracy were already found out, and that conſequently there could be no further Execution: Yet it ſoon

soon appeared, to the great Aſtoniſhment of every body, that all the Tortures made uſe of at *Moskow*, had not been near effectual enough to diſcover the whole Truth in that Affair, nor would they have been able to draw more Light from the remaining Priſoners, had not the whole Myſtery been unravelled by intercepted Letters, which were found ſewed up in the Clothes of certain Perſons. The *Czar* therefore ſaw himſelf neceſſitated to eſtabliſh a ſecond High Court of Juſtice, and to this End to convoke the chief of the Ruſſian Clergy with all poſſible Speed to *Petersbourg*. They being all arrived in June, and the *Czar* having beſides eſtabliſhed another Court conſiſting of ſecular Perſons, *viz.* the Miniſters, Senators, Governors, Generals, and the ſuperior Officers of his Guards, his Majeſty for eight ſeveral Days lay during ſome Hours on his Knees, imploring God, with abundance of Tears, to inſpire him with ſuch Thoughts as the Honour of his holy Name, and the Welfare of the Ruſſian Nation required. And ſo, on the 25th of June, the Seſſions of this criminal Court were opened in the Hall of the Senate, whither his Czariſh Majeſty repaired with the whole Clergy, and the ſecular Judges, after firſt having cauſed ſolemn Service to be performed in the Church of the *Holy Ghoſt*, to implore God's Aſſiſtance in this weighty Affair. The whole Aſſembly having taken their reſpective Places at ſeveral Tables, the Doors and Windows were ſet open in order to give free Admittance to all ſorts of Perſons. Upon this the *Czarewitz* was brought into Court, under the Guard of four Under-Officers, and proceeded againſt in the manner as is set forth in the *Acts* or *Registers of Inquisition*, published afterwards by Authority in the Russian Language. A translated Abstract thereof was communicated to me at *Petersbourg*, which, being joined to the other Pieces annexed to these Memoirs, I shall mention no further Particulars as to those judicial Proceedings, but refer to the said Paper it self, to satisfy the Reader's * Curiosity.

July 1718. The Czarewitz sentenced to Death. The Assembly of the Clergy having declared their Opinion in Writing, that the *Czarewitz* had deserved Death, and the Court of secular Judges established by the Czar, for examining and judging this Cause, having pronounced a formal Sentence, condemning the *Czarewitz* to Death, a new Session was held on the 6th of July in the Morning, and the *Czarewitz* brought out of the Fortress into Court, under the Guard of the foresaid four Under-Officers, where he was obliged to repeat the Confession of his Crimes, and to hear the Sentence of Death signed by the secular Judges, read to him, after which he was sent back into Custody.

The Czar takes leave of his dying Son. The next Day, being Thursday the 7th of July, early in the Morning, the News was brought to the *Czar,* that the violent Passions of the Mind, and the Terrors of Death, had thrown the *Czarewitz* into an apoplectick Fit. About Noon another Messenger brought Advice, that the Prince was in great Danger of his Life; whereupon the *Czar* sent for the principal Men of his Court, and caused them

[* *This Piece being afterwards published entire at the* Hague *in* French, *has been here annexed in* English, *it appearing more correct and intelligible than the* High-Dutch.]

to stay till he was informed by a third Messenger, that the Prince being past Hopes, could not outlive the Evening, and that he longed to see his Father. Then the *Czar*, attended by the foresaid Company, went to see his dying Son, who, at the Sight of his Father, burst out in Tears, and, with his Hands folded, spoke to him to this Effect: That he had grievously and heinously offended the Majesty of God Almighty, and of the *Czar*; that he hoped not to recover of this Indisposition, and even if he should, yet he was unworthy of Life; therefore he begged his Majesty, for God's Sake, only to take from him the Curse he laid upon him at *Moskow*; to forgive him all his heavy Crimes; to impart to him his paternal Blessings; and to cause Prayers to be put up for his Soul. During these moving Words the Czar and the whole Company almost melted away in Tears; his Majesty returned a pathetick Answer, and represented to him in a few Words all the Offences he had committed against him, and then gave him his Forgiveness and Blessings; after which they parted with abundance of Tears and Lamentations on both Sides.

At five in the Evening came a fourth Messenger, being M. *Oczakoff*, Major of the Guards, to acquaint the *Czar*, that the *Czarewitz* was extremely desirous once more to see his Father; the *Czar* at first was unwilling to comply with his Son's Request; but was at last persuaded by the Company, who represented to his Majesty, how hard it would be to deny that Comfort to a Son, who, being on the Point of Death, might probably be tortured by the Stings of a guilty Conscience;

The Czarewitz dies.

but

but when his Majesty had just stept into his Sloop to go over to the Fortress, a fifth Messenger brought the News, that the Prince was already expired.

His Funeral. On the 9th of July the Corpse being laid into a Coffin, covered with black Velvet, and a Pall of rich Gold Tissue spread over it, was carried from the Fortress, attended by the Great Chancellor, and several Persons of the first Rank, to the Church of the *Holy Trinity*, where it was laid in State. Four Officers of the Guards were in waiting near the Corpse, and gave Leave to a vast Number of People, who crouded in to kiss the Hands of the Deceased. On the 10th of July the Corpse continued to lie in State, and the Preparations for the Funeral being finished, it was on the 11th in the Evening carried from the Church of the *Holy Trinity* back to the Fortress, where it was deposited in the new Burying-Vault of the Czarish Family, and put next to the Coffin of the Prince's late Consort. The *Czar*, the *Czarina*, and the chief Nobility of the Court followed in Procession. The *Czar*, as well as the rest of the Mourners, carried each a small Wax-Taper lighted in their Hands; but they wore no Mourning-Cloaks, and the Ladies were only dressed in black Silks. Those who assisted at the Funeral, related, that the Czar was bathed in Tears during the Procession and the Service at Church, where the Priest had chose for the Text of his funeral Sermon the Words of *David: O my Son Absalom, my Son, my Son Absalom.*

A new Ship launched. A costly Man of War of 90 Guns was launched, being built by the Czar himself and his

his Ruffians only, without the Help of any outlandifh Mafters or Ship-Carpenters, the Workmanfhip of which was univerfally admired. She went off with good Succefs, under the repeated *Huzza*'s (the Englifh Acclamation now introduced among the Ruffian Sailors) of above twenty thoufand Spectators, which the Czar himfelf ufhered in by giving a Sign with his Hat, whereupon as many Perfons as the Ship could hold, had Leave to go on board her. The Czar himfelf afterwards went alfo on board, and was very favourably received there by the Vice-Czar of *Moskow, Peter Fedrowitz Romadonofsky*, and was prefented by the Admiral with two Silver Tankards, in Confideration of his great Skill; for which Favour this illuftrious Shipwright returned particular Thanks to the Vice-Czar, and afterwards fate down to Table, with no other Company but his eight Englifh Mafter-Builders, fhewing a great deal of Content and good Humour during the Meal, as well as afterwards all Night long. The young Prince, *Peter Petrowitz*, was carried on Board, and his Health drunk by the Company.

On the 20th of July the *Czar* went to *Cronflot*. The Fleet fitted out for the Service of that Year, confifted of two and twenty Men of War, and was divided in three Squadrons, the firft of which was commanded by the Great-Admiral *Apraxin*, the fecond by the Vice-Admiral *Peter Michailof*, (for this is the Name which the Czar bears in the Fleet) and the third by the Rear-Admiral Prince *Alexander Menzicoff*. The Fleet is fince increafed to about forty Men of War, and

The State of the Czar's Navy.

and three hundred Gallies. The Ships indeed were as good as could be defired, and were abundantly provided with all Neceffaries; but the old Complaint ftill continued, that the Sailors were not yet skilled in their Bufinefs; for though there had been about two thoufand German Sailors diftributed among the Fleet, yet many of the old ones being gone off, there were not able Hands enough for working the Ships in an Engagement. Two Regiments of the Guards were embarked on thofe three Squadrons, to be tranfported to *Finland*, in order to enforce the Negotiations of the Ruflian Plenipotentiaries in the Ifle of *Aland*, where a Treaty had been fet on Foot in the mean Time. This Fleet put to Sea on the 27th of July.

Count Reenfchield exchanged.

On the 31ft Count *Reenfchield* arrived from *Cafan* after having been nine Years Prifoner of War. He was conducted to *Abo* in *Finland*, to be exchanged there for the two Ruffian Generals, *Gollowin* and *Trubetskoy*, who were taken Prifoners in the Year 1702, in the Battel of *Narva**.

Auguft, 1718. New Works in Livonia.

In Auguft we travelled fixty German Miles over Land to *Reval*, to meet the Czar. His Majefty was already arrived there, but put to Sea again on the 12th of the faid Month, after having firft taken a View at *Dagheroe* on the Coaft of *Livonia*, of a Place which had been propofed to him to make a Harbour of it; as alfo at *Reval*, of a large and pleafant Spot of Ground, where he refolved to build a Pleafure-Houfe with fine Gardens; both

[* *Count* Reenfchield *died in* Sweden *the* 9th *of Feb.* 1722. N. S. *being* 72 *Years of Age.*]

The Present State of Russia.

which expensive Works were begun and carried on with so much Diligence, that in the Year 1719, when I came again to *Reval*, they were near half finished.

I was adviced from *Petersbourg*, that the Prince and General *Dolgoruki* had been deprived of the Order of the Elephant, which was remitted back to the Court of *Denmark*, and that he was sent into Exile to *Casan*: Having obtained Permission to take his Leave of the *Czarina*, he endeavoured in a moving Speech to justify himself of the Crimes laid to his Charge, and at the same time complained, that he had nothing in the World but the Clothes on his Back. The *Czarina* gave him a favourable Hearing, and afterwards sent him a Present of two hundred Ducats to his House. *Prince Dolgoruki's Disgrace.*

The *Czar* having made no Enterprize in this Sea-Campaign, he returned to *Petersbourg*, where we arrived from *Reval* on the 15th of September. In a Village not far from *Narva* I found a Peasant lying at the Point of Death in the midst of the High-Road; he was fallen sick being on the Works of *Strelnamuse*, and had made shift to come so far by begging along the Road in his Way home. There was not one of the Inhabitants of the said Village, who would assist him with the least Comfort, and those who passed by did not so much as cast an Eye upon him. I sent for some Brandy, as the best Refreshment for a *Russian*, and obliged two old Women who were walking by, to make him take it, and with the greatest Difficulty and a Piece of Money, at last persuaded a Soldier to call the Priest of the Village to assist this dying Man *Septemb. 1718. An Instance of Inhumanity.*

in

in his laſt Minutes; but he excuſed himſelf on account of the Harveſt-time and his Houſhold-Affairs, till after ſeveral Meſſages, and my threatning him with acquainting the *Czar* with this unheard-of Inhumanity, he at laſt vouchſafed to come, though with a very peeviſh Look, and too late; for the Peaſant was juſt breathing his laſt. After ſome ſhort Prayers he cauſed the Man's Mouth to be broke open, and gave him the Sacrament in a Spoon, which being done, he went directly away, without either concerning himſelf about the Corpſe, or ſo much as exhorting the People who ſtood by, to perform the Offices of Charity on this miſerable Object; but rather ſhewing, by an ill-natured and four Countenance, that he owed me but little Thanks for having put him to ſo much Trouble. Whether or no any body took care of the Corpſe after my being gone, in order to get it buried, is more than I can tell.

Advices from the Caſpian Sea and Aſtracan. A Captain arrived from *Aſtracan* at *Peterſbourg* with the Confirmation, that the *Calmucks*, inhabiting the Coaſt of the *Caſpian* Sea, ſtill continued to oppoſe the Ruſſian Enterprizes, that they had beheaded the Prince *Alexander Bekewitz* in the publick Market-Place, put his Head upon a Pole, and cut off ſixteen hundred Men of the two thouſand Ruſſians lately ſent out againſt them; that conſequently the Deſigns of diſcovering the Gold Sand, raiſing Forts near the *Caſpian* Sea, and eſtabliſhing a Trade with the Aſiatick Provinces, were as yet like to meet with almoſt inſuperable Difficulties. The City of *Aſtracan* had been almoſt deſtroyed by the Fire, and hardly a third Part of the Houſes were
pre-

preserved. The said Captain further related, that the French Ambassador, who had been till then residing at *Ispahan*, was expected at *Astracan* in his Return to *France* by the way of *Poland*.

The Bishop of *Kioff*, who was charged by several Depositions in the last grand Inquisition, was ordered to be brought to *Petersbourg*; but he died on the Way, as it is believed, by a poisoned Draught, which he took to escape a shameful Death. Prince *Dolgoruki*, who had been lately disgraced and exiled, was arrived near *Casan* on the Estate of the rich *Stroganoff*, where he is to end his Days. He departed from *Petersbourg* in a shabby black Coat, with a long Beard, and his own Hair, which had disfigured him to that Degree, that it was hard to know him again. *Alexander Kikin*, who was executed at *Moskow*, had left behind him an unfortunate Widow, once renowned for her Beauty; but now living in a miserable Condition at *Petersbourg* with ordinary People, in a poor smoaky Room, where she had been lying-in, and must certainly have perished for Want, had not Admiral *Apraxin*, with the Connivance of the Court, supplied her with Subsistence and Clothes in her pressing Occasions.

The melancholy Fate of several of the late State-Prisoners.

A Russian Priest at *Petersbourg* took into his Head, to trick credulous People out of their Money, by making them believe a certain Picture of the holy Virgin worked Miracles, and accordingly People had already flocked for some Months to his House. Though he carried on this Trade with great Circumspection in the Night time, and took all imaginable Care in recommending Secrecy to

October 1718. An Impostor punished.

to his simple Customers, yet the Czar got Information of it. The Priest was sent for to Court, and in the mean time his House was searched, and the miraculous Image fetched away, which the Czar caused to be brought to him, in order to see whether it could perform Miracles in his Majesty's Presence. But the Priest, at the Sight of it, threw himself to the Czar's Feet, and confessed the Imposture, for which he was carried to the Fortress, and suffered heavy corporal Punishment, and was afterwards degraded from his Office, in order to be made an Example to his Brethren, not to offend against the wholesome Laws introduced by the Czar against Superstition and false Miracles, and to warn them against keeping up the Spirit of Bigottry among the Russians, who are naturally inclined enough that Way.

Superstitions among the Russians. There is a Picture of the Virgin *Mary* at *Moskow*, the miraculous Power of which, if any Man should have pretended to call into Question but a few Years ago, he would have been torn to pieces by the Populace, who firmly believe that the same was painted by St. *Luke*, and consecrated by the holy Virgin her self with these Words: *My Grace and my Power be with this Picture.* The Introduction of painted Images is by some ascribed to *Basilides*, but some Russians attribute it to St. *Damascenus*. They give the first Place to our Saviour, and the next to his Mother; then follow the Multitude of the heavenly Host, who in their Opinion intercede with God for the Salvation of Mankind. Among those Saints, St. *Nicholas* of *Bari*, and St. *Sergius*, receive the greatest and almost divine Honours.

The Present State of Russia.

Honours. They have peculiar tutelary Saints for every sort of Affliction and Concern. In remote Places where the Czar's Orders are not yet so strictly obeyed, the Superstition of the common People is still so great, that if one sees his Neighbour prosper in matter of Trade, Husbandry, Education of Children, and the like, he borrows the proper Saint of him for an Acknowledgment in Money, and places him in his House, where he does him all imaginable Honour, in order to obtain of him good Success in his Undertakings. Others take their Saint along with them into the Corn-Fields, and if any Stranger coming to the House, happens to ask for the Saint, the good Woman or the Children will tell him, that he is gone to take a Walk in the Fields. The Pilgrimages to the Bones and Relicks of Saints begin to grow very much out of Use in *Russia*, since the *Czar* himself does not much mind that religious Ceremony. His Majesty also endeavours, by his Example, to bring his Russians off from their rigorous Fasts, considering this sort of Devotion has proved pernicious to an infinite Number of his Soldiers, Seamen, and Labourers; and it has often happened, that when the Army incamped in Places where there was Plenty of Cattle, they had their Lent to keep, and when that was over, they found themselves in other Places where there was want of every thing, consequently this Superstition was the Cause that the Troops could not take sufficient Care of themselves, nor make use of those wholesome Provisions, which they had met with before. And though the Russians begin to throw off several of their former Customs in other

other respects, yet they pertinaciously stick to their Lent and Fasts; and it happened at my Time, that several old Russians of Note being under great Indispositions which obliged them to make use of Flesh for their Support, would not venture to break their Fast without having first obtained a Dispensation from the Patriarch at *Constantinople* himself, which they sent for with the utmost Secrecy: For the like Remittances of Money made thither on such Accounts, are rigorously prohibited, the Czar being sensible of what prodigious Sums his Dominions were drained by the Applications made to that See, particularly once on a certain Occasion under the Reign of the Czar *Fedor* or *Theodor*, when the Patriarch of *Constantinople* was sent for to *Moskow* to give Sanction by his Authority to a Regulation made by the Russian Patriarchs for the Laity, to cross themselves for the future only with two Fingers, to which they absolutely refused to submit, but continued to make use of the first three Fingers as symbolizing the Holy Trinity. However they were at last forced to conform, excepted some who merely on that account separated from the Russian Church, and joyned with the *Roskolnicks*, (of whom mention is made above) maintaining their own Method of crossing themselves with such Obstinacy, that no Tortures nor even the Fear of Death are able to make them change it.

pag. 70, & 82.

Precautions against Fire.

A Fire broke out in the German *Slaboda*, but was soon extinguished through the admirable Regulations, the like of which are hardly to be met with any where else in the World. The building of *Petersbourg* having cost

The Present State of Russia.

cost the Czar such immense Sums, and his Heart being so much set on the Preservation of that Place, and yet the greater part of the Houses being at present built only of Wood, his Majesty takes all imaginable Care to prevent Dangers arising from Fire, and with this View has assigned to all his Officers Military and Civil of all Degrees, certain Employments and Functions in case of Fire, to which is annexed a monthly Salary. The Czar not only has taken upon himself such a Function for which he receives his monthly Pay, but even goes to work in Person on such Emergencies, climbing with the most eminent danger of Life on the Tops of the Houses which are on Fire, to encourage his Russians by his Example to follow and assist him. It is owing to these good Regulations that all the Fires that have hitherto happened, how dangerous soever, were always extinguished, before four or five Houses could be burnt down.

On the 9th of *November* * the Anniversary of the Birth of Prince *Peter Petrowitz* was celebrated with extraordinary Rejoycings and Pomp, which ended with an Entertainment in the Evening.

The *Knees Massalsky* † was sentenced to Death for embezling above eighty thousand Rubels of the Salt Revenue; but he died the Day before he was to be executed. His Corpse having been forthwith buried without the Czar's Knowledge, Orders were given for

Novemb. 1718. Anniversary of the young Czarewitz. Male-administration punished.

[* *He was born* November 8. 1715. *See pag.* 108.]
[† *See above p.* 78.]

taking it up again, and hanging it on the Gallows.

Grievances of foreign Merchants.
Notice was given to all the foreign Merchants at *Petersbourg* to pay the Cuſtom for Merchandize imported during the laſt three Years, in German Specie Dalers, which the *Czar* takes but at the rate of fifty *Copecks*, tho' they are intrinſically worth ninety and better. The ſaid Merchants had till then flattered themſelves with Hopes that the Czar would either entirely remit to them the Duties of thoſe three Years, or at leaſt abate great part of them, in Conſideration of the vaſt Expence and Loſſes they had been at in ſettling the Trade at *Petersbourg*; but they found themſelves ſo far miſtaken in their account, that on the contrary the Court exacted the Payment of the ſaid Duties by military Execution without allowing the leaſt Reſpite to the Merchants, ſome of whom were actually put under Arreſt. Thoſe Specie Dalers thus taken in only at the rate of fifty Copecks a piece, being carried to the Mint and recoyned with Allay, and given out again upon the foot of 130, the Profit which thereby accrues to the Czar's Revenue amounts to no leſs than eighty *per Cent*. which method of drawing foreign Silver into *Ruſſia* was then made uſe of, becauſe their own Silver Mines were not yet in a Condition of ſupplying that Defect.

A Board eſtabliſhed for opening Mines.
However at preſent his Czariſh Majeſty begins to reflect what Treaſure may in all Probability be ſtill hidden under Ground in his own Dominions, and as he has newly eſtabliſhed a Board *(Collegium)* for opening and improving Mines, no Pains are ſpared to compaſs

The Present State of Ruſſia.

compaſs the intended End, as may be ſeen from the following Abſtract of a Letter from *Petersbourg*, dated the 12th of *December*, 1720.

"His Czariſh Majeſty continues in his in-
"defatigable Care for the Welfare of his Peo-
"ple and for the Improvement of his Do-
"minions. Among the ſeveral Boards which
"he has eſtabliſhed for the Adminiſtration
"of publick Affairs, he has alſo erected
"a peculiar Board of Commiſſioners for
"Mines, which he has filled with Perſons
"of Merit and Experience who have an ar-
"dent deſire of diſcovering and improving
"thoſe Riches which Nature has hid in the
"Mountains of *Ruſſia*; and the better to
"ſhew his Subjects the way of judging of
"the ſeveral ſorts of Oar, and ſeparating the
"pure Metal from the terreſtrial Parts or
"Droſs, his Majeſty has cauſed divers ſorts
"of Ovens and other Works to be ſet up for
"the ſmelting of Oar, in order to inſtruct
"young Ruſſians in the practical part of that
"Science.

At the ſame time the new Board of Fi- *As alſo a* nances took all poſſible Care to put the Czar's *Board of* Revenue upon a better foot, firſt of all by *Finances.* applying proper Remedies againſt the many Abuſes and Frauds committed in the collecting of them. It had been propoſed to his Czariſh Majeſty to imitate the Maxim and Method of the ancient Romans in appointing three or four Governors or chief Magiſtrates in each Province, independant of each other, free from all Ties either of Relation or Friendſhip, and rather divided by different Intereſts and perſonal Animoſities, that ſo

they

they might controul and check each other in their respective Administration. The Czar seemed to like this Maxim, and accordingly was to nominate those Governors on the first opportunity.

New Orders for peopling Petersbourg.

The Czar being also desirous of seeing *Petersbourg* in a Condition to be a Place worthy of his Residence both as to Regularity and Perfection, issued an Order to all the Nobility of his Dominions that every one of them should send next Spring a good number of his Peasants to *Petersbourg*, for carrying on the several Works there. Remonstrances were thereupon made by some of them, representing that at this rate the increase of *Petersbourg* would prove the ruin of numbers of Villages, but those Objections had no Weight with the Czar.

Decemb. 1718. Two Generals exchanged and rewarded.

In *December* arrived at *Petersbourg* the two Russian Generals *Gollovin* and *Trubetzkoy*, who having been Prisoners in *Sweden*, had been exchanged for the Swedish General Count *Reenschild*. The first was made Knight of the Order of St. *Andrew*, and the second appointed Governor of *Smolensko*, where he lives at present with his Lady and three Daughters, who having been Prisoners with their Father at *Stockholm* from their tender Years, had improved so much by a good Education, that upon their Return into *Russia* they distinguished themselves far above any other Ladies in their own Country.

A merry way of punishing a backward Scholar.

General *Gollovin* has a Brother who is Major-General and a great Favourite of the *Czar*, to whom he had given Proofs of his Fidelity and Bravery on divers Occasions. Some Years ago the *Czar* sent him to *Venice* to learn
Languages

The Present State of Russia.

Languages and the Art of building Ships; but he had such an Aversion to both, that he hardly stirred out of his Chamber during a Stay of four Years in that City. When he returned, and the *Czar* found that he did not know so much as an Italian Word, or how to handle a Tool for Ship-building, his Majesty to punish him, though without any Mark of Disgrace, declared him, for Jest-sake, Surveyor of his Ships by the Titles of *Knees Baas* (Lord Master-builder) and ordered his Picture to be drawn with a Compass and a Ruler in his Hand, surrounded with divers Tools and the different Parcels of Timber, of which a Ship is composed.

On the 20th of *December* several Persons concerned in the late *Czarewitz*'s Flight were publickly executed, there being a Concourse of an immense number of Spectators. They were, *Abraham Fedrowitz Lopuchin*, the late divorced *Czarina*'s own Brother; *James Pustinoi*, the late *Czarewitz*'s Father Confessor; *Ivan Affonassief* his Master of the Horse and Confident; *Dubrofsky* a Gentleman of his Court; and *Voinow* Steward of his Household, together with four more of his Servants. When they were brought to the Place of Execution, their Sentence was read to them, pursuant to which they were all to be broken upon the Wheel, but the same was mitigated with reference to the first five, to be beheaded with the Ax, and as to the other four, their Lives were spared. The Father Confessor suffered first, then *Affonassief*, next *Lopuchin*, and afterwards the two remaining, who were obliged to lay their Heads on the same Block and in the Blood of

The late Czarewitz's Relations and Servants executed.

those who had suffered before them. Prince *Czerbatoff* who had been very intimate with the late *Czarewitz*, was pardoned as to his Life but publickly *knouted*, and had afterwards his Tongue cut out and his Nose cut off. The other three also suffered the *Knout* instead of Death; one of them who was a *Polander* and had served the *Czarewitz* for Interpreter, underwent his Punishment with the utmost Reluctancy and Cowardice, nor could he even be brought to undress till they pulled off his Clothes by Force. But all the *Russians* submitted to their Fate with a great deal of Resignation, and those who suffered Death, expected their Turn in fervent Devotion without saying any thing to the Spectators. The Corpses lay for some Days exposed to publick View in the Market-place with their Heads under their Arms, after which they were twisted upon Wheels.

Several Particulars concerning the Persons that suffered.

And so the Proceedings of the Grand Inquisition occasioned by the late *Czarewitz's* Flight, were closed with this bloody Spectacle. Many Persons of high Rank as well as of lower Degrees had been involved in the unhappy Fate of that Prince. His Uncle *Abraham Lopuchin*, *Alexander Kikin*, the Bishop of *Rostoff*, *Pustinoi* Father Confessor to the late divorced *Czarina*, another *Pustinoi* the *Czarewitz's* own Confessor, the Bishop of *Kioff*, (who is believed to have poisoned himself) and most of his principal Servants lost their Lives by his Fall. His own Mother, his Aunt the Princess *Mary*; the *Czarewitz of Siberia*, Lieutenant-General Prince *Dolgoruki* and his Brother the Senator, the Prince *Louoff*, were disgraced and exiled.

Lieutenant-

The Present State of Russia.

Lieutenant-Colonel *Lopuchin*, the Princess *Trecurva*, the Princess *Galizin*, the Prince *Czerbatoff* were punished with the *Knout* and *Batogs*, and many of the other Accomplices sent to the Gallies. *Abraham Lopuchin* had been thrice married; first to a Daughter of the late Vice-Czar *Romadonofsky*; a second time to the Sister of Prince *Kourakin*; and last to the Daughter of a certain Russian of great Distinction; who shortened her own Life by a violent Death soon after her Husband's Execution, leaving behind her two Children.

An Hour after the abovesaid Execution the Czar went into the Senate who were assembled on this Occasion, and declared to them, that having now justly punished the High-Treason committed against his own Person and Government, he was resolved to call to an Account and bring also to condign Punishment those Bloodsuckers who had enriched themselves with the Spoils of their Country. Accordingly he established a High Court of Justice who were to give Sentence pursuant to the Martial Law which is severer in *Russia* than any where else in the World. Before this Tribunal were brought the Prince *Menzikoff*, the Grand Admiral *Apraxin*, his Brother the Senator, Prince *Dolgoruki* President of the Senate, and several other Persons, to answer to the heavy Charges preferred against them by the *Czar's* Council or *Fiscal*. *Another High Court of Justice established for inquiring into Mismanagements of publick Affairs.*

In the mean time the Privy-Councellor M. *Tolstoy* was honoured with the Knighthood of St. *Andrew* in Consideration of his many Services; Captain *Romanzoff* was made Major of the Guards, and had a Present or Grant *Promotions at the Russian Court.*

Grant of some thousand Boors. Major *Oczacoff* was rewarded with a Brigadier's Commission and a like number of Boors. The *Czar* when he made those Promotions declared that they had deserved those Favours by their faithful Services, and it is to be observed here that the two former were the Persons who brought the *Czarewitz* from *Naples* back to *Russia*, and that the latter commanded at all the Executions which were made at *Moskow* and *Petersbourg* last Year. The Government of *Siberia* was taken from Prince *Gagarin* and restored to the Prince *Czircassi*. The Prince *Galitzin* who was then Governor of *Riga* was by the Czar appointed Governor of *Astracan*, and the Government of *Riga* given to the Prince *Repnin*.

January 1719.
Dr. Areskin dies and is magnificently buried.

Doctor *Areskin* the Czar's first Physician and titulary Councellor, being lately dead at *Alonitz*, his Corpse was sent for to *Petersbourg*, from whence it was carried in Procession with great funeral Pomp on the 4th of of January 1719. to the new Monastery *Alexander Nefsky*, seven Werfts from *Petersbourg*. The Czar himself assisted at the Funeral; in the House where the Corpse lay in State the Minister of the Reformed Church made a funeral Speech in Low-Dutch in Praise of the deceased: His Majesty hereupon gave some Marks of the Esteem he had had for the deceased, and at the same time shewed particular Favour towards his Relation Sir *Harry Stirling*, who was come to *Russia* under the Czar's Protection to see the Doctor's last Will put in Execution. The Corpse was carried on the Shoulders of the Physicians and the principal Surgeons who wore long
Mourning

Mourning Cloaks, and was followed by a numerous Proceſſion and two hundred Flambeaux, as far as the Bridge of the *German Slaboda*. From thence the Funeral proceeded upon Sledges to the aforeſaid Monaſtery, Soldiers being ranged on both Sides of the Way leading from the Gate to the Chapel, with lighted Flambeaux in their Hands. The Czar himſelf followed the Corpſe carrying a burning Taper in his Hand according to the Ruſſian Cuſtom, as far as the Vault, which was built between two others in which the Corpſes of the late Princeſs *Natalia*, and a certain Dutch Rear-Admiral were depoſited. All the Company among whom were both the Lutheran and the Reformed Miniſters, were preſented with Pieces of Crape and a golden Mourning Ring on which was ingraven the Name of the Deceaſed and the Day of his Death, and afterwards they were all ſplendidly entertained. The Deceaſed by his laſt Will had bequeathed to his Mother, Brothers and Siſters all his ready Money; to the Czar's eldeſt Princeſs his Eſtate in Land and his Boors; to the Hoſpital at *Edinburg* the Money ariſing from his Moveables that were to be ſold. The Czar made a Preſent of his Library to Dr. *Blumentroſt* the younger, who is now firſt Phyſician to his Majeſty, as the elder is to the Czarina.

The beginning of January Prince *Menzikoff* was ſummoned before the High Court of Juſtice, to hear the Sentence read which had been drawn up againſt him, importing, that whereas he was found guilty of having embezled the Treaſury committed to his Truſt, he ſhould deliver up his Sword in Expectation

The Reſult of the Enquiry into Male-adminiſtration.

tion of further Punishment. He submitted to the Sentence and went to his own House to be there under Confinement. At his coming out of the Court he met the President of the Senate Prince *Dolgoruki*, who had been summoned to the same End: But this old Knees knew to plead his own Cause with so much Eloquence that the Judges thought fit to make Report to the Czar before they proceeded to give Sentence. General-Admiral *Apraxin* went in next, and was acquainted with the following Resolution, that whereas his Czarish Majesty had been informed how he had managed the publick Treasure, Sentence was given against him, that he had forfeited all his Estate and Dignities, and that he was likewise to remain under Confinement in his own House till further Orders. Whereupon he delivered his Sword and withdrew. After such a severe Sentence nothing less could be expected than that Offenders of so high a Rank would be at least turned out of all their Employments. But it happened otherwise to every Body's surprize; for the Czar was prevailed upon by the Remembrance of their former Merits and faithful Services, as also by repeated Intercessions made in their behalf, that he restored the Prince and the Admiral to his Favour, after they had thrown themselves at his Feet, on Condition however of paying severe Fines.

Rear-Admiral Paddon's Death and Funeral.

Mr. *Paddon*, an Englishman, and Rear-Admiral in the Czar's Service, died suddenly, and was most honourably interred, the Czar, all the foreign Ministers, all the Sea-Officers, &c. attending the Funeral. The Esteem which the Czar had had for this Gentleman,

tleman, may be collected among other things from this Circumstance, that his Majesty followed his Corpse a-foot from the House where it had lain in State to the new Church on the other Side of the River *Neva*, which lies a good League off. That new Church was consecrated on the Anniversary of the Battel of *Pultava*, and dedicated to St. *Samson*, which Saint is in great Repute in the Russian Legends on account of his Affection and Hospitality towards Strangers, for which Reason the said Church has been assigned for a Burying-place to the Foreigners. The Deceased's Widow received a Gratification of one thousand Rubles to defray the Expences of the Funeral, and was allowed for her Subsistence half her late Husband's Salary during Life.

The Son of the late unfortunate Hospodar of *Walachia Cantacuzeno*, strangled at *Constantinople*, having made his Escape with his Mother out of *Turkey*, retired to *Russia* and put himself under the Czar's Protection who gave him an Officer's Place in the *Preobrazinsky* Guards. He was greatly assisted in his Occasions by his Uncle *Demetrio Cantimir*, late Hospodar of *Moldavia*, of whom I have made mention above, to which I shall here add a few more Particulars relating to his Person. In the Year 1712. when the Czar made the Expedition on the River *Pruth*, he being in hopes the same would be more successful than it proved in the Event, offered *Moldavia* to the Czar, who has since allowed him a yearly Pension of twenty thousand Rubels, besides the Estates in *Russia* and *Ukraina* which he gave him as a Present. He

of the Walachian Prince Cantacuzeno and his Uncle Cantimir, Hospodar of Moldavia.

styles

styles himself Hereditary Prince of *Moldavia*, and claims the Title of *Most Serene Highness*. The *Czar* has a great Regard for him, as being persuaded that if in the abovesaid Expedition he had taken the Hospodar's Advice (who was bred at the *Ottoman* Court, and is thoroughly acquainted with their Politicks) he should not have missed the Conquest of *Moldavia* and *Valachia*. Besides this, he is a Gentleman of great Learning, versed in many Languages, and a Member of the Society of Sciences at *Berlin*. He has composed a Turkish History in Greek and Latin, containing many secret State-Maxims of the *Ottoman* Porte, which he has dedicated *Manibus Leopoldinis*, to the Memory of the late Emperor *Leopold*, in Token of his being a Well-wisher to the Roman or Western Empire. That History is still in Manuscript, and expects a Publisher *.

Russian Ambassador returns from Persia.   *Artemon Wolinsky* who had been sent Ambassador to *Persia*, returned to *Petersbourg*; all that could be learnt concerning his Embassy was that he had had six times Audience of the King of *Persia*, and was dismissed with all possible Marks of Honour; but as to the Success of his Negociation, particularly as to his Proposals concerning Commerce, nothing could be known.

Mineral-Waters discovered in Astracan.   Another Mineral Spring was discovered in the Kingdom of *Astracan*, and Dr. *Schauber* who had been sent to enquire into the nature of it, returned to *Petersbourg* by the Way of *Moskow*.

[* *It is at present translating into the Russian Language, and to be printed by the Czar's Orders.*]

The Present State of Russia. 251

The beginning of February the Czar went to the Mineral Waters of *Alonitz*, accompanied by the Czarina and the Dutchess Dowager of *Courland*. His Czarish Majesty being resolved to send an Ambassy to *China*, M. *Ismailof*, Major of the Guards, was nominated to go thither, and M. *Lange* who had already once performed that long Journey, as has been mentioned above, received Orders to accompany him thither. The Presents which they were to carry with them to *China*, consisted for the greater part of curious Turners Work of the Czar's own making, his Majesty being a great Master in that Art. M. *Ismailof* is a Cousin of the Gentleman of the same Name, who in the Year 1701. was sent to the Court of *Prussia* to congratulate the King on his Coronation, from whence he went to the *Danish* Court.

February 1719. The Court at Alonitz.

According to the freshest Advices from the Missionaries in *China*, that Nation had revolted against their Emperor, on account of new Imposts which had clogged their Commerce. A Latin Letter written by a Jesuit from *Ispahan* to *Petersbourg*, which was communicated to me, gave an Account that *Persia* laboured under the like Difficulties, after the Death of the *Can of Scamachi*; the Arabians being then in War against *Persia*, and the Inhabitants suffering great Misery for want of Trade and Money, the King of *Persia* began to think himself in great Danger of losing his Crown. The Poverty of that Kingdom was such, that he *Shach* had ordered the Tombs of wealthy People to be broke open and the Corpses to be robbed of their Jewels and other precious Ornaments. The Silk Trade,

Advices from China and Persia.

Trade, which formerly had been in the most flourishing Condition, was run to such a decay, that last Year they had few or none of their rich Stuffs at all to send to *Russia*.

Scarcity of Money and Decay of Trade in Russia.
Money was no less scarce in *Russia*; the Merchants at *Archangel*, *Moskow* and *Petersbourg* could hardly find any though at 15 *per Cent*. Interest and upon sufficient Security. This was the Effect of Monopolies and new Manufactures, which were so far from answering the intended Design, that they had caused last Year only on the Duties of the Port of *Riga* a Deficiency of eighty thousand Rubels. The new coined Rubels were essayed by Order of the Board of Trade, and found defective both as to Allay and Weight, which obliged them to represent to the Czar the great Prejudice that must thereby accrue to the Publick. The Czar was not unacquainted with the Baseness of the new Coin, but as the Mines were not near yet in a condition of yielding Gold and Silver enough, there was no other Method for raising the immense Sums that were required every Day. Another thing which proved also very destructive to Trade, was the lowering of foreign Ducats, which are at best taken at 190 *Copecks*, whereas the *Russian* Ducats go for full, though their intrinsical Value is much less by reason of the great Allay mixed with the Gold.

New Projects.
The Czar caused divers Models to be made of the new Fortifications and Repairs of *Slutelbourg*, *Narva*, *Revel*, *Pernaw*, &c. the better to judge of the Strength of those Works. At the same time the German Architect *Matrenove* (who is since dead) finished the Model

The Present State of Russia.

del of the Observatory to be built on *Wassily-Ostroff,* the great Island in the River *Neva* at *Petersbourg:* In the same Building are to be lodged the Library, the Cabinet of natural and Anomatical Curiosities, and the Globe of *Gottorp.*

The Generals Czeremetoff and Lewenhaupt die. The Russian Field-Marshal-General *Czeremetoff* died in *Poland,* as also the Swedish General *Lewenhaupt,* in his Captivity at *Moskow,* so that the latter was frustrated in his Wish, to out-live the Issue of the Northern War.

A Missionary arrives from Astracan; his Account of the State of the Christian Religion in Persia. A Capuchin Missionary, by Birth an *Italian,* above sixty Years of Age, was then at *Moskow,* where he had already waited some Weeks for the Czar's arrival there, being in Hopes of obtaining Leave to build a Church at *Astracan* for the Roman Catholick Congregation, which is reported to consist already of ninety Families, who are partly *Austrian* Gardeners and *Bavarian* Soldiers who were taken Prisoners in the Swedish Service. This Capuchin had been formerly a long time in *Persia,* and very often on the Brink of Death: He was said to be a Man of Learning and well skilled in Physick, by which Art chiefly it is that those Friars insinuate themselves in *Persia*; they are frequently sent for to sick Children in order to cure them, which opportunity they take to baptize them; they keep a Book in which they register the Names of those Children, of whom they report that after their Recovery they preserve a grateful Remembrance towards their Benefactors. For instance of which the said Missionary related, that being once in Punishment for his having made a secret

Convert

Convert so severely beaten on the Soles of his Feet that he had almost died of it, a certain Mahometan, (whose Name stood in the foresaid Register, though it was unknown to himself, and that he constantly professed Mahometanism) not only interceded in the Friar's behalf, but also secretly contributed to a Fine the latter was to pay amounting to five thousand *Seckines* or Venetian Ducats, and from that time maintained a strict Friendship with the Christians out of an hidden Impulse of his Conscience, as the Friar would have it. The secret Professors of Christianity among the *Persians* meet once a Year at least at some House where the Friars are, and perform their Devotion with the utmost Privacy, and though at their Baptism they engage to live only with one Woman in Wedlock, yet to save outward Appearances they are obliged to have more than one, and to observe all the Ceremonies of the Mahometan Religion. There have been great Disputes between the Jesuits and the other Ecclesiastical Orders, whether those People might be connived at in doing so, which Differences have put the Christian Religion in those Parts in great Danger. The Grand Treasurer of the Kingdom of *Persia* who died two Years ago, is said to have been one of those secret Converts. It is on the account of such Proselytes the Missionaries often endure the most violent Persecution to the great hazard of their Lives, in case one or other of them chances to disclose his new Faith; for the *Georgians* and others who are born Christians have nothing to fear in *Persia* on account of their external Worship,
provided

The Present State of Russia. 255

provided they pay their Taxes and forbear talking againſt the Mahometan Religion.

After the Death of the King of *Sweden*, and the breaking off of the Negociations in *Aland*, extroardinary Preparations were made in *Ruſſia* for the enſuing Campaign, for the better forwarding of which two *Pricaſes* or Boards were eſtabliſhed, which were to amaſs a great Sum of Ducats to be taken in at the rate of 195 *Copecks* a piece. All the Corn in the Store-houſes was ſeized for the Czar's Uſe, and a Proclamation was publiſhed ordering all ſorts of Perſons to give in an account of the Salt in their Poſſeſſion, to be delivered to the Czar for a ſettled Price, on Penalty of Confiſcation of the Salt concealed, and being rigorouſly puniſhed. Some Ruſſian Merchants received Orders to furniſh Sheep-skins to the value of ſeven thouſand Rubels, to be delivered into the Parchment Manufacture for making Cartridges and Charges, it being believed that the Gunpowder preſerved itſelf better in Parchment than in Tin or Paſte-board. The Czar had taken the Reſolution to make the enſuing Summer a powerful Deſcent in *Sweden* with twenty ſix thouſand Men, as the only Means to force that Crown to a ſpeedy and reaſonable Peace. During thoſe Preparations the Princeſs *Ulrica* who had been elected Queen, notified in Form to his Czariſh Majeſty by a Letter the Death of the late King, declaring at the ſame time that ſhe was willing to reſtore the former Friendſhip and good Neighbourhood between the two Nations, and that to this End ſhe would ſpeedily ſend her

Warlike Preparations againſt Sweden.

Councellor

March 1719.

The Death and honourable burying of an old English Servant.

Councellor and Minister M. *Lilienstet* to the Isle of *Aland* in order to resume the Negociations of Peace.

Mr. *Cravat*, an Englishman, who had served the Russian Court seventy Years as Translator, and had already long ago received a Pension as a Gratuity in Consideration of his decrepit Age, died ninety Years old, and was buried the 23^d of March, which Funeral the Czar honoured likewise with his own Presence, and the Attendance of his whole Court.

A Court Jester to be King of the Samoieds.

The titular Count and Mock-Master of the Ceremonies, *La Costa*, a Portugueze, well versed in several Languages, had by his Humours and Jests so well diverted the Court in their late Journey to the mineral Waters of *Alonitz*, that the Czar in Regard of his uncommon Capacity gave him Hopes of being declared King of *Samoiedia*, a Post of Honour which is always filled by a Court Jester. His Coronation was to be solemnly performed as soon as four and twenty Raindeer and so many Samoieds sent for from that Country, should be arrived.

The War with Sweden renewed, and justified by a Manifesto.

The Russian Forces were at that time on their March from all parts where they had been in Winter-Quarters. They were to rendezvous one part near *Petersbourg*, and the other near *Reval*, to be transported to *Finland* to reinforce the Army there, which this Campaign was to consist of fifty thousand Men, and was to act against *Sweden*. At the same time a Treatise written by way of *Manifesto* was published in Russian, being printed at *Petersbourg*, which was drawn up by one of the best Pens

The Present State of Ruſſia.

Pens in *Ruſſia* [*], and contained a ſpecial Account of the principal Tranſactions during the preſent Northern War, the chief Intent of which was to prove that the Countries the Czar had conquered of *Sweden* during that War, *Finland* only excepted, had been wreſted from *Ruſſia*, to which they had formerly belonged. A Deduction or State of the Caſe (mentioned above) drawn up in Latin by a learned Swediſh Officer in *Siberia* relating to the Poſſeſſion of *Carelia* and *Ingria*, had given occaſion to the Ruſſian *Manifeſto* or Refutation of the Swediſh Aſſertions. Both thoſe Writings are annexed to this Work. *See p.* 104.

M. *Schafiroff* Secretary of the Privy-Council, Brother to the Vice-Chancellor, when he was rummaging among the old Records and Papers of the Archives, found a Letter of Confederacy written by the Emperor *Maximilian* to the Czar *Baſilius*, and as the former therein gives to the latter the Title of Emperor, his Czariſh Majeſty ordered the Original to be ſhewn to every Body [†], and a Copy *An old Letter found relating to the Title of Emperor of Ruſſia.*

[* *The Vice-Chancellor Baron* Schafiroff.]
[† About the ſame time, as alſo but lately upon the Czar's aſſuming the Title of Emperor, this Piece was inſerted in the *Dutch* and other News Papers. In *London* it was publiſhed in the *Poſt-Boy*, *July* 17. 1718, with this Introduction.

When the old Records in the Chancery of Muſcovy, *relating to the Ambaſſadors of that Empire, were ſearched and regiſtred, they found in them an original Letter from his Imperial Majeſty the Emperor* Maximilian, *ſigned with his own Hand, with the Golden Bull or Signet Manual, which his Imperial Majeſty had writ to the Czar and Great Prince of all* Ruſſia Baſili Ivanowitz, *Father to* John Baſilides *of glorious Memory, which Letter was writ in the old German Tongue and was*

a Copy of it was given to me in *High-Dutch*, which is to this Effect:

"According to the Will of God, and our Love, We, *Maximilian*, by the Grace of God, elected Roman Emperor, always Augmenter of the Empire, King of *Hungary, Dalmatia, Croatia*, &c. Archduke of *Austria*, Duke of *Burgundy, Britany, Lorrain, Brabant, Stiria, Carinthia, Carniola, Limbourg, Luxembourg*, and *Gueldres*; Count of *Flanders, Habspurg, Tyrol, Pfiert, Kybourg, Artois*, and *Burgundy*; Count Palatine of *Haynault, Holland, Zeland, Namur*, and *Zutphen*; Marquess of the Roman Empire and of *Burgau*, Landgrave of *Alsatia*, Lord of *Friesland*, the *Wendish Mark, Portenau, Salins*, and *Malines*, &c. &c. &c. We have conceived Love, and entered into everlasting Alliance and brotherly Friendship with our Brother, the Great Lord *Basili*, by the Grace of God, Emperor and Dominator of all the *Russias*, and Grand-Prince of *Wolodimir, Moskow, Novogorod, Pleskow, Tweer, Jugoria, Permia, Wiatkie*, and *Bulgaria*, &c. Dominator and Grand-Prince

---

was sent in the Year 1514, *in which the Title of all* Russia *was given to the abovementioned Czar* Basili Iwanowitz. *This now being a curious Piece, will serve to maintain without Contestation the said Title to the Monarchy of all* Russia, *which high Title was given them many Years past, and ought to be valued so much the more, because it was writ by an Emperor, who by his Rank, was one of the first Monarchs in the World. His Czarish Majesty has ordered the said Letter in the original* German *Tongue, Word for Word, as also the Translation in the* Russian *Language, to be copied and printed here in* St. Petersbourg, *the tenth of May* 1718.]

"of

The Present State of Russia.

"of *Novogorod* of the Low Country, and of *Czernichow, Refan, Wolosk, Rzeva, Biela, Roſtow, Jareſlaw, Belozero, Udoria, Obdoria,* and *Condeſch,* &c. &c. We shall be with him in Fraternity, Fealty, and Friendship, as long as we live, and our Children with your Children in Friendship, and in Fraternity and Fealty as long as it pleases God. And he that becomes a Friend to Us, *Maximilian,* King of the *Romans* and of *Hungary,* and to our Imperial Majesty, he shall also be a Friend to you, Great Lord, *Baſili,* by the Grace of God, Emperor and Dominator of all the *Ruſſias,* and Grand-Prince, and whosoever is our Enemy shall also be your Enemy; and he that becomes a Friend to You, Great Lord *Baſili,* by the Grace of God, Emperor and Dominator of all the *Ruſſias,* and Grand-Prince, he shall also be our Friend, and whosoever is your Enemy shall also be our Enemy; and if you our Brother, Great Lord, *Baſili,* by the Grace of God, Emperor and Dominator of all the *Ruſſias,* and Grand-Prince, should want our Assistance against your Enemies, then will we assist you in Truth according to this our Letter, as God shall help us; and when we shall want your Help against our Enemies, then shall you likewise help us in Truth according to this our Letter, as God shall help you. And since your and our Enemy, *Sigiſmund,* King of *Poland,* and Grand-Prince of *Lithuania,* has done Us and You great Injustice, and stands against the Teutonick Order, and holds unjustly some Castles in *Pruſſia,* and intends to ruin the

"Laws

"Laws of the Teutonick Order in the Country of the Prussians, and to oppress them, in like manner unjustly holds of your Dominions the Castle of *Kiow*, with some other of you Russian Castles, we shall be united against this our Enemy, *Sigismund*, King of *Poland*, and Grand-Prince of *Lithuania*, and do our Business with our Enemy as far as God helps us, &c. We, *Maximilian*, King of the *Romans* and of *Hungary*, and our Imperial Majesty shall now begin on our Side to do our Business with *Sigismund*, King of *Poland*, and Grand-Prince of *Lithuania*, as far as God helps us, and still do our Business with him in Truth, without Fraud, according to this our Letter to you, to recover the Castles of the Teutonick Order in *Prussia* which he unjustly keeps under him. And since you Great Lord *Basili*, by the Grace of God, Emperor and Dominator of all the *Russias* and Grand-Prince have begun to do your Business with your Enemy the King of *Poland*, and Grand-Prince of *Lithuania*, you shall also do your Business with him still as far as God helps you, in order to recover your paternal Inheritance, and before either of us shall march against our Enemy, we shall send to each other, and we shall do our Business jointly against our Enemy. When we *Maximilian* King of the *Romans* and of *Hungary*, and our Imperial Majesty, shall march against the King of *Poland* and Grand-Prince of *Lithuania*, or send our Princes and Captains into his Country, then we shall let you know it, upon which your self also
"shall

"shall march against him, or send your
"Princes and Captains with your Forces in-
"to his Country, and you shall do the Bu-
"siness in conjunction with us, and if you,
"our Brother, Great Lord *Basili*, by the
"Grace of God, Emperor and Dominator
"of all the *Russias* and Grand-Prince shall
"march against our Enemy, or send your
"Princes and Captains, and you then let us
"know it, then shall we in Truth, and ac-
"cording to this our Letter, be joined with
"you against our Enemy, or ourself shall
"march against him, or send our Princes
"and Captains with our Forces into his
"Country. And when by reason of the
"great Way we could not so soon let you,
"our Brother, know, and we should march
"against the King of *Poland* and Grand-
"Prince of *Lithuania*, or send our Princes
"and Captains with Forces into his Coun-
"try, and you, our Brother, come to know
"it, then you, our Brother, Great Lord *Ba-
"sili* by the Grace of God Emperor and
"Dominator of all the *Russias* and Grand-
"Prince shall likewise be united with us a-
"gainst him, your self march against him,
"or send your Princes and Captains with
"Forces into his Country. In case you, our
"Brother, Great Lord, Emperor and Domi-
"nator of all the *Russias* and Grand-Prince
"should march against him, or send your
"Princes and Captains into his Country, and
"in case neither we nor you should know it
"by reason of the great way, and we shall
"come to know to it, we shall likewise our
"self march against him, or send our Princes
"and Captains with Forces into his Coun-
"try,

"try, and if God grants us his Mercy, and
"if God grants us his Affiftance againft our
"Enemy the King of *Poland* and Grand-
"Prince of *Lithuania,* and we recover our
"Caftles, which our Caftles he now unjuft-
"ly holds under him, then fhall we ftill be
"united with you againft our Enemy, or
"any other that becomes Lord of the Coun-
"try of *Poland* and the Grand-Principality
"of *Lithuania,* and againft all our Enemies.
"And in cafe the Bufinefs with our Enemy
"fhould not go according to our Opinion,
"then fhall we ftill be united with you a-
"gainft him, or any other that becomes Lord
"of the Country of *Poland* and the Grand-
"Principality of *Lithuania,* and againft all our
"Enemies for all our Life-time. The way
"through your Country is free to our Mef-
"fengers and Merchants without any hinde-
"rance, in like manner the way through
"our Countries is free to your Meffengers
"and Merchants without any hinderance,
"and upon all thefe Terms above-mention-
"ed which are contained in this Letter. We
"*Maximilian* by the Grace of God King of
"the *Romans,* and of *Hungary,* and our Im-
"perial Majefty, of *Dalmatia* and *Croatia,*
"&c. &c. Archduke of *Auftria,* Duke of
"*Burgundy, Britany, Lorrain, Brabant, Sti-*
"*ria, Carinthia, Carniola, Limbourg, Lux-*
"*embourg,* and *Guelders,* Count of *Flanders,*
"*Habfpurg, Tyrol, Pfiert, Kybourg, Artois,*
"and *Burgundy,* Count Palatine of *Haynault,*
"*Holland, Zeland, Namur,* and *Zutphen,*
"Marquis of the Roman Empire and *Bur-*
"*gau,* Landgrave of *Alfatia,* Lord of *Frife-*
"*land,* the *Wendifh Mark, Portenau, Salins,*
"and

" and *Malines*, &c. &c. to you, our Bro-
" ther, Great Lord *Basili*, by the Grace of
" God Emperor and Dominator of all the
" *Russias* and Grand-Prince of *Wolodimir*,
" *Moskow, Novogorod, Pleskow, Tweer, Ju-*
" *goria, Permia, Wiatkie,* and *Bulgaria*, Do-
" minator and Grand-Prince of *Novogorod* of
" the Low-Country, and of *Czernichow, Re-*
" *san, Wolosk, Rzeva, Biela, Rostow, Jare-*
" *slaw, Belozero, Udoria, Obdoria,* and *Con-*
" *desch*, &c. to greater Confirmation we
" have kissed the Cross, and we have affixed
" our Seal to this our authentick Letter.
" Given in our City *Gemünde* * the fourth
" Day of the Month of *August* after our
" Lord's Nativity in the one thousand five
" hundred and fourteenth Year, of our Ro-
" man Reign the twenty ninth, of the Hun-
" garian the twenty fifth.

MAXIMILIAN.

By His Imperial Majesty's Order,

P. *Sernhern* †.

The first of *April* was this Year celebrated to the Czar's great Diversion, who was pleased to make that Opportunity serve to collect a Present of some hundreds of Rubels, for the strong *Samson*, as he was called, newly arrived from *Germany*. His Majesty had gi-

April 1719. *April-Mirth.*

[* *This Place in all other Copies is called* Brundenau, *but it will be hard to find a City of that name in all the Austrian Dominions.* Gemünde *is situate in* Upper Austria *on the River* Traun *near a Lake called* Traun-See.]

[† *Other Copies have* Serkern.]

ven Orders to all Persons of Distinction, the Czarina Dowager and her Princesses not excepted, to appear at the Play-house to see the famous *Samson* perform the Feats of his prodigious Strength. Pit and Boxes were soon filled, so that many were obliged to go back for want of room. The Expectation of the Spectators being raised by long Preparations made on the Stage, they already grew impatient to see the Shew begin, when a Machine was let down from the Clouds with this Inscription in Capital Letters: *APRIL.* The Harlequin appeared afterwards, and having in a merry Complement ridiculed the Company for being thus come on an *April* Errand, thanked them for the Present, and invited them to come again next Day for better Diversion. The Year before the Czar had pleased himself with another sort of Humour on the like Occasion. He had ordered an old House to be set on Fire on the first of *April*, in the Night-time, in some remote part of the Town, and the Drums to be beaten. He went to the Place himself very much delighted to see his Soldiers running full speed in great Numbers to extinguish the Flames, after which he caused some Barrels of Beer and Brandy to be given among them to reward them for their Pains.

Of a Man of extraordinary Strength. The Proofs the said *Samson* gave of his surprizing Strength, were by many Russians looked upon as the Effects of Witchcraft; even the Bishops themselves were possessed with that Notion, and seemed persuaded, that it would be impossible for that Sorcerer to lift up a Bench with his Teeth as he used to do, if a Russian Clerk should sit down upon it

with

with the Book of the Gospels. The Czar moved by this Simplicity, made some of the principal Clergy come upon the Stage, to convince them that there was nothing supernatural in *Samson*'s Performances. The Vice-Czar of *Moskow Romadonofsky* helped the Czar to lift up an Anvil and lay it on *Samson*'s Breast, who lay suspended in the Air only supported under his Head and Feet, and in this Posture large Pieces of Iron were broken with Hammers upon the Anvil standing on his Breast. *Samson* took also a Stick between his Teeth, which the Czar endeavoured with both Hands to pull out, but in vain, and even without being able to make *Samson* move from his Place. Then he took the same Stick across his Mouth, and, as I believe with the design to complement the Czar on his own natural Strength, he bid two strong Fellows pull on both Ends, but they both together did not shew near so much Force as the Czar, on the contrary *Samson* led them about the Stage like weak Children. Upon my discoursing with his Czarish Majesty on the Cause of these Performances, he said he was convinced the real Strength of the Man had more share in the effecting of them, than Art.

The young Prince *Peter Petrowitz*, who had been declared presumptive Heir to the Crown, died on the 6th of *May*, which unexpected Death occasioned great Affliction and Grief at Court. Though he was but about four Weeks younger than the young Grand-Prince the late Czarewitz's Son, and that all imaginable care was taken of his Health and Education, yet he always remained

May 1719. *The Death and Funeral of the young Czarewitz.*

mained weakly and puny, and never equalled the other in that Vivacity and Forwardnefs he fhewed in fpeaking, walking, and even performing already his Exercifes. He was buried on the 8th following with great Solemnity. The Proceffion began with a general Difcharge of the Artillery: Firft marched the Officers of the Grenadier-Guards with their Company confifting of 240 Men with their Arms reverfed; the fuperior Officers were all dreffed in black, with Crapes in their Hats and on their Swords; the Subalterns and Soldiers had only Crapes on their Headpieces: Then followed fifty Men of the *Preobrazinsky* Guards with Flambeaux, and after them went the Singers and the Clergy chanting by turns their ufual Service. The Coffin as well as the Bier were covered with black Velvet edged with Gold-lace, the Regalia lying on the Top. The Czar was attended by the chief Nobility of his Court in long Mourning-Cloaks, who were followed by his Minifters of State and of thofe of foreign Powers, as alfo all Military and Civil Officers in great numbers, likewife in long Mourning-Cloaks. The Proceffion went on foot to the River *Neva*, where the Corpfe was put into the Mourning-Sloop attended by the chief Mourners; the reft of the Company were carried in feveral other Sloops to the Monaftery of *Alexander Nefsky*, where Obfequies being performed according to the Rites of the Ruffian Church, and the Corpfe depofited, the Czar returned in the Mourning-Sloop, and ftreight repaired to the Czarina who was almoft comfortlefs at the Lofs of her only Son, but the Czar fhewed a great

deal

deal of Resignation and Constancy under this Affliction.

This mournful Incident prevented the launching of a new Man of War of ninety Guns, which was to be on the said 8th of *May*, and for which all things were prepared, as also the celebrating of the Wedding of one St. *Jean*, a Giant-like Frenchman, whom the Czar had brought with him from *Paris*, the Bride being an exceeding tall *Finlandish* Woman; but those Diversions were put off till another time by reason of the Mourning. *A Giant Couple to be married.*

Intimation was made to the Foreigners who had taken Employments in the Offices or Boards newly established by the Czar, speedily to resolve and declare whether or no they would ingage in the Czar's Service for Life. Many of them were unwilling to serve upon those Terms, but insisted on their Capitulations, by Virtue of which they were at Liberty to leave the Service after a certain Time. But as the greater part are *Swedish* Subjects and Prisoners, they made no Exception, considering that some of them were apprehensive of a troublesome Enquiry at home into their respective Behaviour, and that others had no Probability of changing for the better. *Foreigners obliged to engage in the Czar's Service for Life.*

Notification was made to the several Jesuits, who upon the Recommendation of the Imperial Court, had been admitted and lived some Years at *Petersbourg*, *Moskow*, and *Archangel*, to depart the Czar's Dominions on account of the Differences depending between the Imperial and Russian Courts: At *Petersbourg* Father *Engel* and his Brethren were e- *The Jesuits ordered to depart the Czar's Dominions.*

ven put under a Guard, and the Councellor of the Chancery *Stepanoff* was fent to feize their Papers in order to be examined. The Czar's Order relating to this Affair was affixed at the Door of the Roman Catholick Church, to this Effect:

" His Czarifh Majefty having always main-
" tained good Friendfhip with the Imperial
" Court, till the Imperial Refident *Pleyer*
" began a dangerous Correfpondence with
" the Ruffian Subjects, his Majefty found it
" neceffary to defire he might be recalled;
" which being done accordingly, the faid
" Refident was allowed to ftay four Weeks
" and above at *Petersbourg*, and to continue
" his Correfpondence, whereas on the con-
" trary the Ruffian Refident at *Vienna Wef-*
" *felofsky* and the Agent at *Breflaw* were ob-
" liged inftantly to retire out of the Empe-
" ror's Dominions. Which unfriendly Be-
" haviour of the Imperial Court has induced
" his Czarifh Majefty to ufe Reprifals, and
" therefore all Jefuits are earneftly command-
" ed by Virtue of thefe Letters Patents to
" quit the Ruffian Dominions within four
" Days after having Notice given them, the
" World being fufficiently apprized of their
" dangerous Machinations, and how com-
" mon it is for them to meddle with poli-
" tick Affairs.

However the Roman Catholick Congregation at *Petersbourg* obtained Leave to fend for Friars of other Orders, provided they claimed no Protection from the Imperial Court, and came from Provinces free from any Sufpicion. The Italian Capuchin who for fome time had been endeavouring to obtain

tain Leave to build a Church and a Convent at *Aſtracan*, met with greater Difficulties on the part of the Ruſſian Clergy, than he had at firſt imagined.

Admiral-General *Apraxin* received his Orders and Inſtructions from the Czar concerning the intended Tranſport of the whole Army to *Finland*. At firſt were to be ſhipped off twenty thouſand Foot and ſix thouſand Dragoons, in twenty eight Ships of the Line, 180 Gallies, and 300 flat-bottomed Veſſels. The Admiral had the command in Chief of the landing on the Swediſh Coaſt, and kept the ſame on Shore during the whole Campaign. *The Forces deſigned for a Deſcent in Sweden.*

Major-General *Henning* ſet out on a Journey to *Germany*, *France*, and *Italy*, in which Countries he was to take Draughts of all ſorts of curious and uſeful Machines, and to get Models of them made. The Czar defrayed the Expences of this Journey, which was to laſt two Years, and the Major-General was among other Things to take an exact View of the foreign Mines and Works, and to engage in the Czar's Service as many of the Workmen as poſſible. *An Officer ſent abroad for making Improvements in Arts.*

On the 30th of *May* (11. *June*, N. S.) the Anniverſary of the Czar's Birth-day was celebrated with the uſual Solemnities, the Court being out of Mourning for that Day, the Joy of which was conſiderably heightened, during Dinner, upon the arrival of a Captain-Lieutenant who came Expreſs from *Reval* with Advice that Captain *Chapuzeau* had taken and brought into the Harbour three Swediſh Privateers, one of 52, another of 24, and a third of 12 Guns. The Courier who carried *Rejoycing on the Anniverſary of the Czar's Birth-day.*

carried this welcome News, was upon the Recommendation of the Czar, as Vice-Admiral, declared Captain by the Vice-Czar of *Moskow*. On this Occasion the Vice-Chancellor Baron *Schafiroff* was honoured with the Order of Knighthood of St. *Andrew*, which proved no small Mortification to those Persons who had made it their Business for a good while to undermine that Minister's Credit with the Czar. Towards Evening the Czar with the whole Court repaired to the Admiralty, where a new Man of War of sixty six Guns was launched, on board of which the Company drank very hard afterwards.

June 1719. The Czar prepares to put to Sea. On the 2^d of *June* the Czar set out for *Peterhoff* in order to enter on the intended Expedition against *Sweden*, and was followed in the Afternoon by thirty Gallies which had near five thousand Men on board, and were saluted in their Passage with the Discharge of the Artillery, and other usual Marks of Honour at Sea.

A Calmukish Ambassador, and his strange Behaviour. In *June* arrived at *Petersbourg* the Ambassador of *Bustucan*, a *Calmuckish* Prince, who was at War with his own Father. His Credential Letters were directed to the Grand Admiral *Apraxin*, because his Brother had been formerly Governor of *Casan* and *Astracan*. The Audience he had of the Admiral was so comical, that I cannot omit mentioning several Particulars. After having made his Complement by word of Mouth, he delivered to the Admiral his Present, consisting in all but of a Sugar-loaf and a Piece of Silk; then he took out of his Pocket a Letter all rumpled, which was read and explained by the Interpreter: The beginning of it ran thus:

thus: *If thou art well in Health, I am; If I am well in Health, thou art:* The reft was made up of nothing elfe but fuch extravagant Stuff. The Lines were written not horizontally, but perpendicularly from Top to Bottom, and at the End of the Letter was feen the Impreffion of a Seal of red Colour. This Ceremony being over, the Admiral inftead of an Anfwer caufed a Bowl of Brandy of a middling fize to be prefented to the Ambaffador, who, to his great Surprize, returned it and defired a bigger; accordingly a huge filver Bowl was brought in, filled with as much of the fame Liquor as might have fuddled two or three fturdy Ruffians, but the Ambaffador gulped it all down to the laft Drop without fo much as making a wry Face upon it, though thofe who ftood by were afraid the quantity of that hot Liquor would ftifle him, however he appeared not in the leaft concerned, on the contrary he made reafonable Anfwers to the Admiral's Queftions. At Table this Barbarian gave fufficient Proofs, that he was not ufed to Dainties, for he left the beft Difhes, as alfo Bread, untouched, and chofe the coarfeft and hardeft Victuals, fhewing himfelf withal very much difpleafed that his Interpreter, whom he had brought with him from *Saratoff*, was left ftanding by with a hungry Stomach; but as notwithftanding no body took notice of the Fellow, the Ambaffador with both his Fifts took out of the Difhes that ftood next to him, as much as he could grafp, and very liberally made his Interpreter, who ftood behind him, fhare of his own Meal. This ftrange Behaviour kept the Company in a continual laugh, but the
Ambaffador

Ambassador little heeded it, and called for a Pot of Mead which he emptied at one Draught with a frightful Grimace, and afterwards licked his Lips like a Monkey. He had hardly dispatched this, but he took a Quart of Brandy mixed with one third of French Wine, held it to his Mouth, and having first smelled at it, did not leave off pulling till he saw the bottom. So much Liquor could not but at length overcome him, so that he began to puff and blow through his Mouth and Nostrils, but as the Admiral offered to talk with him upon the State Affairs of his Country, and to concert some Measures with him relating to his Commission, this Barbarian had so much Sense left, that he excused himself, and told the Admiral that it was not proper to settle Matters of Consequence in a drunken Fit, but that would be the Business of the next Morning. Dinner being over, the Admiral put a Ducat into his Hand to hire himself a Boat to carry him to his Lodging. He was well pleased with the Present, but before he parted with the Company, he took a Pye which had been left untouched, and gave it to his Interpreter, and so they jogged on together to the Market-place where they sate down upon the Ground and made a new Meal of it, devouring it with a more than canine Appetite in the midst of a Crowd of Spectators, whom the odd Behaviour of those Strangers had drawn together. The indifferent Treatment which those *Calmuckish* Ambassadors meet with in *Russia*, is not much to be wondered at, for that Nation know but little what is good, and the Admiral's Brother, when he

was

was Governor of *Aſtracan*, uſed to pay to the Tartarian Ambaſſadors that came thither five Copecks a Day for their Allowance, purſuant to the ancient Cuſtom of *Ruſſia*, which Sum however he afterwards raiſed to the double of it out of his own Liberality.

Several Particulars, which I learned at *Peterſbourg*, concerning that Nation, are contained in the Deſcription a late anonymous Author * has given of them, which therefore I will inſert here:

A Deſcription of the Calmuckiſh Nation.

"Between the Sources of the Rivers *Tobol* and *Oby*, as far as *Jamuſchowa Ozer* (Lake) live the *Calmucks*, a numerous and powerful Nation, who poſſeſs the Country lying between *Mungalia* and the *Wolga*, as far as *Aſtracan*, and are divided into innumerable *Hordas*, each of which has its ſeparate Can. The chief of them is *Otchiurti Can*, who pretends to be deſcended from the great *Tamerlane*. He is very powerful, yet pays a yearly Tribute to the *Ruſſians*, as well as to *Yousbec* (*Usbeck*). It is ſaid he keeps a magnificent Court, is ſerved in Gold Plate, and dreſſed in Silver Tiſſue.

"As to their Religion, they are not circumciſed like the Mahometans, they eat no Pork, and ſay that St. *Nicolas* is their God. They have a holy Man, whom they call their Patriarch (probably *Dalai Lama*, as others relate) to whom they go every Year in Pilgrimage, to pray and repent of their Sins.

[* In *The preſent State of* Siberia *in* High-Dutch, *Nuremberg*, 1720. *in* 8vo. He has taken this Account from *Iſbrand Ides*'s Travels, and Father *Avril*'s Travels into divers Countries of *Europe* and *Aſia*.]

"The

"The Lake *Jamuschowa Ozer* abounds with good and hard Salt, and lies under the Jurisdiction of the *Calmucks*. The *Russians* go every Year with twenty or twenty five *Doschenicks* (a sort of Vessels) up the River *Irtis*, under a Convoy of two thousand five hundred Soldiers, and afterwards travel Part of the Way by Land to the said Lake, where they hew off the Salt which sticks like Pieces of Ice on the Shore, and lade their Vessels with it. But seldom a Year passes without Skirmishes with the *Calmucks* upon that Account, who will not allow their Salt to be carried away, though they are not able to hinder it.

"Sailing from *Jamuschowa Ozer* down the *Irtis*, they meet with a Town called *Tara*, on a small River of the same Name. This is the last Russian Frontier Town bordering on the Territories of *Bustu Can*, a *Calmuckish* Prince.

"The Inhabitants of that Country are called *Barabinsi*, extending from the Town of *Tara* Eastwards to the River *Oby*, opposite to the River *Ton*, and the Town of *Tomskoy*. The Country, which is called *Barabu*, is not at all mountainous, but level, on it grow Cedars, Larch-Tees, Birches, Firs, and Bushes, and it is watered with the finest Brooks of clear Water. It is travelled over both Winter and Summer, though chiefly in Winter, and as the *Oby* is not then passable, Travellers go to *Siberia* this Way by *Tomskoy* and *Jeniseiska*. The Inhabitants or Tribe of *Barabinsy* are a sort of *Calmucks*, who pay a Capitation, one half to the Czar, and the other half to *Bustu Can*.

" *Can.* They have three *Taifchi* or Gover-
" nours among them, who levy the Taxes
" for the Czar, which confift in nothing but
" Furs; the firft is called *Karfagaz,* who car-
" ries his Portion to the Town of *Tara*; the
" fecond, *Baikifch,* delivers his at the Caftle
" of *Teluwa*; and the third, *Baiduk,* at *Ku-*
" *lenba,* another Caftle. They are a fierce
" and warlike People; they live in wooden
" Houfes raifed a very little from the Ground
" like the *Siberian* Tartars; they do not make
" ufe of Stoves, but have in their Houfes a
" fort of Chimneys or Smoak-holes, which
" they fhut when their Wood is burned, and
" warm themfelves by the Coals as long as
" the Heat lafts. They have no Towns, nor
" any fixed Habitations; in Summer they
" live in Tents and Huts, which they can
" fet up and take down very eafily. In Win-
" ter they dwell in their warm and wooden
" Houfes. They breed Cattle, and love A-
" griculture, they fow Oats, Barley, and
" Buck-wheat; but Rye and Rye-bread they
" do not value at all; if any is offered them,
" they feem to like the Tafte of it well e-
" nough, yet they chaw it fo awkwardly and
" roll it upon their Tongues, as if it was
" fomething filthy, at laft they fpit it out,
" and fcrape their Tongues, as if it was a
" thing they could not refolve to fwallow.
" They fteep their Barley in Water, dry it
" a little, then threfh off the Husk, after
" which they fry it in a very hot iron Pan or
" Kettle till it becomes as hard as Bone, that
" it crafhes between their Teeth, and this
" ferves them inftead of daily Bread. They
" alfo eat *Saranna,* or Bulbs of yellow Lil-
" lies

"lies, dried, ſtamped, and boiled with Milk,
"as a ſort of Milk-pap. They drink *Kumis*,
"a ſort of Brandy drawn off from Mares-
"milk, as alſo *Karaza*, or black Tea, which
"is carried thither by the *Bulgarians*. The
"Habits of Men and Women are after the
"*Mungalian* and *Calmuckiſh* Faſhion; they
"marry as many Wives as they can main-
"tain. Their Arms are thoſe common to
"the greateſt Part of the Tartars, *viz.* Bows
"and Arrows. They keep great Numbers
"of Cattle, Horſes, Camels, Cows, and
"Sheep. Hogs they neither keep nor eat.
"They catch every Year great Quantities of
"furred Animals, Sables, Martens, Squirrels,
"Ermins, Foxes, Hyenas, Beavers, Minks,
"Otters, and the like, in which they pay
"their Tribute. When they go a hunting,
"they carry their *Shaitans* along with them.
"Theſe are rough Images, as well carved
"in Wood as they can do it with a Knife;
"they cloath them in a Stuff-Dreſs of all
"ſorts of Colours, much like that of the *Ruſ-*
"*ſian* Women. Theſe Idols they place up-
"right in ſmall Caſes, and carry them upon
"particular Sleds. To this wooden *Shai-*
"*tan* they offer up their firſt Capture of what
"ſort of Beaſt ſoever it prove. When they
"have taken a great deal of Game, they
"return joyful home, mount the Idol in
"his Caſe to the higheſt Place of the Hut,
"and hang him behind and before with Sa-
"bles, Martens, and all ſorts of Furs, in Ac-
"knowledgment for having proſpered their
"Hunting, and theſe rich Furs muſt hang
"there to rot and be ſpoiled, they believing
"it a moſt unpardonable Crime to take off
"or

"or sell any of these dedicated Hides;
"whence it is that we daily see so many fine
"Skins about these Images eaten up by the
"Worms.

The Czar having ordered the whole Fleet to weigh Anchor, and put to Sea, we departed from *Petersbourg* on the 18th of June for *Reval*, where we stayed all the Summer, during which the Czar made the famous Descent in *Sweden*, when he burned several Towns, Villages and Forests, and destroyed some Copper-Mines. *The Descent on the Swedish Coasts*

Little or nothing remarkable happened during that Time at *Reval*, but the Advices we had from *Petersbourg* contained the following Particulars. The Swedish Prisoners, who had been sent for from *Siberia* to *Petersbourg*, to be employed in the new-established Offices or Boards of War, State, Justice, Finances, Admiralty, Mines, and others, had Hopes either of obtaining their entire Liberty, or being employed on the Lands in *Livonia*, after having sworn Allegiance to the Czar. Some Passengers coming from *Petersbourg* told us, that the new *Scout* or Master of *Police* there, was very rigorous in exercising his Jurisdiction over the Ears and Noses of the Offenders, and that a Woman of the Town had been punished with three Lashes of the *Knout* at each Corner of the Street. Our Surprize to hear such severe Punishment inflicted on a Sister of a Trade, which otherwise enjoys perfect Liberty in *Russia*, abated upon hearing that it proceeded from her having peppered some hundreds of the *Preobrazinsky* Guards, who, being unable to march on their Duty with the rest, were obliged to stay *Advices from Petersbourg during the Czar's Absence.*

stay behind at *Petersbourg* in order to be cured. As for the rest, the new Regulations of *Police*, a thing unheard-of in *Russia* before, had already produced a very good Effect, particularly as to the Safety of the publick Streets, and they have since introduced a nightly Watch after the Method of *Hambourg*. The Jesuits at *Petersbourg* were released of their Confinement, but Father *Engel* was obliged to promise upon Oath, never to revenge himself. Among their Papers had been found a Letter of Father *Frantz*, in which he had ridiculed a Russian Candidate for a Bishoprick, which had given great Offence to their Clergy. However, they were not allowed to depart *Petersbourg* before the Court had received Advice from *Moskow* and *Ukraina*, what Information they had drawn from the Papers of the Jesuits there. The Capuchin Friar, who, as we have mentioned, sollicited the free Exercise of the Roman Catholick Religion at *Astracan*, had in the mean time taken Possession of their Church at *Petersbourg*, and writ to *Poland* and other Countries to send him Assistants.

New Regulations in Finland.

At *Reval* Orders arrived from the Czar for six Noblemen nominated by his Majesty, and so many Secretaries, all Natives of *Esthonia*, forthwith to repair to *Abo* in *Finland*, where they were to receive further Directions from Count *Douglass* the *Lands-Höfding*, or Lord-Lieutenant of that Province. Those Gentlemen obeyed these Orders with the utmost Reluctancy, which forced them away from their native Country where they had Estates and Families, into another, to the Laws and Customs of which they were perfect Strangers.

On the other Hand, as there were in *Finland* but too many of the Natives of good Families, able Persons, and well versed in the Affairs of their own Country, it was judged the Czar did not think fit to trust them with publick Employments, and that he had some particular politick View in the Change he was going to make in the Administration of *Finland*. The Czar's Pretensions till then extended no further than the keeping only of *Wybourg*, *Kexholm*, and *Savolax* with their respective Territories, which together make up the best Part of what is called *Finland* in general, and have been hitherto governed by none but *Russians*. But the Grand Dutchy of *Finland*, properly so called, of which Count *Duglass* is *Lands-Höfding*, or Governor, is divided into four Lieutenancies, and the Multiplicity and Weight of Business being such that he is not able to manage all, the Czar with an Intent of putting the Revenue of the said Grand Dutchy upon a better Foot, sent for those Gentlemen from *Reval*, who were to divide those Lieutenancies between them, and to administer them in Quality of *Lagemans* (or High-Sheriffs) which is an Employment given only to Persons of noble Extraction. Many were of Opinion that these new Regulations were a politick Contrivance for inforcing the Negotiations at *Aland* by making the *Swedes* apprehensive that in case they did not speedily yield up to the Czar his Conquests from *Riga* to *Wybourg*, he might retract his former Offer of restoring *Finland*, properly so called, and insist on keeping all.

A new Harbour projected.

We were told at *Reval*, that the Czar before he went over to *Hango*, had been at *Roger-wik*, to view the Situation of the Harbour that was to be made there, and that he had left Orders to an Italian Ingineer to begin the Work, which if it succeeds will render that Haven, which is capable of one hundred Ships, one of the best in the World, besides that the Entry of it will be much more convenient than at *Reval*, where they want two different Winds in coming in. But as the Mouth of the Harbour of *Rogerwik* is above a Cannon-shot wide, and that it is extremely deep, the Inhabitants believe that the vast Expence which will be required, will make the Design come to nothing.

July 1719. Church Affairs.

The Bishop of *Pleskow*, whose Name is *Proskopowitz*, was by the Czar promoted to the Episcopal See of *Dorpt* and *Reval*. The Archbishop of *Rezan Stephen*, is, as I mentioned above, *Exarchus Sedis Patriarchalis*, Vicegerent of the Patriarchal See; then follow the Archbishops of *Starodub*, *Fibaisky*, &c. next the Bishops of *Pfusky*, *Sarsky*, *Susdal*, *Rostoff*, *Tweer*, *Novogorod*, *Kioff*, *Pleskow*, *Cafan*, *Astracan*, *Tobolsky*, *Reval* and *Carelia*. The rest of the Clergy are the *Archimandrites* and *Igumenes*, (Abbots and Priors) *Popes* and *Protopopes* (Priests and Arch-Priests). Of preaching they all know nothing, consequently the People are but indifferently instructed, and live in a gross Ignorance. But the Czar having in his Travels observed the Usefulness of preaching as to the Instruction and Morals of the People, has since sent several Priests to follow their Studies at *Kioff* and other Places, in order to be able to preach, and

The Present State of Russia.

and there is actually now among others one *Theophylactus*, a Grecian Monk at *Petersbourg*, who almost every Day gives Proofs of his Learning and Eloquence; but as to Controversies, they as well as the rest of the Clergy abstain from them, and leave every Religion as it is.

In the Year 1717, when the Czar was at *Paris*, some Doctors of the *Sorbone* or Faculty of Divinity of the University there, delivered to him a Project in Latin of uniting the two Churches of *Rome* and *Russia*, by observing a certain Moderation on both Sides. I have inserted the said Project among other Pieces which are annexed to this Book. But the Impossibility * of bringing about such an Union is plain to every one who is acquainted with the Doctrines of both Religions, and the Maxims of the present Government in *Russia*. It is the Czar's Interest, that his Clergy be brought out of that profound Ignorance in which they live at present, and that they acquire solid Learning, in order to imprint in the Minds of their Flocks a desire of Knowledge, and notions of true Religion; that they preach up to them the Necessity of obeying God and their Sovereign; but abstain from Controversies and Disputes, and

Of the Project of the Sorbone for uniting the Russian Church and that of Rome.

---

* [The *Question, whether there is any Possibility of reconciling the two Churches, in Point of Doctrine, is discussed in a small Treatise published at* Jena 1719. 4to, *with this Title*: Ecclesia Romana cum Ruthenica irreconciliabilis; seu scriptum aliquod Doctorum quorundam Sorbonicorum Augustissimo Russorum Imperatori ad utriusque Ecclesiæ unionem ei suadendam exhibitum, modeste expensum & animadversionibus illustratum à Jo. Francisco Budeo, Theol. Doct. & Profess. Publico Ordinario.]

content themselves with teaching plain Doctrine and inforcing the Practice of good Morals. But to admit the Roman Catholick Religion would be opening a Door to endless Disputes, which could not fail disturbing that Civil as well as Ecclesiastical Tranquillity which has been hitherto maintained in *Russia*, and endangering the Security which the Czar has procured to himself with respect to the Russian Clergy, as well as their blind Dependants the Peasants. Besides the Popish Religion would prove a Bar to the Introduction and Improvement of Sciences in *Russia*, which the Czar has so much at Heart, and has already put in Practice with so much Applause by inviting to his Dominions so many able Men from all Parts of the World without distinguishing Religions, which End he also pursues by sending young People, particularly Students of Divinity, to foreign Universities. Neither is it probable that the Czar after having suppressed the Patriarchal Authority in *Russia*, will subject himself and his Dominions to a far greater Dependency either on the Pope, or a general Council, and part with that Supremacy, or (to adapt the Phrase more to the Form of the Russian Government) that despotick Power he has acquired over the Clergy and the whole Church. It is needless to mention the Difficulty concerning the Marriage of Priests which is looked upon in *Russia* as sacred, and other controverted Points, about which both Churches are never likely to agree; I shall only say thus much to conclude the whole Matter, that the Czar never had any such Union in his

The Present State of Russia. 283

his Thoughts, but rather caused the Reports that had been spread about it, to be declared false and groundless.

In *August* we returned to *Petersbourg*, where we met with some Deputies from *Riga* and *Reval*, who were sent by the Magistrates of those two Towns to represent several Grievances, whereby their Trade to *Finland* was obstructed. The Magistrates of *Riga* were till then maintained by the Czar in the Enjoyment of their great Privileges, and even the several Members of the Senate, or common Council were owned and treated as Nobles pursuant to a Charter granted them in the Year 1660, by the Queen of *Sweden Hedwig Eleonora*, during the Minority of her Son *Charles* XI. in Consideration of the brave Defence that Town had made three Years before against the numerous Russian Army who besieged them.

_{August 1719. Affairs of Livonia.}

Before my departure from *Petersbourg*, the State of the Russian Forces was communicated to me as it stood in the Year 17.17, which was as follows:

_{The State of the Russian Land-Forces.}

Regiments of INFANTRY.

	Batall.
1. Preobrazinsky	4
2. Semonofsky	3
3. Ingermanlansky	3
4. Astrakansky	2
5-9. *Five Regiments of Grenadiers*	10
10. Moskoffsky	2
11. St. Pieterburgsky	2
12. Trojetskoy	2

CAVALRY.

1. Squadron } of Prince
2. Squadron } Menzicoff.
3. *Life-Guards.*
4-7. *Four Regiments of Grenadiers, of four Companies each.*

Regiments.
8. Moskovsky
9. Kiovsky
10. Sibirsky

13. Le

INFANTRY.		CAVALRY.	
13. Le Fort	2	11. Novogorodsky	
14. Butirsky	2	12. Ingermanlansky	
15. Kiowsky	2	13. Aſtrakansky	
16. Narwsky	2	14. Kaſansky	
17. Jareſlavsky	2	15. Niſegorodsky	
18. Novogorodsky	2	16. Reſansky	
19. Smolensky	2	17. Archangelsky	
20. Kaſansky	2	18. Tiulsky	
21. Sibersky	2	19. Wologdagsky	
22. Pleskovsky	2	20. Jereſlawsky	
23. Roſtovsky	2	21. Roſtofsky	
24. Ludsky	2	22. Ludsky	
25. Wologodsky	2	23. Pleskovsky	
26. Gallitzky	2	24. Narvsky	
27. Czernikoffsky	2	25. Nevsky	
28. Newsky	2	26. Tweersky	
29. Wolodimirsky	2	27. Kargapolsky	
30. Wasky	2	28. Oloridsky	
31. Wibursky	2	29. Wolodimirsky	
32. Schlüſſelburgsky	2	30. Troitzky	
33. Koporsky	2	31. Nove-Troitzky	
34. Woronsky	2	32. Azoffsky	
35. Reſansky	2	33. Wetsky	
36. Azoffsky	2	34. Tobolsky.	
37. Archangelsky	2		
38. Tobolsky	2		
39. Pernovsky	2		
40. Belgorodsky	2		
41. Niſegorodsky	2		
42. Welika-Ludsky	2		

Thoſe Regiments Infantry as well as Cavalry are not alike as to the number of Men, ſome containing 1200 Men and better, but upon an Average the Forces of the preceding Liſt may be reckoned to amount to ninety

The Present State of Russia.

ninety thousand Men. But the whole State of War has been changed these two or three Years past, and the Troops have since increased to about one hundred thousand Men. I have already mentioned above that the *Black Regiments*, as they are called, who are a sort of Militia, ought to be reckoned apart, as also the *Tartars, Calmucks,* and *Cosacks*. Many of the Swedish Prisoners have listed among the *Black Regiments* at *Casan* and other Places, others work on the Fortifications, and one half of them are dead, so that few of them are like to return to their own Country. To judge of their Number, it will be sufficient to mention, that only after the Battel of *Pultava* when General Count *Lewenhaupt* surrendered Prisoner with the Body under his Command to Prince *Menzicoff*, near *Perewoloczin*, on the 30th of *June*, O. S. 1709. the number of those Prisoners pursuant to an exact List amounted in all to 15753 Men.

That Month a Woman Dwarf was brought to Bed, and added a new Member to the Society or Species of those Diminutives of Mankind, whom they take particular care in *Russia* to propagate by marrying them together, so that there is scarcely a Man of Quality but keeps a Man or Woman Dwarf for his Lady. In the Year 1710. the Czar was pleased to add to the Solemnities of the Nuptials between Princess *Anne*, his Niece, and the late Duke of *Courland Frederick William*, the Diversion of a Wedding of a Couple of Dwarfs, which Humour I think deserves a Place in this Account of the Russian Court, though it happened before the time

The Russian Humour of keeping Dwarfs and marrying them together.

of my Arrival there. The Solemnity of the principal Marriage of the illuftrious Couple being performed on the 11th of *November*, N. S. the 13th of the fame Month was appointed for celebrating the Dwarf-wedding. The Day before, two Dwarfs of well proportioned fhape and finely dreffed drove about in a little Chaife with three Wheels, drawn by a good Horfe adorned with Ribbons of divers Colours, to invite the Guefts, two of the Waiters appointed for the Wedding riding before on Horfe-back, likewife well trimmed, after the way of the Country. On the Day appointed in the Morning Bride and Bridegroom were married in the Church of the Fortrefs according to the Ruffian Rites. A very little Dwarf marched at the Head of the Proceffion, as being the *Marfhal*, that is to fay, the Conductor and Mafter of the Ceremony, carrying a Staff on which hung a large Taffel of Ribbons, the diftinguifhing Sign of his Office. He was followed by the Bride and the Bridegroom neatly dreffed. Then came the Czar attended by his Minifters, Kneefes, Boyars, Officers and others; next marched all the Dwarfs of both Sexes in Couples. They were in all feventy two, fome in the Service of the Czar, the Czarina Dowager, the Prince and Princefs *Menzicoff*, and other Perfons of Diftinction, but others had been fent for from all Parts of *Ruffia* howfoever remote. The Proceffion was clofed by a vaft number of Spectators. At the Church the Couple took their Place in the midft of the Company: The Prieft asking the Bridegroom, whether he would take his Bride to be his Wife, he anfwered with a loud Voice, addreffing

dreffing himfelf to his beloved: *You and no other*. The Bride being asked whether fhe had not made any Promife of Marriage to another than her Bridegroom, fhe anfwered: *That would be very pretty, indeed*. However when the main Queftion came to be asked, whether fhe would have the Bridegroom for her Husband, fhe uttered her *Yes* with fuch a low Voice as could hardly be heard, which occafioned a good deal of Laugh to the Company. The Czar in Token of his Favour, was pleafed to hold the Garland over the Bride's Head, according to the Ruffian Cuftom. The Ceremony being over, the Company went by Water to the Prince *Menzicoff*'s Palace. Dinner was prepared in a fpacious Hall, where two Days before the Czar had entertained the Guefts invited to the Solemnity of the Duke's Marriage. Several fmall Tables were placed in the Middle of the Hall for the new-married Couple, and the reft of the Dwarfs, who were all fplendidly dreffed after the German Fafhion. The Bride and Bridegroom fate each at a feparate Table under fmall Canopies of Silk. Over the Bride and her two Bridemaids that fate overagainft her, hung three Garlands of Laurel; there hung alfo one over the Bridegroom's Head. Between the two Bridemaids fate a little Carver who in Acknowledgment for his Trouble was prefented by them with a Cocarde, which Favour he returned to each in a Kifs. This little Company were attended by one *Marfhal*, and eight Deputies, or *Under-Marfhals*, all Dwarfs, who wore each a Cocarde of Lace and Ribbons on the right Arm in Token of their Office, in the Management

nagement of which they acted with so much Dexterity, Mirth, and Noise, as afforded a great deal of Diversion to their Superiors. On one side sate the Czar, the Duke of *Courland*, the several Russian and foreign Ministers, the Generals; on the other the Dutchess of *Courland*, the Princesses her Sisters, and the principal Ladies of the Russian Court; then the several Kneeses, Boyars, and Officers Russians as well as Germans. They were placed along narrow Tables which went around the four Sides of the Hall, sitting with their Backs to the Wall, in order to have a full View of the sporting Dwarfs in the middle of the Room. The first Health was proposed by the little Marshall, who with his eight Deputies stept before the Czar's Table, holding in one Hand their Staffs, and in the other the Glasses, and after having made a Bow to the Ground, they emptied them under the Sound of the Musick which was in the next Room. Some small Pieces had been mounted behind the House to be fired on each Health, but this was countermanded by reason of Prince *Menzicoff*'s youngest Son being then a dying, who actually expired the same Day. After Dinner the Dwarfs began to dance after the Russian way, which lasted till eleven at Night. It is easy to imagine how much the Czar and the rest of the Company were delighted at the comical Capers, strange Grimaces and odd Postures of that Medley of Pigmies, most of whom were of a Size, the mere sight of which was enough to provoke Laughter. One had a high Bunch on the Back, and very short Legs; another was remarkable by a monstrous

monstrous big Belly; a third came waddling along on a little pair of crooked Legs like a Badger; a fourth had a Head of a prodigious size; some had wry Mouths and long Ears, little Pig-eyes, and Chub-cheeks, and many such other comical Figures more. When these Diversions were ended, the new married Couple were carried to the Czar's House, and bedded in his own Bedchamber.

The expensive Works of the new Canal near the Lake *Ladoga* were already begun when I left *Russia*, twelve thousand Men being employed on them every Day. It is to be observed, that there is a Communication between the Lake *Ladoga* and the River *Wolga*, by a Canal from the River *Tweer*, which falls into the River *Wolga*, to the River *Emsta* which falls into the River *Wolkofa*, which discharges itself into the Lake *Ladoga*. All Timber for Ships, Corn, and the *Persian* Commodities coming by the way of the *Caspian-Sea*, were hitherto brought to *Petersbourg* by the said Canal. But the Navigation on the Lake *Ladoga* being so dangerous, that every Year some hundreds of *Karbasses* and other Russian Vessels were cast away, to the great Loss of his Czarish Majesty and the Merchants, it was resolved after a long Deliberation, to make a Canal out of the River *Wolkofa* along the Shores of the said Lake for eight German Miles, into the River *Neva* near *Sleutelbourg* to the End the Ships might have no need of crossing the Lake. I am credibly informed, that this Work is in such Forwardness as to be ready next Summer (1721) and that consequently the Trade between

Of a new Canal, and the Communication between the Baltick and the Caspian-Sea.

tween the *Baltick* and the *Caspian Sea,* between all *Russia* and *Persia* will be upon a sure foot, though still with this Inconveniency that the Ships coming from *Casan* must be near two Years in their Way, first by going against the Stream, and then by waiting in that Canal of Communication between the *Wolga* and the *Wolkofa,* by reason of its low Water, till the Rivers swell and furnish Water enough for the Sluces. By this Project things are brought to that Pass, that the Undertakers are able to furnish all the Oak that is necessary for building a Man of War of sixty or seventy Gun, from *Casan* to *Petersbourg,* at the Rate of twelve or fourteen thousand Rubels; and as all other Materials and Stores whatsoever, which are required for the building or fitting out of Ships, are either produced or wrought in the Czar's own Dominions, it is easy to imagine that his Fleet stands him in much less than it may cost any other Sea-Power. In order to man his Ships he uses the following Method for training up to Navigation Recruits of Seamen. They are put on board the Boyers, of which there are now about one hundred at *Petersbourg,* to learn the working of a Ship; after some Months Experience they are sent to the Fleet, and their Places in the Boyers supplied with fresh Recruits. Those Boyers partly belong to the Czar, but most of them to the great Men of his Court, or to the Merchants. The Signal of three Guns being given from the Fortress, all those Vessels are obliged on a certain Penalty, to sail down the River in order to exercise the

Men,

Men, which happens as often in the Week as a fair Wind prefents, and the Czar is pleafed to divert himfelf with reviewing that Nurfery of his Fleet.

In *September* 1719, I left *Petersbourg* and fet out on my return for *Germany*, and fo I fhall end here my Account of what I have obferved in *Ruffia* during my ftay at that Court, though I could have added many Particulars more, which certain Confiderations and Circumftances obliged me to pafs over.

Conclufion.

A

DESCRIPTION

OF THE

City of *St. Petersbourg,*

AND THE

Town and Castle of *Cronflot,*

With feveral Obfervations relating to thofe Places and the Neighbouring Country.

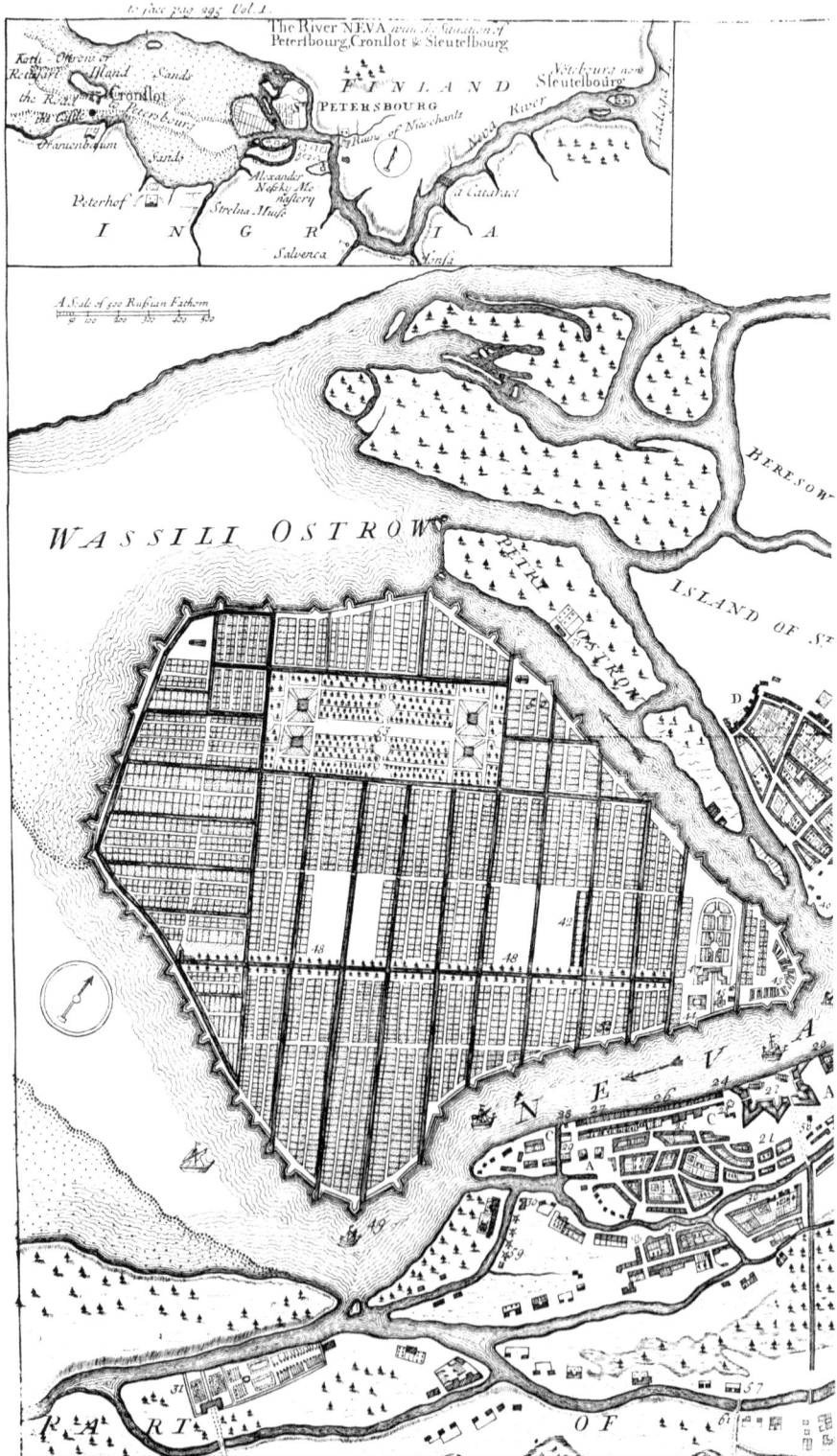

Explanation of the Copper Plate.

A. The Admiralty Ifland.
B. The Ruffian Slaboda.
C. The German Slaboda.
D. The Tartarian Slaboda.
E. The Ruffian Slaboda on the other fide of the Water.
 1. The Fortrefs St. *Petersbourg.*
 2. The Ruins of *Nie-Schantz.*
 3. The Arfenal.
 4. The great Brew-houfe.
 5. The late Czarewitz's Houfe.
 6. The Gun-foundery.
 7. General *Bruce*'s Houfe.
 8. Boyars Houfes on an Arm of the River.
 9. The Czar's Summer-Refidence.
 10. Water-Works.
 11. A Meadow-field.
 12. The Czarina's Garden and Summer-Houfe.
 13. The Poft-Houfe.
 14. The Elephant's Houfe.
 15. The Finlandifh Scheren.
 16. The Finlandifh Lutheran Church.
 17. The Roman Catholick Church.
 18. The Czar's Winter-Refidence.
 19. The High-Dutch Lutheran Church.
 20. Houfes of the great Officers of the Admiralty.
 21. A large open Place.
 22. The Admiralty Yard.
 23. The Admiralty Church.
 24. Prince *Menzicoff*'s Inn.
 25. The Rope-yard.
 26. Copperfmiths Houfes.
 27. The Admiralty Forge.

28. The

28. The Slaughter-House.
29. The *Ambare*, or great Store-House.
30. Boyars Houses.
31. *Catharinen-Hoff*.
32. Senators and Boyars Houses.
33. The new Chancery.
34. The Russian Church of the Holy Trinity.
35. The *Lawks*, or Shops.
36. The great *Kaback*, or Tap-House.
37. The Printing-House.
38. The Tartarian Rag-Fair.
39. The Market for Provisions.
40. The new Slaughter-House.
41. The Physick-Garden.
42. The new Street in the Prince's Island.
43. Boyars Houses.
44. Prince *Menzicoff*'s House.
45. The Prince's Church.
46. *Salavioff*'s House.
47. The Prince's Garden and Pleasure House.
48. The *Perspectiva*.
49. The Passage in the River, through which Ships go in and out.
50. Prince *Menzicoff*'s Farm.
51. The late Crown-Princess's Farm.
52. The Government's Chancery, now burnt down.
53. A Place designed for publick Walks.
54. Magazins.
55. Hospital.
56. Field-Marshal *Czeremetoff*'s House.
57. Major-General *Du Pré*'s House.
58. A *Kaback*, or Tap-House.
59. Saw-Mills.
60. The Monastery of *Alexander Nefsky*.
61. The only passable Way by Land to *Ingria* and *Livonia*.

A DE-

A DESCRIPTION

Of the CITY of

St. PETERSBOURG,

WITH

Several Observations relating to it.

HEN I wrote the foregoing Account, it was not my Design to enter upon a particular Description of *Petersbourg*; but as the Plan of that City which was lately published in *Germany*, only relates to the State of it as in the Year 1716. since which time to the present 1720. many substantial Alterations have been made, I was desired to add to my foresaid Account of *Russia* an exact Description of that Place; in compliance to which Desire I am now going to relate many Particulars not yet mentioned, of a City which may be called a Wonder of the World, was it only in consideration of the

few

few Years that have been employed in the raiſing of it.

His Czariſh Majeſty from his younger Years ſhewed a particular Inclination for Shipping and Sea-affairs. At *Moskow* he was always navigating and making uſe of Sails on the Rivers there, as far as the Situation of that Country would admit. But when Fortune ſeconded his Arms ſo far that in the Year 1702. he took *Nôtebourg* (now called *Sleutelbourg)* and the Year following *Nie-Schantz* (or *Schantz-ter-Nie)* a trading Town in *Ingria,* having obſerved that about a German Mile further down, the River *Neva (Nie)* forms ſeveral Iſlands, the conveniency of that Situation inſpired him with Thoughts of building a Town there, in order to get footing in the *Baltick*. His Army was thereupon ordered to encamp there, ſo that the Infantry ſtood on the Territory of *Finland,* or properly *Carelia,* and the Cavalry on that of *Ingria*. A ſmall Fort was raiſed on the Place where at that time only ſtood two poor Fiſhermens Huts, but where now ſtands *Petersbourg*. The Czar himſelf went with ſome Sloops to view the River down to the main Sea, and ſent other Veſſels to examine and found the Coaſts on all Sides. As they ſpied ſeveral Swediſh Ships cruiſing in the Sea, a Detachment of about one thouſand Men were ordered for the Iſland *Retuſari,* or *Rutzari,* (on which now lies *Cronſlot)* where they took Poſt. The *Swedes* endeavouring to diſlodge the Ruſſians again by continually firing upon them from one of their Ships, the Ruſſians retired and hid themſelves behind a great quantity of large Stones lying on the Shore;

Shore; which made the *Swedes* believe that they had quite retired to the other Shore of the Island, under the Cover of the Bushes and made off in some Vessels; upon this Supposition the *Swedes* landed with the Design of maintaining so advantagious a Post, but they were so warmly received by the Russians, that they were obliged to retire to their Ships with the Loss of some of their Men, and to put to Sea again. After this Rencounter the Czar maintained the Possession of that Island, and afterwards made a Harbour there and built a Fort upon it, with a pretty large Borough, which is now famous under the Name of *Cronslot*, of which mention shall be made more at large hereafter.

The Czar being more and more pleased with the Situation of the neighbouring Country, which actually is one of the most agreeable that is to be found in those Parts, resolved not only to build a Fortress on the River *Neva*, as he designed at first, but also to make his chief Dock there for building large Men of War. The River being very deep near the Place where the Fort or Citadel stands at present, *viz.* Fourteen or fifteen Fathoms, or ninety Foot, and the neighbouring Territory round about being all Morass, which makes the place inaccessible, the Czar pitched upon the several Islands formed by the River, in this manner that the Fortress should be built on the small Island marked in the Plan with N° 1. and the Town partly on the other Islands, partly on the Continent.

This Resolution was no sooner taken, but Orders were forthwith issued, that next Spring a great number of Men, *Russians, Tartars,*

tars, Cosacks, Calmucks, Finlandish and *Ingrian* Peasants, should be at the Place to execute the Czar's Design. Accordingly in the beginning of *May* 1703. many thousands of Workmen, raised from all the Corners of the vast Russian Empire, some of them coming Journies of 200 to 300 German Miles, made a beginning of the Works on the new Fortress. There were neither sufficient Provisions for subsisting such a number of Men, nor Care taken to furnish them with the necessary Tools, as Pick-axes, Spades, Shovels, Wheel-barrows, Planks and the like, they even had not so much as Houses or Huts; notwithstanding which the Work went on with such Expedition, that it was surprizing to see the Fortress raised within less than five Months time, though the Earth which is very scarce thereabouts, was for the greater part carried by the Labourers in the Skirts of their Clothes, and in Bags made of Rags and old Mats, the Use of Wheel-barrows being then unknown to them. It is computed that there perished on this Occasion very nigh one hundred thousand Souls, for in those Places made desolate by the War, no Provisions could be had even for ready Money, and as the usual Supplies carried by the Lake *Ladoga* were frequently retarded by contrary Winds, those People often were in the utmost Misery. This Fortress was afterwards from time to time inlarged, and in the Year 1704. a Crown-work added to it, as also some Redoubts (which however are said to be now in a decaying Condition) the whole being projected and directed by the Czar himself.

At the same time that they were going on with the Fortress, the City also by degrees began to be built, and to this End Numbers of People both of the Nobility and the trading Part of the Nation were ordered to come from *Russia* to settle at *Petersbourg* and to build Houses there, all which was executed with such Forwardness, that in a short time the Place swarmed with Inhabitants. The Boyars and others of the Nobility brought along with them numerous Retinues and many Servants. The Merchants and Shop-keepers found their Account at this new Place, where every thing was excessive dear. Many *Swedes*, *Finlanders*, and *Livonians*, not being able to subsist in their Towns and Villages, which were ruined and many of them destroyed by Fire, and not knowing where else to go, were obliged by Necessity, to mingle with the greater number of People. All sorts of Artificers, Mechanicks, and Seamen with their Families were drawn to *Petersbourg*, in order to encourage Shipping and settle a Commerce by Sea. Many Labourers being *Russians*, *Tartars*, and *Calmucks*, having served the Time prefixed by their Sovereign, and being unwilling to return so far home, engaged with the Boyars who were building Houses every Day, and got sufficient Work to get their Bread by; some thousands of them even built Houses for themselves, and settled at *Petersbourg*, the rather because every body was allowed to build on what Place he liked. All those Circumstances together very much contributed to the sudden peopling of *Petersbourg*, which now hardly yields to any in *Germany* as to

the

the number of Houses and Inhabitants: For there are reckoned at this time sixty odd thousand Houses in that City, among which however, it must be owned, are many poor and small ones, which in two Hours time may be taken to pieces and put up again in another Place, which is particularly the case in the *Tartarian Slaboda*, in the *German Slaboda* South-west of the Dock, and in the *Finlandish Scheren*, about the Finlandish and Roman Catholick Churches.

The Fortress, or Citadel, lies in the midst of the City of St. *Petersbourg*, surrounded on all Sides by the River *Neva*, as appears in the Plan (N° 1.) There was on that Place a small Island before, called *Hasen-holm*, in Finlandish *Jenneszari* (Hare-Island) but as at high Water it was quite over-flown, the Ground of it has been raised and inlarged with Earth carried thither to that End, but it is to be apprehended that the Water may yet rise above it in case the Wind should blow for some time South-west, this being the Wind which is extremely dangerous to this new City, as shall be said hereafter. The Figure of the Fortress (as may be seen in the Plan) is an oblong and irregular Hexagone: The opposite Bastions are like each other, except the two middlemost, in such manner that of four Bastions every one has one *Oreillon*, one of the middlemost Bastions towards *Carelia*, or *Finland*, has two *Oreillons*, and the other middlemost that lies over-against it, where the River is broadest, has none at all. I have related above, that at first the Fortress was only raised of Earth, but in the Year 1710, the Czar began to have it changed into strong

and

The Present State of Russia.

and thick Walls; that Side which looks towards *Carelia* is quite finished, but towards the River People are still at Work. The Wall from the Ground to the Parapet is thirty Foot high, and is so well furnished with Iron and Brass Guns that the firing a Round takes up a pretty good while; in the Flanks which are somewhat short, there are strong Casemates one above the other, arched within and without, but not vaulted, instead of which they are only covered with strong Beams for a Fence against Bombs. Part of them are let out to Merchants to keep their Wine and other Goods in them. The Fortress has two Gates; that which looks down the River, is not yet finished, but that above is now brought to Perfection and is of fine statuary Work. On the Outside stands a Statue of St. *Peter* bigger than the Life, with two Keys in his Hand, very well contrived. There is also an Inscription in Russian, marking the Foundation of the Fortress and the Year 1703. Within over the Gate is the great black Russian Eagle with the Crowns on his two Heads, holding in his right Claw the Scepter, and in the left the Globe. Lower down stands St. *Nicholas*, the great Patron of the Russian Nation. I do not remember that they have as yet given a Name to that Gate, though in all Probability it will be called St. *Peter*'s Gate. Before this Gate lies a Ravelin from which there is a fine Bridge built over that Arm of the River with two Draw-Bridges. The said Arm of the River between the Crown-work and the Fortress serves for a safe Harbour to the Gallies and other small Vessels where they lie ranged in

order

order during the Winter. Through the Fortress they have cut a Canal which is to have a Communication with the broad part of the River, but as yet unfinished. On one of the Bastions they hoist every Day after the Dutch manner the great Flag of the Fortress which is of several Colours, fastened to an high Pole standing on a Cross-foot of Timber. On publick Days, or great Festivals which they call *Prasnik*, they display in its room another large yellow Flag, which represents the Russian Eagle grasping with his Claws and covering with his Wings the four Seas, *viz.* The *White*, the *Black*, the *Caspian*, and the *Baltick*, to denote that his Czarish Majesty's Dominions border on those Seas, though now it is otherwise with respect to that of the *Black Sea*, since the Peace made with the Turks in the Year 1710.

After having described the Fortress, I should also give the Particulars of its Buildings within. But those few that have been begun are every Day altered, so that nothing certain can be said of them before they are finished, besides that the Place is so narrow that there is no room for large Edifices. However there stands a *Cathedral* in it which is near finished; the Steeple belonging to it is pretty high, built all of Stone with four Rows of Pillars each upon the other, with great Arches, contrived by the Italian Architect *Tressini*. Within hangs a Chime which the Czar caused to be made in *Holland* with great Expence. The principal Office of State, or *Great-Chancery*, as they call it, is a wooden House in which the Senate used to meet, and the Privy-Council was held, but since the new *Chancery*,

The Present State of Russia.

(N° 33.) was finished all Papers and publick Records have been lately removed thither, nor does the Senate any more assemble in the Fortress. Entering through the upper Gate in the Courtine at the Right there stands the *Dispensary*, one of the finest that can be seen any where, both with respect to the most exquisite Drugs with which it is furnished, as especially the curious Gally-pots, which are all of fine *Chineze* Porcelaine and have cost many thousands of Rubels. Among the Drugs which *Russia* produces, *Rhubarb* is one of the most principal. They dig it in *Siberia* in great quantity. The Russians at first were unacquainted with the value of that Drug, which they used to sell for one *Grive* (or ten Copecks) a Pound. But a certain Merchant of *Hambourg* having contracted with the Czar for thirty thousand Rubels to have the Monopoly of it, sold it at *Hambourg* and in *Holland* for eight Rixdollars. A Russian at *Hambourg* hearing of the great Profit of this Trade, made Report of it to the Russian Court, who forthwith gave Orders to dig for abundance of Rhubarb in *Siberia*, and sent a whole Ship's Cargo of it to *Holland*; but the *Hamburgher* having timely Intelligence of it, made haste to put off his Stock at eight *Grosch*, or $\frac{1}{3}$ of a Rixdaler the Pound, which was the Occasion that the Russian Rhubarb remained upon their Hands and lay to rot at *Amsterdam*, the rather because the Dutch had since taken Care to provide themselves with that Drug from the *East-Indies*, so that they can now do without that from *Russia*. Besides those Buildings there is at present nothing else remarkable in the Fortress;

Fortress; a few wooden Houses are in it, which are but in an indifferent Condition, nor does any body live there besides the Governour, some Officers, the Apothecaries, and about two hundred common Soldiers.

Round about the Fortress lies the City of *Petersbourg*, partly on the several Islands, and partly on the Continent; it is of so large an Extent, that it rather resembles a Landskip of many Boroughs than a City. It is a good German Mile long, and very near as broad. The Houses are built very close together; and as very little is left of the good and dry Ground, those People who are continually arriving to settle there, are obliged to look out for Places to build on in the Morass, which renders the new Streets exceeding dirty, particulary in Spring and Autumn.

Up the River (in the Plan N° 2.) is the Place on which formerly stood *Schantz-ter-Nien* (the Fort of *Neva*) on the Corner between that great River and a little one that runs into it, of which I do not remember the Name. Of that Fort there is hardly so much as one Stone left.

That Part of the City lower down, (Lit. B.) which is called the *Russian Slaboda*, tho' situate on the Continent, yet has on the Country side a deep Morass, which leaves but one Passage to the City, as appears by the Plan, (N° 61.) by a bad Road, which forms, as it were, another Island, or Peninsula. But from the Arsenal (N° 3.) up the River along the Banks there is a rising Ground, which with that on the opposite Side of the River near the great Brew-house (N° 4.) are the only dry and elevated Places of *Petersbourg* that on high

high Water are out of Danger. In this Part of the Town lives the Czar, as did alſo the late Czarewitz (N° 5.) with his Conſort, and the Princeſs *Natalia.* There is alſo the *Gun-foundery* (N° 6.) where great numbers of Braſs Cannon are caſt every Year. Next to it, (N° 7.) the Maſter the Ordnance M. *Bruce* has cauſed a Stone Houſe to be built, which is not very large, but well contrived. There are other Houſes along the River, and in the firſt Street that runs parallel with it, in which live ſome Boyars; the reſt are inhabited by other Ruſſians of divers Degrees, for which Reaſon this Part of the Town is commonly called the *Ruſſian Slaboda.* Lower down along the Banks of the ſmall Arm of the River (N° 8.) ſtand ſeveral Noblemens Houſes, which they are inlarging or augmenting every Day. Six thouſand Houſes and upwards have been built towards the Fields ſince the Year 1717. The Houſes generally ſpeaking are all of Wood, Beam upon Beam, rough without, and ſmoothed within by the help of a Hatchet: The Roofs are made of thin Splinters of Fir, ten or twelve Foot long laid one near the other, and Laths nailed acroſs over them. Thoſe who will have a better Fence again the Rain, lay large Pieces of very thin Bark of Birch under the Splinters, which never rot, and keep out the Water tolerably well, but are dangerous by reaſon of their eaſily taking fire. Others cover their Roofs with large ſquare Turfs laid over the ſaid Splinters, which as long as they are freſh, remain green and keep the Houſe pretty dry within. Beſides thoſe common Houſes, which make but one Room

and

and one Story, there are many others of Carpenters-work and divided into Apartments: For inftance, that of the late Czarewitz and of his Confort, that of the Princefs *Natalia*, and others, which are all covered with Pantiles. But fince the Czar has commanded all his great Men who live in this Part of the Town, to build Stone Houfes on *Waffili Oftroff*, or the Prince's Ifland on the other fide of the River, and that many have begun to build there, it is probable no Expences will be laid out for the future in embellifhing this Part of the Town, but things be left as they are, except that common People may go on with building there. On the other Side of the faid Arm of the River (N° 9.) ftands the Czar's Summer-Habitation (for he refides there in Summer.) It is built of Stone, fmall indeed but well contrived. The Houfe ftands in the Garden which confidering its Situation and the fhort time fince it was raifed, is perfectly well contrived and cannot be found fault with. In the Year 1716. a Canal was dug round the Garden, and on all Sides Arbours fet up facing the Walks, and fine Statues of white Marble placed in them. In this Garden is a Plantation or Nurfery of Oaks, which thrive according to Wifh, a thing fo much the more remarkable becaufe not only the neighbouring Country, but all the Northern *Ruffia* does not produce that fort of Trees, whence it appears how far things may be carried by Induftry. There are alfo in this Garden a Green-houfe, Water-works, (N°. 10.) and particularly a Grotto, which when finifhed, will yield to no other whatfoever. Next

The Present State of Russia.

to the Garden lies a large Meadow-field (N° 11.) in which they have planted an Orchard. Over against on the other Side of another small Arm of the River (N°. 12.) are situate the Czarina's Garden and Summer-house, and down along the Water the Habitations of her Servants, and her Stables. The House it self is only of Wood, but the Apartments are noble and full of Pictures. Nor does the Garden want Verdure or any Ornament that can be desired. As there is a large Spot of Ground behind, which lies empty, there is no doubt but it may in time become the best Part of the Town, the rather because there is no other Passage into the Country but that way.

I am now proceeding to the principal *Slaboda* on the River, which is properly called the *Admiralty Island*, (Lit. A.) but commonly goes by the Name of the *German Slaboda*, (Lit. C.) because most of the Germans live in that part of the Town. The Post-house stands about (N° 13.) and next to it (N° 14.) in the middle of a Meadow the House formerly built for the Persian Elephant, in which now is kept the Globe of *Gottorp*. Over against stand several fine Houses, among which that built by the Marshal *Alzovioff*, has cost twelve thousand Rubels. The Corner in that part of the Town (N°. 15.) is called the *Finlandish Scheren*, because it is for the greater part inhabited by *Finlandish* and *Swedish* Exiles. Here is also the Finlandish Lutheran Church (N°. 16.) which is but a wooden House, as is likewise the Roman Catholick Church, (N°. 17.) but the Design now is to change the latter into a Stone Building, and to build many Roman Catholick Churches

more,

more, as alfo Convents, the Czar having given Leave to the Jefuits to return into his Dominions, and promifed largely to fupply them with Neceffaries for building. If one excepts two or three hundred Houfes in this Place, the reft are but poor Huts crowded together more like Cages than Houfes. It is remarkable that not one Street of *Petersbourg* has a Name: If one aks for another's Houfe, they give him Direction by defcribing the Place, or naming fome Perfon that lives thereabouts, till they hit upon one that he knows, and then he may go thither and inquire further. From the Poft-houfe down along the River ftands a long Row of Houfes, one of them (marked N°. 18.) is the Czar's Winter Habitation and his ufual Refidence, a Stone Building two Stories high. It had formerly the Profpect over the greater part of the City, the Fortrefs and the Prince's Houfe, and even towards the open Sea by one Arm of the River; but fince they have made a Wharf or Key along the Banks, and built Houfes upon it, (as fhall be hereafter mentioned) the Street in which the Czar's Refidence ftands, has loft all that Profpect, and they have built another Houfe for the Czar on the faid Wharf. Round about the Czar live all forts of People, Ruffians as well as Germans, but moft of the latter who have taken up the Streets that lie neareft the Czar's Refidence. The High-dutch Lutheran Church (N°. 19.) a wooden Structure in the Form of a Crofs, ftands not above three hundred Paces from the Back-fide of the Czar's Refidence. Further down South-Eaft the faid Church (N° 20.) are the Habitations of the great Officers

of

The Present State of Ruſſia.

of the Admiralty. Five of thoſe Houſes are large and built of Stone, the others which are as yet of Wood are likewiſe to be tranſformed into Stone Buildings, for which the Materials lie ready. The Back-Street which ends into the large Place (marked N°. 21.) is inhabited by Ruſſians and Germans indiſtinctly, though there are more of the latter, but further to the Left of the ſaid large Place there live none but Ruſſians; the Houſes are ſmall and placed at random without any regularity. In the midſt of the Admiralty Iſland is the great Admiralty-yard, (N°. 22.) or *Wharf* (as they call it) where the large Men of War are built, of which there are commonly ſeven or eight at once upon the Stocks. In the Year 1716, this Yard was taken in with a Ditch, and a Rampart with a Parapet raiſed behind it, ſo that there are now two Fortreſſes at *Petersbourg*. The ſame Year they built within the Yard two large Store-houſes of Carpenters-work, in which is a great quantity of all ſorts of naval Stores. Other Materials, as Timber, Anchors and the like, lie on the Place round the Yard. The Iron Cannon, with which the greater part of the Ships are armed, lie on the Wharf. The Czar has cauſed Iron Cannon to be caſt at *Alonitz* on the Weſt-ſide of the Lake *Onega*, which are four and twenty Pounders as fine as may be ſeen any where; they are ſmooth, and ſo neatly worked that they may vie with Braſs Cannon, beſides that they ſtand the Trial and are as durable as others of Braſs of the ſame weight and ſize. In the Year 1715. ſome Iron Cannon were brought from *Siberia* where they had been

been caſt. In outward Appearance they exceeded the others, and were as ſmooth as if they had been poliſhed, but they burſt in the Trial of the double Charge. Probably the Siberian Iron is not ſo good as that of *Alonitz* which is ſaid to have a Mixture of Gold and Silver. As for heavy Artillery and ſmall Arms the Czar has ſuch Store of both as are not inferior to thoſe of any other Power whatſoever. South-weſt of the Admiralty-yard ſtands the Admiralty Church (N° 23.) whither the Court goes to divine Service. It is of Wood and but ſmall, for which reaſon it is to be taken down, and another to be built on the large Place. Next to it (N° 24.) ſtands Prince *Menzicoff*'s Inn, a long Building of Carpenters-work, covered with Pantiles. But as it is not yet fitted up for the Reception of Strangers, there live in it at preſent ſome German and French Manufacturers and Artificers, particularly the Handicraftsmen who came from *Dantzick* in the Year 1716, for whom the Czar pays Houſe-rent to Prince *Menzicoff*. Behind this Building is the Rope-yard (N°. 25.) which furniſhes the Fleet with Ropes and other Neceſſaries. Next to it live the Copperſmiths (N°. 26.) and lower down on the Water-ſide is the great Admiralty Forge (N°. 27.) in which there are thirty odd Furnaces. All along this ſide of the River from the Poſt-houſe down as far as there are any Houſes, the Banks are lined with thouſands of Piles and Stakes driven into the Ground, behind which all is filled up with Rubbiſh and Earth, upon which the Houſes are to be built cloſe to the Water, and the Foundations of them

railed,

The Present State of Russia.

raifed, the Ground there being low, and very much expofed to high Water. On this Key ftand actually above thirty large Stone Palaces. That of the Great Admiral *Apraxin* is the moft fplendid, and contains above thirty Apartments: The others belong to the Vice-Admiral *Cruys*, General *Jagozinsky*, General *Czernichoff*, and other great Officers of the Court, and give that part of the City a fine Afpect from the Water-fide. Somewhat lower (N°. 28.) is the Slaughter-houfe which furnifhes this part of the Town with Meat in abundance; further down along the Water (N°. 29.) ftands a great *Ambare* or Storehoufe, near which they build Gallies, between twenty and thirty every Year. The number of thofe Gallies is now increafed to three hundred, which the Czar is refolved conftantly to keep up, at leaft in time of War. They are of different Sizes, the largeft carrying three hundred Men and five Guns, and the fmalleft one hundred and fifty Men and three Guns. This Fleet of Gallies is able without the Affiftance of a Fleet of Men of War, to tranfport an Army of thirty thoufand Men with one thoufand Pieces of Cannon to any Place where it is required. On the South-fide along the fmall Arm of the River (N°. 30.) ftand the Houfes and Gardens of fome Boyars, particularly of the Great Admiral, of the late Commiffioner of the Admiralty *Kikin*, and of *Peter Matweoff*, formerly Ambaffador at feveral foreign Courts. To this Part of the City may be reckoned the Czarina's Garden and Pleafure-houfe *Catharinen-Hof* (N°. 31.) The Garden is not much advanced, becaufe it is often overflowed and ruined

ruined by the Water; however it is pity that no care is taken to improve it, and to guard it againſt that Inconvenience, for it has as fine a Situation as any Place about *Peterſ-bourg*. The Houſe is but of Wood, and the Apartments are ſmall and very low.

Thoſe *Slabodas* or Suburbs are at preſent all paved, beſides, they have made a paved Road the Length of a good *Engliſh* Mile out of Town, through a Moraſs which was hardly paſſable before. The whole City is as it were ſunk in a Moraſs, and every where ſurrounded with Wildernefſes and Buſhes, except the great Place (N°. 21.) which is free from Buſhes, and dries up in good Weather. However, the cutting down any Wood about *Petersbourg* is prohibited on ſuch ſevere Penalties, that two Years ago a certain Colonel underwent the *Knout*, and twenty or more Peaſants run the Gantlet, (a Puniſhment introduced in *Ruſſia* among other Novelties) becauſe the former had not only for himſelf made uſe of a Foreſt, notwitſtanding the Czar's Prohibition, but even for a certain Sum given Liberty to the ſaid Peaſants to fell Trees in it. This Prohibition is the Cauſe that Wood is exceſſive dear at *Petersbourg*, as being fetched far off, ſo that in a large Family, if they have not in Time laid in Proviſion for firing from *Finland*, they may eaſily in twenty four Hours time, burn up as much Wood as will coſt them two or three Dalers. The Canals that were begun to be cut in the Year 1717, are already in ſuch Perfection, that a Man may almoſt at his own Door ſtep into a Boat, and from thence be carried into the *Neva*, and further into the main Sea. It is a
good

good Diverfion on Holidays to fee one hundred and more Sloops rowing and failing together in Emulation of each other, which Shew is the more fet off by the handfome Drefs of the Watermen.

That Part of the City which ftands on the Side of *Finland*, is of a large Extent, and though the North-fide behind the *Tartarian Slaboda*, (Lit. D.) is but indifferently inhabited, yet it is not quite empty, for there are large Farms and Gardens that take up the Place, till it be built upon with Houfes. For this Reafon it is not marked in the Plan. The principal Buildings ftand about the Water; in the Corner (N°. 32.) are the Houfes of the Senators and chief Boyars; moft of them are of Wood, yet they are fpacious and full of Apartments. But the Great Chancellor Count *Golofkin*, the Vice-Chancellor Baron *Schafiroff*, the Knees *Gagarin*, formerly Governor of *Siberia*, and other Men of Quality, have raifed magnificent Stone-Palaces along the Shore. Next to the Houfes of thofe Boyars (N°. 33.) there is the new *Chancery*, or Office of State, a long Building all of Carpenters Work, now finifhed, in which the nine Boards or Offices newly eftablifhed, ufe to affemble, and the foreign Ambaffadors have their Audiences.

Notwithftanding thofe Buildings are fo liable to Fire, yet the Regulations that have been made againft it, are fo ftrict and well obferved, that, though there fcarcely paffes a Week without a Fire breaking out in fome Part of the Town, there is feldom above a couple of Houfes burnt down, how great foever the Danger may appear. There are
Watch-

Watchmen appointed, who keep Guard on the Steeples Night and Day: So soon as one observes any Fire, he tolls a Bell after a particular Manner, in which he is immediately followed by the rest all over the Town, and the Drummers go up and down beating Alarm. Upon this Notice there appear thousands of *Plotnicks* (or Carpenters Boys) of whom all Ends of the Town are full, with Hatchets in their Hands, running full speed to the Fire, and all Soldiers, of what Rank soever, are obliged, on severe Penalties, to repair to the Place. The Czar himself, when in Town, is usually one of the first, or the Prince *Menzicoff*, the Governor of the Fortress, and other Generals and superior Officers. It is a common thing to see the Czar among the Workmen, with a Hatchet in his Hand, climbing up to the Top of the Houses that are all in Flame, with such Danger, that the Spectators tremble at the Sight of it. Considering therefore that a good Command in such Cases is of more Effect than hundreds of Hands, there is a speedy Stop put to the raging Element by pulling down in a Minute the two Houses standing next to the Fire, and as the Engines arrive in the mean time, the Flame is soon quite extinguished.

Near the *Chancery* (N°. 34.) stands the Russian Church of the *Holy Trinity*, which, next to the Cathedral and Prince *Menzicoff*'s Church, is the largest and finest at *Petersbourg*. It has a sort of Chime which is but indifferent, and is played with Hands every Hour. Then come the *Lawks*, as they call it, or the Shops (N°. 35.) which is the Market-Place, where the whole Trade of *Petersbourg*

tersbourg is carried on, and all sorts of Merchandize are sold, no body being allowed to lay in or sell any Goods any where else. It is a very spacious Building two Stories high of Carpenters Work, covered with Pantiles, having a large empty Yard within. The Building is all along within separated by a Wall, so that there are two Rows of Shops, one facing the Street, and the other the Yard, and so many Galleries going round before the Shops to shelter the Buyers from the Rain. All those Shops in both Stories are well furnished. The House is the Czar's own, to whom the Shopkeepers are obliged to pay large Rents, but no body is allowed to live in it, and for Security there are Centinels placed on the four Corners and four Gates. As all selling of Merchandize in private Houses is prohibited, the Trades-people and Merchants, who are of twenty and more different Nations, are obliged either to be themselves in the Day-time in their Shops, or to keep their Servants there, which occasions such a Bustle of the Carriages arriving by Water and Land from all the Islands and Corners of the City, and such a Crowd of People about the House, that one has Difficulty enough to get through. This Market was formerly kept in a Place about one hundred Paces further off backwards, and consisted only of poor Huts made of Wood and Planks; but in the Year 1710. in July at Night it was burnt down to the Ground in about an Hour's time, and most of the Goods were either consumed or stolen. In the Room of it there stands at present a Row of Huts, in which the Russian Pastrycooks sell their paltry Cakes, which they call *Pyrogs*.

Pyrogs. Going to the Bridge that leads into the Fortress, one meets at the Left (N°. 36.) the principal *Kabak,* or Tap-House, where they sell Wine, Beer, Brandy, Tobacco, and Cards, for his Czarish Majesty's Account, for that sort of Trade belongs solely to him throughout his Dominions. At the Right, (N°. 37.) is the Printing-House, a great Curiosity in these Parts, for there are few or no Russian Books, of what sort soever, to be had for Money. The old Russian Letters being hardly legible, and their Writing much perplexed with Abbreviations and strange Characters, the Czar has taken particular Care to remedy this Inconvenience by introducing, instead of the ancient Scrawl, a neat and legible Print, in which the Bible, and many other useful Books, have been published. Going by the Fortress one comes to the Tartarian Rag-Fair, (N°. 38.) opposite to the Crown-work. The Goods are sold there very cheap, either in the open Streets, or in two Rows of Shops; they consist in second-hand Suits of divers Nations, basten Shoes, old Iron, Pack-thread, old Cord, wooden Sadles, with proper Housings to them made of Felt, and other such Curiosities. Those Shops generally have most Customers, and the Throng thereabouts is such, that he who chances to come among them, ought well to look to his Purse, Sword, and even Hat and Peruke, and, for the better Security, carry them in his Hands. At my time a certain Officer of the Grenadier Guards, who is a German, once returned from that Place without either Hat or Peruke, and the very same Day a Woman of Fashion had the like Misfortune in losing

her

The Present State of Russia.

her Head-Dress there. Two Tartars on Horseback had met the said two Persons at different Places, and, whipping off their respective Head-ornaments with great Agility, left them exposed to the Laughter of the Mob, and even within their Sight offered their Spoil to Sale. Behind this **Rag-Fair** lies the *Tartarian Slaboda*, (Lit. D.) inhabited by *Tartars*, *Turks*, *Calmucks*, and many the like Nations, among whom there is such Variety of fine House-keeping as far exceeds the Way of Life practised among the Inhabitants of the Out-skirts and By-lanes of *Rome*, *Paris*, or *London*. On the River beneath the Fortress, (N°. 39.) stands the *Muitnoy-Dwor*, or Market for Provisions and Houshold Goods. It is a spacious square Building, though not quite so large as the Market above-mentioned. In the two Sides of it which look to the Street, are sold all sorts of Necessaries for House-keeping, *viz.* Peas, Lentils, Beans, Grout, Oatmeal, Meal, Bacon, wooden Wares, Pots, and the like. The other two Sides facing the Water are Storehouses for Meal. The House is of Wood, and covered with Splinters after the Russian Way, which makes the Shopkeepers greatly apprehensive of Fire. Not far from thence (N°. 40.) is the new Slaughter-house raised on Piles above the Water; but as the Foundation of it is too low, it is to be feared that such a wooden House will hardly stand the Shock of another great Flood, like that which happened in September 1715. * when the

---

[* *Another such Inundation happened on the sixteenth of November, N. S.* 1721. *when the Water stood ten Foot higher than ever before, and occasioned almost irreparable Damage.*]

Wind blowing hard South-West, the Waters fwelled fo high, that a *Carbus* (a pretty large Veffel with two Mafts) was carried againft the Houfe, and, when the Waters fell, was left there on the Foundations or Key of it. The Part of the Town North-weft the Slaughterhoufe and the Market for Provifions, is called the *Ruffian Slaboda on the other fide of the Water* (Lit.E.) It is moft altogether inhabited by mean People, except along the River, where there ftand fome good wooden Houfes; as, for Inftance, that of the Vice Governor, of the *Land-Richter*, (a German Word, adopted by the Ruffians, fignifying the Judge of the Country) and thofe of fome other Officers of the Chancery. The Government's Chancery (the chief of the whole Country) that formerly ftood on the Prince's Ifland, (N°. 52.) being burnt down to the Ground in the Winter of the Year 1716. has fince been removed to this Part of the Town, and rebuilt there. On this Ifland is alfo the Phyfick-Garden, (N°. 41.) a large Spot of Ground, but without any great Curiofity. The Banks being there higher than in other Parts, and there being befides a Sand-Hill in the Garden, which is never overflowed by by the Water, the Germans have chofen this Garden for their Burying-place. However, Corpfes are not fo fafe there, but that they often are dug up by Thieves, who, after having ftript them of the Clothes in which they were buried, throw them by to lie there till another Burying happens, or the Relations of the Deceafed come to know it, and bury them a fecond time. For this Reafon fome Germans bury their Dead in their Yards, particularly their Children, or, if they be Perfons of good Circumftances, cumstances, they place a Guard near the Grave in the Phyſick-Garden till the Dead and his Clothes are forgotten. In the Year 1715. ſome Thieves attempted to dig up the Corpſe of a German, who had been Court-Muſician, and had been enterred two Days before: They had already broke the Coffin to pieces; but as they went the wrong Way to work, and endeavoured to pull the Corpſe out by the Legs, they could not gain their End, but were obliged to go away: The next Morning ſome Ruſſian old Women ſeeing the Legs of the Dead reaching out of the Grave, were frightened at it, and told the Neighbours, that one of the dead Foreigners was riſing again, which Rumour made his Friends put him under Ground a ſecond time.

Waſili-Oſtrow is a large and fine Iſland, of which the Czar has made a Preſent to the Prince *Menzicoff*, who lives upon it with his Family and Servants. But as the Czar afterwards took a particular Fancy in the Situation of it, which it ſeemed he had not minded at firſt; he reſolved, that the true City of *Petersbourg* ſhould be built upon it in a regular Order. Accordingly he cauſed ſeveral Draughts to be made of a new City, to be raiſed on the Compaſs of that Iſland, and having met with one to his liking, he approved of it, by putting his Sign-manual to it, ſo that the new City is to be built after that Model. Purſuant to this Reſolution the Streets and Canals were laid out and marked with Poles in the Year 1716, proper Palaces were alſo ſhared out for the Houſes to be built, and an Order iſſued, enjoyning the Czar's Subjects to build and ſettle there. This Order has had ſo much Effect,

Effect, that many Persons have made a Beginning: The Street (marked in the Plan with N°· 42) is actually built on both Sides, and other Streets laid out, the Houses of which, though only of Wood, yet are for the greater Part covered with Pan-tiles, and of better Condition than those that stand in the other Parts of the Town. Many Persons of Quality have already built their Stone-Palaces there, and others have sent the Materials for theirs thither, pursuant to the Czar's Orders. They have for the greater Part pitched upon the Corner of the said Island, (N°· 43.) where they have got Places measured out, on which they intend to build, for which Reason several Saw-Mills, that stood there before, have been taken down, and removed to other Places. To judge by the Draught, it may become a considerable Town in Time, and render *Petersbourg* one of the largest Cities in *Europe*, the rather because all that is already built, is to remain so as it is. And though the greater Part of the said Island is still covered with a thick Wood and Bushes, except a small spot of Ground cut out and laid open, this will prove no Obstacle to the Czar's Will and Intention, at whose simple Command so many thousands of People must be ready to put his Designs in Execution. The whole Islands to be taken in, and fortified with a Line of Breast-Works.

The first remarkable Thing on the said Island, is the Prince's House, (N°· 44.) It is to be observed, that by the plain Name of the Prince, is only meant the Prince *Menzicoff*; for it is not the Custom in *Russia*, neither among the Natives nor Germans, nor even at Court,

Court, to ſtyle any Perſon *Prince*, but in Ruſſian, as well as in High-Dutch, *Knees*. But as the Prince *Menzicoff* is a Prince of the holy Roman Empire, and yet there is no other Appellation for him in Ruſſian but *Knees*, he is always ſtyled *Swetlieſhe Knees*; that is to ſay, *the moſt ſerene Prince*, in Diſtinction of all other *Kneeſes*, who bear the Title of *Waſhe Siatelſtwo*, i. *your High-born Lordſhip.* Germans therefore, and other Foreigners, if they mention the Prince, are to be underſtood to mean the Prince *Menzicoff*. But to return to his Houſe, the ſame is built of Stone after the Italian Manner, three Stories high, and covered with large Iron Plates painted red. It has Wings behind and before, is all vaulted underneath, and as for the reſt, provided with every thing that is requiſite in a fine Houſe. It has a great Number of Apartments furniſhed with rich Houſhold Goods, particularly of Silver and Plate. In the middlemoſt Story is a ſpacious Hall, in which are uſually kept all great Entertainments, and the Weddings of Kneeſes or Boyars. Againſt the Houſe, over a ſmall Canal, is the Prince's Church, (N°. 45.) built of Stone, with a pretty Steeple, which has a ſort of a Chime that is but indifferent. About twenty two Years ago, when there was no Thought of *Petersbourg*, the Prince cauſed a ſumptuous Church and Steeple to be built in the City of *Moskow*, and to be provided with a Chime, which is ſtill ſubſiſting there. His ſaid Church at *Petersbourg* is neatly contrived, and has a Gallery going round on the Out-ſide. Within are ſome Figures carved of Wood, and another ſort of a Gallery, both which things are

not

not very customary in *Russia*. There is, besides, in this Church a Pulpit, in which Sermons are preached now and then in Russian, a thing very extraordinary, and entirely new in this Country; for the Russian Priests never preached before, but contented themselves with performing Mass. But this Precedent shall be followed for the future, and the Intent is, not to admit ignorant Persons any more into Ecclesiastical Orders, who have no other Learning, than merely being able to read, but to chuse such Subjects as have more Knowledge, and are able to preach Sermons to their Congregation, to instruct them in the Word of God. The next large House by the Church (N°· 46.) was built by the Prince's Master of the Horse, *Fedor Salavioff*; it is of Stone, and covered with large iron Plates, the finest House in *Petersbourg*, excepting the Prince's Palace, and that of the Admiral. The two foremost Rows of Houses joyning to it, are to be pulled down, to make Room for the Boyars, and other Persons of Distinction, to whom Places have been assigned here, as was mentioned above. But the two hindmost Rows, where the Houses are built after the Manner of *Holland*, though but of Wood, are to remain, and a Canal is to be dug in the midst of the Street, which will be the more easily done, because the Ground there is very low and marshy. Next come the Prince's Garden and Pleasure-House (N°. 47.) The Gardens are very large, as appears by the Plan; however, there is but little in them, except that the Arbour-work of the Walks on both Sides is finished, and Hedges and Trees planted along them. The
House

House in it is but of Wood, two Stories high, yet built after the Italian Manner, and has noble Apartments. Side-ways of the Garden the Prince has caused a Lane to be cut out, extending to the Shore, which they call *Perspectiva*, (N°. 48.) At the End of it stands a wooden House with a Steeple, that can be seen from the opposite Continent, and very far at Sea, and serves the Seamen for a Mark to steer their Course by in sailing up and down the River, the Channel of which runs close by the said Steeple. The Stream having many Turnings, and there being not Water enough on either Side for the Ships, they have a very dangerous Passage in sailing through the many Buoys into the open Sea. For this Reason the foreign Merchant-Ships cannot quite go up to *Petersbourg*, but cast Anchor before the Buoys, a League from the said Steeple, till they are laden by the Help of other Vessels. Large Men of War are carried out into the Sea between two floating Machines, which the Dutch call *Camels*, before they are rigged, or provided with any thing that is heavy. The Entry and Turning of the River where it is deep, is marked in the Plan with N°. 49. Behind the Garden, along the Water, there live at present the Prince's Architects, Gardiners, and Mechanicks: But Time will shew whether they will be left in the Possession of so convenient Places. Further North-west (N°. 50.) is the Prince's Farm, which is stocked with all sorts of tame Fowl for his Kitchen. Over-against, on a particular Island (N°. 51.) the late Crown-Princess (the Czarewitz's Consort) had another such Farm of her own, next to which a Garden was begun, with a pretty
wooden

wooden House belonging to it, which was already finished. But as this Island is liable to be quite overflowed at high Water, it is probable the Garden upon it will be neglected, unless they resolve to secure it against those frequent Inundations, by a Dike drawn round the Island. The said Prince's Island is covered all over with a Forest of Fir, Birch, and Alder Trees, and the Ground of it is very marshy, which Inconveniency they are in Hopes may be remedied, by the great Quantity of Earth which is to be dug out of the many Canals that are to be cut into the Island.

As to the River *Neva*, I must add here, that the same is extremely deep all along till it opens into a Bay, where it has great Turnings, and grows shallower, with many Sands on both Sides, which render the Stream very narrow; but about a League further into the Bay, it comes to a sufficient Depth again. For this Reason large Ships cannot come up with their Cargoes, but are obliged to lie at Anchor in the Bay, where they are laden and unladen. The Stream is as rapid as the *Rhine*, and its Current may be very plainly observed above a League into the Bay, thence it runs on less sensibly in a very crooked Channel, till it comes to the Streights near *Cronslot*, where it forms again a very rapid Current, particularly towards the Southern Shore, the Force of which is observed a good Way into the Gulph of *Finland*. The Breadth of this River at *Petersbourg* is sometimes but 700, sometimes even 1600 Paces, and as it is extremely deep between the Islands, it is hardly practicable to build a Bridge over it.

It

It has been several times proposed to make a Bridge of Pontons; but the Czar would never consent to it, because it is his Intention to bring his Subjects to learn Navigation by any Method. There are about twenty Boats on the River for carrying over the Passengers; the Money they pay for their Fare, comes into the Czar's Coffers. The Watermen are ignorant Peasants, who, after being first paid their Fare, go to work with their Sails, (for they are forbidden to make use of Oars) but so unskilfully, that a Passenger cannot but be uneasy, considering besides the Rapidity of the Current, and the frequent Tempests that happen. Among the great Number of Persons that lost their Lives in this manner, were, the Polish Minister M. *de Kôningsek*, Major-General *Kirchner*, one of the Czar's first Physicians, and many others. People that are in good Circumstances keep Sloops and Sailors of their own, and foreign Ministers have been since allowed by the Czar, Sloops with four able Watermen each, who are permitted to row, and are paid by the Ministers themselves. A certain Russian Ingenier once proposed to the Czar, to build a Stone-Bridge over that large River, which, according to the Model he gave in, was to consist only of one Arch; but this wild Project was exploded by the foreign Architects; and the Czar, who has a better Judgment of Things of that Nature than to think it practicable, made a Jest of it, by putting the poor Inventor off with Hopes of executing it on another Opportunity.

Late Advices from *Petersbourg* say, that all the Inhabitants in general, who live on the
Ingrian

Ingrian Side, in the *Slaboda* where the Czar's Palace stands, have received Orders to build on the Prince's Island, and to settle there, which, considering the Expences they have already been at in building, will be very disagreeable, and a great Hardship to them.

On the said *Ingrian* Side is a large empty Grass-Field, which would make a very good Market-Place. There the Peasants, Journeymen, and other common People, particularly Boys, meet on Sundays and Holidays, and after having fuddled themselves in the neighbouring *Cabacks*, or Tap-Houses, divide in two Parties, and fight and box for Diversion sake, in the most barbarous Manner, that the Ground lies full of Blood and Hair, and many of them are carried off lame. When they fall on, they make such a dreadful and wild Noise, that they may be heard a Mile off. Those Disorders are connived at by the Government, with this View, that the young People may use themselves to fighting and boxing, and make afterwards the better Soldiers.

It has already been mentioned, and it may be judged from the Plan, that the Situation of *Petersbourg* is very low, and the Ground marshy every where. Hence it is, that the whole Town, from that Part where the River divides it self, down to the Sea, is exposed to great Dangers of Inundations. Since it was founded, it has suffered already twice, when abundance of People and Cattle were lost, and great Damage done, particularly in the Year 1715, when the Water washed away most of the Bridges and Fortifications, and stood so high, that they went in Boats up and

and down the Streets. The neighbouring Parts of the Town are likewife fo marfhy, that on the South-fide it is acceffible but by one Way, which divides it felf in two Roads not far out of Town, which are fo bad, that in Spring and Autumn one may count the Horfes by Dozens that perifhed in the Mire. At length they were obliged to mend that Road; accordingly a Year ago they raifed a Dike reaching to the furthermoft Branch of the River, which Work being but flight, was of no long Duration. But the Road to *Jamfchiki-Slaboda,* a Mile long, is all paved.

To fpeak now in general of the Soil about *Petersbourg,* and the neighbouring Country, the fame is fo cold, by reafon of the great Quantity of Water, Moraffes, Forefts and Wilderneffes, that there is feldom a good Harveft to be expected, particularly in a wet Year, when nothing at all comes to ripen. Turnips, white Cabbage of an indifferent Sort, Cucumbers, and Grafs for Cattle, is the chief Product of thofe Parts. Yet, all forts of Cattle, particularly Sheep, Swine &c. are very thin; for the War and bad Times have deftroyed the greater Part of them, and the prodigious Confumption occafioned by the vaft Number of the Inhabitants of *Petersbourg,* hinders the Propagation of the few that remain. For not only *Peterfbourg,* but likewife all the neighbouring Country, would certainly be famifhed, was it not for the Supplies of Provifions, efpecially of Meal, fent thither from *Novogorod, Pleskow, Moskow,* and even from the Kingdom of *Cafan,* which are carried to *Peterfbourg*

bourg in Winter on thousands of Sleds from Places lying above two hundred German Miles off, and in Summer by Water on the Rivers *Swirri* and *Wolkofa*, and the Lakes *Onega* and *Ladoga*. If those Supplies happen to be only a little retarded by some Incident or other, every thing grows excessive dear, and all the Country suffers very much; for it is to be observed, that *Petersbourg* is the reverse of other great Towns in this respect, that instead of drawing its Provisions from the adjacent Country, it supplies the Country with Necessaries of Life. To give a true Idea of this Country, the Reader must be informed, that it is not like others, where one meets sometimes with large Forests, someimes open Fields again, with Towns and Villages within Sight of each other, and Roads on all Sides for the Communication between them: About *Petersbourg* there are vast and horrid Forests and Desarts, but there are not above one or two Roads in all the Country; if one should happen to miss his Way, (which, however, is hardly possible, there being no By-Roads) he will pass his Time very ill among Bushes and Morasses, till he finds the Road again, nor must he expect to meet with open Fields or Villages. There are indeed here and there some poor Farms in the midst of the Woods, but without regular Roads or Paths leading to them, and the Peasant endeavours to creep through the Bushes as well as he can. To confirm how thin Towns, Boroughs, and Villages lie in those Parts, I will instance *Livonia*, which undoubtedly surpasses all other Countries that lie more North, as to the Goodness of the Soil. That Province which has

has near one hundred German Miles in length, and sixty in breadth, holds after all but five Towns, about fifteen or twenty Boroughs, and Villages in proportion: Whereas *Brabant*, so small a Tract of Land if compared to *Livonia*, is stocked with ten times the Number of Cities, Towns, and Villages. No wonder therefore that the neighbouring Country of *Petersbourg*, being thus all covered with thick Woods, without any open Fields, the fruitful South and West Winds cannot reach nor warm the Soil, consequently the Fruits of the Earth are smothered and nipt by the Cold, and seldom ripen. Besides, the many Morasses with which even the highest Mountains are covered, can never dry up for the same Reason. However, would the Inhabitants clear the Forests, it is probable the Land might be improved there as well as in *Germany*, great Part of which, according to History, was much like these Parts in ancient Times, but, by the Industry of the Inhabitants in politer Ages, was rendered fruitful enough to answer the Exigencies of a good Husband. And even in the few Places near *Petersbourg*, where there are open Fields, it plainly appears, that the Barrenness is not so much owing to the Nature of the Soil, as to the Sloth of the Peasants, who do not trouble themselves much with laying of the Land open to the Wind, and clearing the Ground. Those *Dutch* and *Germans* who live at *Petersbourg*, have accordingly taken great Pains in planting Garden-Fruits, but as the Soil is too marshy, particularly on the South-side of the River, and that, besides, the Seasons have been very moist and cold for

for some Years successively, the Event has not seconded their Intentions. But there is Reason to hope, that, if the Weather should prove better for the future, the Soil will answer the Pains of cultivating, the rather because it begins to dry up pretty well between the Houses, and is now much fitter for Gardening than it was before. Besides, it is observed in the Prince's Gardens on the North Side of the River, where the Ground is sandy and free, and is warmed by the Sun at Noon, that every thing thrives, even the finest Melons, and that the French Dwarf-Trees planted there bear the best Fruit. Excepting what is in this Garden, there is scarcely any Fruit at all in the whole Country; which Defect, however, is likewise owing rather to the Laziness of the Inhabitants, than to the Barrenness of the Soil: For if it was not an old Custom among them to sow their Corn before the Winter comes on, they would hardly venture to bury it under Ground for so long a Time, with the Hazard whether they should ever see it grow up again. It is true, their Winters are so severe, and last so long, that one may be sure to make use of Sleds for six Months together; but then, on the other Hand, the Summer Heats are so scorching, that in two Months time, *viz.* from the middle of June to the middle of August, every thing shoots up and ripens, and whatever does not come to Perfection in that short Space of Time, may surely be given over for lost. I have indeed met about three German Miles from *Petersbourg*, with ripe Cherries in September, but they were very few and sour. As to other good Fruit, *viz.* Plumbs,

Plumbs, Pears, Apricocks, and the like, I doubt whether any body can say he ever saw any of them in those Parts. Strawberries, Billberries, and Blackberries is all they have, and very seldom Currants or Goosberries. But from *Moskow* they are supplied with the finest Fruit and Garden-Fruits, among which are a sort of Apples, in their Language *Nalevi*, many of which weigh ten Oounces, are transparent that the Kernel shines through, and have a Taste like Pippins. Abundance of Mushrooms of divers sorts grow about *Petersbourg*, which the People eat without any Distinction as something very delicious, quite raw, only with Salt and Vinegar: In Autumn they gather them in great Quantities, and without picking them, pickle them in Barrels, and carry them to Market with the Pickle, and so the common People eat them without further Ceremony. This is a Diet very hard to be digested; but as the severe Fasts in *Russia* allow few of the wholesomest Provisions, the Natives are obliged to take up with such Food, and to aid Digestion with Brandy, their usual stomachick Essence. The Czarina-Dowager, Relict of the late Czar *Alexius*, dying in the Year 1715, during Lent, her Body was opened, and it was found, that her Indisposition was chiefly occasioned by eating too much of those pickled Mushrooms, out of Devotion of strictly observing her Fast. During the two Summer Months, which are excessive hot, as is already mentioned, the Sun raises the Vapours in the low and marshy Ground about *Petersbourg*, which occasions almost every Day Tempests of Thunder and Lightning, but they soon blow over,

over, and fair Weather enfues. During the Summer the Sun hardly fets: For though the Body of that Luminary is actually under the Horizon for about three Hours, yet there remains fo much Dawn above, that one may read all Night by it. I was often pleafed to obferve, that in Summer two Hours after Sun-Rife not one Soul was to be feen in the Streets, Doors and Windows being yet all clofe fhut, and the People every where in a profound Sleep. On the other Hand, the Winter Days are fo fhort, that one has but little Comfort during the three Hours that the Sun appears, which, befides, is but feldom feen at all, by reafon of the thick Fogs with which the Air is filled and darkned, to that Degree, that one may juftly fay, that the Winter with them is a long and tedious Night, and what they then call Day, is but a Dawn. In Auguft it begins to grow cold again, and from that Time till May no body is afhamed to wear a good Fur-Coat and Fur-Boots. In Winter it freezes fo hard, that the Beams of their wooden Houfes crack and give a Report like fmall Arms. The Ice in the Rivers, and other Waters, is commonly one Ell and a half thick. It is obfervable, that in Spring when all the Snow is gone, and the Grafs comes up already, yet the Ice, particularly in the Rivers, holds out to the laft, and melts by the Force of the Sun by Degrees, like Metal in a Crucible. The Night-Frofts, however, thicken and ftrengthen it again, fo that for fome Hours in the Morning, Horfes and Carriages may go over it; but in the Afternoon it is not fafe to venture over. At laft towards the End of April, if there happens a pretty warm Day,

the

the Ice difappears as it were at once in lefs than two or three Hours time, and the River is entirely open again. In the Year 1713, I obferved this fudden Alteration with the more Curiofity, becaufe on the firft of May, O. S. at ten in the Morning I had croffed both Arms of the River *Neva* on Horfeback, and at two in the Afternoon the Ice was altogether gone, fo that I might have croffed it again in a Boat. The freezing up of the River in Autumn is not quite fo foon done; however, a couple of Days commonly do the Bufinefs, for when it is once laid over with Ice, which often happens in one Night, People pafs over it, and then they may reft fatisfied, that before May the River will not be open again.

The Inhabitants of the Country about *Petersbourg* were formerly of two Nations: Thofe on the South-fide of the River were *Ingrians*, and thofe Northward *Carelians*, both Subjects to the King of *Sweden*. But at prefent they are a Mixture of divers Nations: For the War and the Plague having fwept away the greater Part of the ancient Natives, their Eftates and Poffeffions were given to Ruffians, who put fome of their own Countrymen, and fome of the remaining *Carelians* into the Villages and Farms, fo that they are now quite blended together, and cannot be any more looked upon as diftinct Nations, except that the Ruffians have the Preference above the reft. There is none of the ancient Families of the Nobility left, for they are either dead, or have removed into other Countries, and difperfed themfelves, confequently the prefent Poffeffors of their Eftates have no reafon to be afraid of any Pretenfions sions or Claims on their Part. The *Ingrians* and *Carelians* are sturdy People, and naturally of a robust Constitution. Their Dress is like that of the *Livonians*, their Shoes are made of Bast, their Coats of a coarse Cloth, which they work themselves; about their Waste they wear a large leathern Girdle, adorned with Brass Buckles, in which they commonly wear a Hatchet behind their Backs, and their Heads are covered with a short Cap without a Brim. They have generally white or yellow Hair, but their picked Beards are of a reddish Colour. Unmarried Women go bareheaded Winter and Summer with short cropt Hair like Boys, so that all the Distinction between them and the Men is, that the latter wear Breeches of Linnen, and the former a Piece of Cloth about their Waste instead of Petticoats. But on Sundays they adorn themselves with white Shells, commonly called Gowries or Blackamores Teeth, little Chains and large Buckles of Iron and Brass, and all sorts of Spangles; for the more it glitters, the greater is their Finery. Their Language is the *Finlandish*, which has no relation with any other whatsoever, though it yields to none as to Richness of Words and Propriety of Turns, which appears by their Hymns, that have a very harmonious Cadence, according to their own Poetry, and may vie with German Rhyme, as to the Choice of the Words, and the Circumlocution and Figures of Speech. Their Way of Life is very poor and miserable; the meanest Peasant in *Germany* lives better than the most substantial among them. Their Food is coarse brown Bread, Pap, and Pudding; and Water

their

their Drink; Meat is what they feldom tafte of.

Their Houfes in general are all of Wood; the Ruffians as well as the Finlanders build them after the following manner. The Carpenter takes the Fir Trees unhewn as they are and piles them up into a fquare Figure, faftening them on the Corners with Dents or Notches without much minding whether one Tree juts out, and another runs in. Such a wooden Box being raifed to a fufficient Height, he gets into it by the help of a Ladder, and cuts his way out again with a Hatchet in the Place where the Door is to be, the Windows he forms in the fame manner, for there is no opening left when the fquare Box is fetting up. Next, to make the Infide fmooth, he planes the Walls with the Hatchet, and leaves the Outfide as it is. Then the Roof-timber is fet up, and thin Splinters nailed upon it, and fo the Houfe is finifhed. The Floor is laid with Planks three Inches thick clofe to one another, yet without faftening them to the Ground with Nails or otherwife, fo that commonly they move up and down when People walk upon them. The Planks that make the Ceiling, are covered with a great deal of Sand to keep the Room warm. The whole Architecture wants no other Tool but a Hatchet, which their Carpenters underftand to handle with more Skill than thofe of any Nation whatfoever. The Doors are fo low that no body can go in without ftooping very low, for they are feldom three Foot high, and on the other hand the Threfhold is raifed from the Ground

two

two Foot at leaſt, a Perſon therefore that goes in, being obliged to lift up one Foot very high, and to thruſt his Head in through the Door ſtooping very low, comes into the Room in a Poſture no leſs comical than that of Harlequin when he appears upon the Stage, and even often thoſe who are not uſed to it, come tumbling into the Houſe with their Heads foremoſt. Generally ſpeaking the whole Building conſiſts but of one Room, with a large ſquare Oven or Stove in it, that is flat above, in which they not only boil, bake, and roaſt their Victuals Winter and Summer, but even ſleep, in it as well as on the Top of it. The Openings that ſerve them for Windows have Shutters before them, which they can puſh one way or another to make the Room light or dark. Some have Saſhes to them, over which they paſte Paper, Rags of Linnen, Hogs-Bladders and the like, to keep out the Air; but People who think themſelves above the common ſort, have ſome ſmall Window or other of Icinglaſs, about a Foot ſquare. As to Beds, that is what they have no Notion of; they make ſhift to wrap themſelves up in Rags, and cover themſelves with their Clothes. Their common way of going to ſleep is like that of the *Ruſſians* in general: When the Room is firſt well heated, ſome go to lie on the Top of the Oven, or on the Benches round it, the remaining part of the Family range themſelves on the ſeveral Planks that are faſtened to the Cieling with Ropes or otherwiſe, to which they get up with Ladders. Each being but one Foot broad or at beſt fifteen or ſixteen

sixteen Inches, one should reasonably apprehend, the People would fall down in their sleep and break their Necks or Bones; but they are so used to it that I have seen with Astonishment about twenty People lying thus over my Head without so much as turning themselves on the other side, and there they sleep as quietly as any other Person in the best Bed. Instead of Candles they burn thin Splinters of Fir, one end of which they put into some Crevice in the Wall or in the Oven, and very often they even take them into their Mouths; and as their usual Work is not very nice, they can easily do it by that Light. The Contrivance of rocking their Children is curious: They fasten to the Cieling one End of a Pole like that of a Turner, on the other End they hang an oblong Basket full of Rags, Hay, and Straw, in which the Child lies; they pull it from time to time, and so the bending of the Pole makes the Basket dangle and dance a good while: When the Child wants Suck, the Mother leans over the Basket and suckles it.

The whole Country being almost nothing but Bushes, Morasses and Forests, there is consequently plenty of Wood, though the greater part of it is good for nothing, as it has neither a right Sap nor Pith, and is not near so good as that in *Germany*. It usually rots in ten or twelve Years time, which makes the Houses very soon decay and stand in need of Props and Repair. The Trees are Fir, Pine, Alder, Birch, Asp and Elm, but all short, wry and knobby Stuff, so that their Woods may rather be called Bushes than Forests.

rests. Nothing can thrive by reason of the dampness of the Morasses, and all the Summer long the Trees cannot be carried out except a few that stand on the Brim of the Morasses. Of Beach and Oak there is none at all, no more than in any of the Northern Parts of whole *Russia*. This obliges the Czar to fetch the Oak for his Men of War from the Kingdom of *Casan*, three hundred German Miles off and upwards, from whence it is carried up the *Wolga* and other Rivers and by the Lake of *Ladoga*, with great Trouble and Expence. There are some Lime Trees in the Woods, but they are small and not to be compared to those that grow along the *Wolga*, in the Kingdoms of *Casan* and *Astracan*, which are as fine and as large as any in the World: They have Boats there hollowed out of one Trunk of Lime Tree, and the Bast made of the Bark of the same is there in such Plenty, that they make vast quantities of Matts of it, which are exported to most of the neighbouring Countries: In *Russia*, particularly on the *Wolga*, and about the Lakes *Ladoga* and *Onega*, they make Sails of it for their Ships.

Of wild Beasts or Game there are others in *Russia*, but Wolves and Bears. The Wolves are there in such numbers, that one can hardly travel two German Miles, be it Summer or Winter, without meeting some. But especially in the Winter time they appear in Herds thirty and forty together; when Hunger spurns them on to do great Mischief; and then it is no new thing to hear that they attack Men and Horse in the Sleds;

The Present State of Russia.

Sleds; Dogs particularly are in great danger, for they catch them even before the Doors of the Houses and Farms. In the Year 1714. a Parcel of Wolves attacked the Centinel standing before the Foundery, and pulled him to the Ground; another Soldier who came to his Assistance, was torn to pieces and devoured by them; the former crawled off in the mean time but died afterwards of his Wounds. Soon after a Woman was devoured by those furious Beasts not far from Prince *Menzicoff*'s House in the Morning, it being already broad Daylight. It happened the same Winter, that a Country Parson near *Ladoga*, took into his Head to go and shoot a Wolf; he put his Horse to a Sled, behind which he had tied with a Rope about two Yards long another small Sled, on which he had fastened a Pig, by the squeaking of which he intended to start some Game for him to kill with his Piece he had with him in the Sled. Thus equipped he went out into the Fields towards Evening; it was not long before his Invention took effect, some Wolves appeared, but in greater numbers than he well liked; his Horse frightened at the sight of them, began to run away, and the unhappy Sportsman had enough to do to manage him so as to make him take his Course back to the Village; the Wolves however galloped after him almost as swift as his Horse and pursued him closely to his very House, where it unluckily happened that the Horse taking too short a Turn into the Yard, overturned the Sled and threw the Parson on the Ground, where he became a Prey to those ravenous Beasts,

Beasts, which in a few Minutes devoured him, leaving nothing behind but the bloody Remains of his Fur-coat. Bears appear also sometimes, but they do less Mischief than the Wolves, for in Summer they may get their Food otherwise, and during Winter they sleep; however now and then they catch some Horse or Cow they meet with. There are Hares enough in the Country but not so good as those in *Holland* and *Bohemia*, for they are smaller, poor, and their Flesh eats dry and tough, and is of no good taste: During Summer they are of a grey Colour like Hares in other Countries, but against the Winter they turn white and remain so till the Grass springs, and then they resume the grey Colour. There are few Foxes, but Lynxes are in greater number, of a good Colour and Skin, though they are not so fine as those in *Siberia*. Elks are found sometimes; but Stags, Roe-bucks, wild Boars and Raindeer are never seen in those Parts. Of wild Fowl there is plenty, particularly of Heathcocks, Morehens, Woodcocks, Snipes of all sorts, wild Geese and Ducks, and if one should want never so many of either sort, one may be sure to find enough in the Market in proper Seasons for a small Price. At a certain Colonel's House I always saw in Winter between two and three hundred Woodcocks in the Yard, which his People had sent him to Town for Provision in his Family. Therefore, as there is such quantity of them, they are slighted and seldom served up on the Master's Table, but given to the Servants. The common Partridges of a red Colour are scarce, but

The Prefent State of Ruffia.

but white ones are in abundance; they are fomewhat bigger than in *Germany*, but commonly poor, nor of fo good a tafte. Thrufhes or Feldifare are never feen in thofe Parts, and as there are hardly any open Fields, as abovefaid, confequently they have but few Larks. All Rivers and other Waters are ftored with well-tafted Fifh: There is particularly one fort in the Rivers, which they call *Harrius*, which is delicious. It is obfervable, that in the Rivers towards North and Weft, that fall into the *Baltick* or *White Sea*, they catch great quantities of Salmon: But in the other Rivers which run South towards the *Cafpian Sea*, there is not one of that fort, nor Trouts neither. On the contrary they yield abundance of *Sterlets*, a fort of Fifh which may be preferred to all others for delicioufnefs, and are not found in the Rivers or Waters that run North. Notwithftanding this Plenty, frefh and alive Fifh are extremely fcarce and dear, for they are not kept in Fifh-pools and Stews like in other Places, but carried to Market falted and pickled, and though they may be fmelt at a great diftance, yet the *Ruffians*, efpecially the common People, eat them with a great deal of Appetite and prefer them to frefh Fifh. They eat them even raw out of the Barrel, or if they boil them they eat the Pickle too, with Bread in it like a Soup. To this they are obliged by frequent Fafts, which make above thirty Weeks in the Year, in which time they dare not tafte neither Flefh nor what comes of Flefh, as Eggs, Milk, Butter, Cheefe, and the like, but muft live upon Fifh, and Linfeedfeed-Oyl inſtead of Butter. Thoſe Perſons who have ſeen foreign Countries have pretty well broke through this cruel Cuſtom of faſting, but the common People, and others who affect an extraordinary Devotion, are ſtrict Obſervers of it, and look upon breaking the Faſt as a moſt heinous Crime. In the Monaſteries they never eat any Fleſh at all the whole Year round.

A DESCRIPTION OF CRONSLOT.

O much may suffice of *Peterf-bourgh*: Next I am to say something of *Cronflot*. By this Name, which properly only belongs to the Castle, is commonly understood the Island of *Retufari* or *Rutzari*, called by the Russians *Kotli-Oftrow*, Kettle-Island. It lies at the End of the Gulph of *Finland*, which Eastward of it forms a large Bay or narrow Sea, reaching as far as the Mouth of the River *Neva*. South of it there is the only Road or Passage up to *Petersbourg*, not much above two thousand Paces in breadth, where it is of a sufficient depth for the largest Men of War: But the Current there runs so strong, that, unless the Wind be very fair, it is hard to come up through it. North of the

the Island no Vessels can pass by reason of the Shallowness of the Water, whence it comes also that the Current is hardly observable on that Side. This Situation renders it a safe Port for the Czar's Fleet, inasmuch as there is but one narrow Inlet, by which it can be attacked, so that *Cronslot* may be justly called the Key to *Petersbourg*. The Island it self is barren and bears neither Corn nor any thing else: Formerly it was not inhabited, except by a few Fishermen; but the Czar being sensible of its advantagious Situation, made it the Port of his Fleet, which not only he fortified with a strong Castle called *Cronslot* or *Cron-Schloss*, (Crown-Castle) but also caused a pretty large Town to be built upon it, which commonly goes by the same Name with the Castle. The Harbour is spacious and deep, being built into the Sea on the South-side of the Island; but towards the opposite Continent the Water by degrees grows so shallow that no Vessels can come on Shore, but People are obliged to land at the long Bridge built for that purpose. Here the Czar's Fleet used to lie at first both Summer and Winter, but being since increased to the number of forty odd Ships of the Line, they have for the greater part been removed to *Reval*, into the Harbour that was made there six Years ago. However *Cronslot* is still the true Harbour of *Petersbourg*, which lies almost four German Miles off. The Castle, which is properly called *Cronslot* or *Cron-Schloss*, stands in the midst of the Sea, about a Cannon-shot from the Island, and a good English Mile from the Coast of *Ingria*, on a Sand-
Bank

Bank which increases every Day by the strong Current which runs through there. The Foundations of it were laid in Winter upon the Ice with Boxes formed of strong Timber and filled with Stone, on which the rest was afterwards built of Earth and Timber. It is in the Form of a round Tower with three Galleries round, one above the other, well furnished with Cannon from top to bottom: But as by reason of its round Figure, they cannot discharge above three or four Guns at once against a Ship that should endeavour to force her Passage through, the Czar once designed to have it pulled down again, and to make a triangular Work of it, to be built more durable, and in such a manner as to fire from it more Guns at once upon a Ship that comes with a hostile Design. Over against on the Island are two Batteries, of ten or twelve Guns each, and the Peers of the Harbour may in case of Necessity be mounted with forty or fifty Guns more, so that this Entry of *Petersbourg* is sufficiently covered and guarded against any Insult, the rather because the Ships in the Harbour are at full Liberty to ply their Guns too. As for what relates to the Town of *Retusari* or *Cronslot* as they call it, the same is already pretty large, considering the short time since it was begun to be built, but the Houses which are all of Wood, lie dispersed, nor is there is so much as a Ditch, or even a Hedge round the Place. The Czar once seemed resolved to have all those wooden Houses changed into Stone Buildings, to the number of six thousand, built in regular Streets, through which Canals were to be cut after the way of *Holland*,

The Present State of Russia.

land, that the Merchants might have their Goods laden and unladen at their very Doors. The best Houses at present are, first, a large Stone Building raised by the Prince *Menzicoff*, which has two Wings, the Ground-floor of which is adapted for Trade and Merchandize, and the two remaining Stories are designed for a Palace. There are four other large Stone Buildings which the Czar has caused to be erected, and are to be let out to Merchants for Store-houses and other Business. The Russian Church is a fine Building, which was finished in the Year 1718. This Place, therefore, being the usual Station of the Czar's Navy, where he has his principal Store-houses, it is easy to imagine, that there are also a good number of Inhabitants; and though Provisions bear an exorbitant Price, there being no planting or sowing, nor breeding any Cattle in the Island, which is altogether supplied from *Petersbourg*, and that sometimes sparingly enough, yet every Day People go to settle there. As for the rest, their way of Life is much the same with that at *Petersbourg*, and as the Inhabitants are a Medley of all sorts of Nations, every one lives according to his own way. In point of Religion they are under no Restraint, but enjoy the same Liberty of Conscience as others do any where in the Czar's Dominions. The Lutherans particularly have the Exercise of divine Service in a private House: Formerly they had a Minister of their own in the Island, but as his Allowance was but small, he took his Leave of them in the Year 1714. It happened some time after that one of the Swedish Prisoners came to *Retusari*, a Native

tive of *Koningsberg* in *Pruſſia*, who had been taken Priſoner in *Poland* as Lieutenant in the Swediſh Service, in which Condition he was kept ſome Years at *Moskow*, till he obtained Leave to make Shift to get a Livelihood ſomewhere in the Country as well as he was able. He chanced to come to *Retuſari* at a time when the Roman Catholick, Reformed and Lutheran Inhabitants were altogether unprovided with Paſtors of their own Profeſſion. In this Conjuncture he took upon him to tender thoſe Flocks howſoever different in their Profeſſions of Faith: He not only preached to them by turns, but alſo adminiſtred the Sacraments to them without Diſtinction; and this he continued for a Year or two, till at length he was informed againſt, and had Inhibition made him: However as he had nothing elſe to ſubſiſt, nor knew where to turn himſelf, they were obliged otherwiſe to provide for him, and ſo he got a Lieutenant's Commiſſion again.

The South Coaſt from *Cronſlot* to *Petersbourg*, is all along full of Country Houſes and Farms. For when the Czar conquered *Ingria* he made Grants of the Eſtates of the former Gentry on the Continent to his Officers and Servants of all Ranks and Degrees, but this Tract along the Coaſt he cauſed to be meaſured and divided into ſeveral Parcels holding five hundred Rods in Front, and running two thouſand deep into the Country, which he diſtributed partly among the Senators and Boyars, partly among the Officers of his Houſhold, and the military Officers, who according to their Fancy and Circumſtances have built thereupon Pleaſure-houſes,

or

or Farms, which render that Situation very agreeable. About a thousand Paces from the Shore the Ground rises to almost an equal Height of sixty or seventy Foot, on the Top of which those Country Houses stand along in one Row, and not only enjoy a fine Prospect from that Eminency for themselves, but also afford a pleasant Sight to those that sail up the Bay, forming as it were an Amphitheatre. That Part of the Land is as good as any where, consisting of arable Ground, Pasture, Meadow-fields, Woods, and affords abundance of Fish, Wild-fowl and divers other sorts of Necessaries. It would be too tedious to enter upon a Description of all those Houses, I shall therefore content my self with giving a short account of only three of them.

The first is called *Oranjen-baum* (Orange-Tree) being a Palace and Garden lying directly opposite to *Cronslot*, and belonging to the Prince *Menzicoff*. The Situation of it is charming. The House is of Stone three Stories high with two long Wings on both Sides, built in the Form of half an Oval. The Garden which lies before the House towards the Shore, is not quite finished. The Sea on that Shore being very Shallow, the Prince for the better Conveniency of landing, has caused a Bridge to be built there, which advances three hundred Paces into the Sea.

A German Mile and a half from thence lies *Peter-Hof*, where the Czar's Gardens and Pleasure-houses are. One of those Gardens lies on the Eminence, and the other six hundred Paces off towards the Water-side on the lower Shore. This once was the Czar's favourite

vourite Place, for which Reaſon he ſpared no Expences nor Pains to make ſomething extraordinary of it. Before the one Houſe at the foot of the Hill a Grotto has been made with double Caſcados, from whence they have dug a very deep Canal into the Sea, on which Veſſels may come up as far as the Grotto at the foot of the Houſe, which ſtands ſixty Foot high on the Hill. This laſt Houſe and the other that ſtands on the Sea-ſide, are built of Stone and finiſhed. Both are not very large, but well contrived, and may paſs for the beſt in the whole Country, next to the Buildings raiſed by the Prince *Menzicoff*. The Situation likewiſe is the fineſt on all that Shore, particularly as to the Houſe on the Hill, from whence one has a full View both of *Cronſlot* and *Petersbourg*, and all thoſe narrow Seas and their Shipping.

A German Mile from thence lies *Strelna-Muiſe*, another Garden and Palace newly raiſed by the Czar. His Majeſty at firſt had but a wooden Houſe there; but as he was extremely delighted with the Rivulet *Strelna*, which there falls into the Sea, he reſolved to make a Royal Seat and Garden of it, that might vie with that of *Verſailles*. The Water on that Shore is likewiſe ſo ſhallow, that formerly even the ſmalleſt Boats could not come up to the Shore: But a certain Major-General, a German by Birth, having raiſed a large Dike or Peer made of Fachines and Earth, twenty Paces in breadth and advancing ſeven hundred into the Sea, all ſorts of Veſſels may now conveniently come up. It was thought at firſt this Work would prove of no long Duration, but ſoon be blown up by the

the ſtrong Current; but it has now for theſe three Years paſt reſiſted the moſt violent Tempeſts, which ruined almoſt all the neighbouring Dikes, Bridges and other Works, ſo that this method of building in the Water is at preſent looked upon as the moſt durable and even the cheapeſt, and eaſieſt to be repaired, and is therefore judged the propereſt for the making of Harbours. The Garden is to be of a vaſt Extent according as it is laid out, and will certainly in time be ſomething very extraordinary, if it ſhould be executed ſo as it is projected in the ſeveral Draughts relating to it, which the Czar ſeems reſolved upon, let the Expence be what it will. Hitherto ſeveral thouſands of Labourers have been employed in levelling the Ground; they have begun to plant thouſands of Lime Trees, and the Hill on which the noble and coſtly Palace is to be built, has been cut out with incredible Pains in the Form of an Amphitheatre.

The End of the Firſt Volume.

For Product Safety Concerns and Information please contact our EU
representative GPSR@taylorandfrancis.com
Taylor & Francis Verlag GmbH, Kaufingerstraße 24, 80331 München, Germany

www.ingramcontent.com/pod-product-compliance
Lightning Source LLC
Chambersburg PA
CBHW052129010526
44113CB00034B/1043